Strains
of Dissent

RHETORIC AND PUBLIC AFFAIRS SERIES

Strains
of Dissent

POPULAR MUSIC
AND EVERYDAY RESISTANCE
IN WWII FRANCE, 1940–1945

Kelly Jakes

MICHIGAN STATE UNIVERSITY PRESS • *East Lansing*

♾ The paper used in this publication meets the minimum requirements
of ANSI/NISO Z39.48-1992 (R 1997) (Permanence of Paper).

Michigan State University Press
East Lansing, Michigan 48823-5245

Printed and bound in the United States of America.

28 27 26 25 24 23 22 21 20 19   1 2 3 4 5 6 7 8 9 10

LIBRARY OF CONGRESS CATALOGING-IN-PUBLICATION DATA
Names: Jakes, Kelly, author.
Title: Strains of dissent : popular music and everyday resistance in WWII France, 1940–1945 / Kelly Jakes.
Description: East Lansing : Michigan State University Press, 2019. | Series: Rhetoric and public affairs series |
Includes bibliographical references and index.
Identifiers: LCCN 2018011222| ISBN 9781611863055 (pbk. : alk. paper)
| ISBN 9781609175849 (pdf) | ISBN 9781628953497 (epub) | ISBN 9781628963496 (kindle)
Subjects: LCSH: Popular music—Political aspects—France—History—20th century.
| World War, 1939–1945—Music and the war. | Popular music—France—1941–1950—
History and criticism.
Classification: LCC ML3917.F8 J35 2019 | DDC 781.640944/09044—dc23
LC record available at https://lccn.loc.gov/2018011222

Book design by Charlie Sharp, Sharp Des!gns, East Lansing, MI
Cover design by Erin Kirk New.
Cover art: "La Chanson des Camps," reproduced with permission from
Fonds ARMA Musée de la Résistance et de la Déportation de Thionville.

Visit Michigan State University Press at *www.msupress.org*

For my parents,
Robert and Jane Jakes

Contents

———•◆•———

Acknowledgments

————— ·◆· —————

In many ways, I began preparing to write this book more than a decade ago as an undergraduate student at Furman University. Having completed the majority of my music major, I decided to take on a second concentration in communication. Early in this coursework, I was fortunate to study with Sean O'Rourke, a wonderful teacher whose classes helped me to make sense of my world and inspired me, really for the first time, to apply myself fully to academic work. He helped me to see that writing about rhetoric and music was not only possible, but also important.

In the years between my days at Furman and the publication of this book, many scholars have helped bring the project to fruition. At the University of Wisconsin-Madison, Robert Asen, Sara McKinnon, Stephen Lucas, Robert Howard, and Karma Chavéz offered invaluable feedback and moral support. I am also grateful to Mary Louise Roberts, whose love of history is truly infectious. Lou taught me to love searching for needles in haystacks and that rigorous research can be creative and fun. Above all, I am indebted to the formidable and fine Susan Zaeske, who always believed in this book and in my ability to complete it. Sue has read and reread many drafts along the way, and I am deeply thankful for her guidance, criticism, and encouragement. I must also thank my graduate student cohort. Keeping up with them during our time as developing scholars helped sharpen my mind just as I was starting to pull the ragged strands of the book together. And special gratitude goes to the brilliant Jennifer Keohane, whose friendship is one of my greatest treasures.

I owe thanks to various other colleagues and scholars who have helped, directly or indirectly, to shape this book. I have benefited from numerous conversations with my colleagues and students in the Department of Communication at Wayne State University. Kelly Young and Katheryn Maguire deserve special mention for their generous mentorship and enthusiastic cheerleading. Rahul Mitra, Stephanie Tong, and Elizabeth Stoycheff made my work life a joy, even on the bad days. I have also had considerable help from editors and reviewers. Raymie McKerrow and several anonymous readers helped me to polish chapter 2, a version of which was previously published in the *Quarterly Journal of Speech*. I am especially grateful to Marty Medhurst and the anonymous reviewers who gave the full manuscript careful consideration and provided honest, fair, and helpful evaluations.

Writing about French popular culture in a bygone era is an expensive endeavor, and I have been fortunate to enjoy a great deal of financial support over the years. As a graduate student at the University of Wisconsin-Madison, I was able to spend large chunks of time in France thanks to money from the Wisconsin Alumni Association, the Chateaubriand Fellowship, and the Graduate Fellowship at CELSA-La Sorbonne. At Wayne State, two internal fellowships provided me with the funds to return to France and expand the project into its current form. Across all these research trips, I was fortunate to work with knowledgeable archivists at the Bibliothèque Nationale, Archives Nationales, Préfecture de Police, Archives du Havre, and Archives Départementales des Bouches-du-Rhône who pulled countless boxes of materials for me and provided suggestions when I encountered roadblocks. Special thanks goes to Anne-Marie Pathé, who made sure to show me everything even remotely related to my research topic at the wonderful Institut d'Histoire du Temps Présent.

Finally, thank you to my family, without whose love and encouragement the project would have been impossible. Daisy, my sweet and stubborn hound dog, helped by instituting compulsory work breaks in the form of long walks and chats with various neighbors. My brother, Will, has kept me humble and well teased but also well traveled. Our sibling vacations have been a source of much-needed rest and fun and I am so happy to be his friend. I am especially fortunate to have supportive parents. They instilled in me the qualities of hard work and self-confidence that are required to complete a long, difficult project, but more importantly, taught me how to lead a happy and fulfilling life. I am most grateful to Cutter, whose delightfully silly side has always been a vital counterweight to all the stuffy seriousness of academic life. He hasn't read many of these pages, but his own work ethic has inspired me to improve my focus, and his generosity of heart has sustained me in moments of frustration and self-doubt. Without him, writing this book would have been a lonely and boring business.

Preface

————•◆•————

The French people . . . sing their defeats, their miseries, their troubles,
as well as their good fortunes or their victories . . . It seems that song has
become the natural expression of its sentiments.
—Léon Deutsch, *La Revue Française*, December 21, 1924

O n December 14, 1940, six months after France's shocking fall to
Hitler's army, cultural critic Jean Laurent penned an inspira-
tional column for the nation's new collaborationist newspaper,
Les Nouveaux Temps. Borrowing playwright Pierre Beaumarchais's observation that, in France, "Tout finit par des chansons" (Everything ends in
songs), Laurent attempted to ease his compatriots' fears about life under
the Nazi regime by reminding them of a shared mode of civic discourse,
the nation's repertoire of traditional songs. Having sustained French citizens across centuries of war and political unrest, these songs, he argued,

were uniquely poised to help the French accommodate themselves to the sweeping sociopolitical changes imposed by the Germans. After all, Laurent observed, popular songs had always "reflected the qualities of our race," eliciting proper feelings of comfort and reassurance no matter whether citizens were "in war or in peace, conqueror or conquered, happy or unhappy." An "essentially French genre," he continued, popular song owed its power to its open boundaries, its resistance to classification. "Like all that touches the collective heart, song has no limits," he wrote. "As varied as the human soul," songs and their performance offered a rich repository of representations from which citizens could draw to pursue a variety of rhetorical ends. "The true author of these popular songs is the people who sing them," he wrote, "modifying them according to their wishes, following their dreams, their ideas, and their loves." Tracing French popular song from its performance in ancient Greek temples, Gaulist settlements, the Sun King's royal court, Revolutionary barricades, and World War I trenches, Laurent closed his article with an observation about song's role in forming popular opinion. "Don't forget," he concluded, "that it is through song that poets leave their ivory towers, go down to the streets, and address themselves to the crowds."[1]

Given the power of song in the French cultural and political tradition that Laurent celebrated, it is hardly surprising that Occupation leaders turned to music as a rhetorical tool to promote collaboration among French citizens. Authorities capitalized on the mass appeal of popular music, hiring famous singers to record songs in support of the new government, banning "degenerate" American jazz from the airwaves, and providing youth with pro-collaboration songbooks.[2] These interferences were intended to coax along abrupt and colossal shifts in France's political ideology and cultural norms, the most significant of which was a radical departure from the nation's republican heritage.[3] Indeed, while the fighting still raged, French leaders disbanded the Third Republic, the government in place since 1870, and granted power to the World War I hero Philippe Pétain. On June 22, 1940, Pétain signed an armistice with Germany that granted Hitler control over three-fifths of French territory, an area that included the most heavily populated and richest portions of metropolitan France. The rest of the country would be controlled by Pétain's small government, headquartered in the spa town of Vichy. Pétain coupled these political changes with sweeping social reforms, introduced to the public through an ideological campaign called the National Revolution. The campaign, marketed extensively through public performances and radio broadcasts of Vichy's new, jubilant anthem, urged French citizens to abandon their alleged obsession with *liberté, égalité, fraternité* and obediently embrace an emphasis on traditional, Catholic duty, represented by the new mantra *travail, famille, patrie* (work, family, fatherland).

Yet, authorities were not the only ones to transform popular music into a weapon in the ideological battle over the nation's future. As Laurent noted in *Les Nouveaux Temps*, French people, whom he recognized as the primary "authors" of French song, possessed musical tools that they could use to rhetorically regenerate and reconstruct their nation. While Laurent never explicitly called citizens to take up musical arms against collaboration, his narration of song's role throughout French history provided a clear reminder of music's potential for resistance. Like the creative troubadours who had repurposed songs to negotiate centuries of conflict, French citizens, he wrote, could mine the repertoire of popular song for symbols to modify "according to their wishes," "dreams," and "loves." "As varied as the human soul," yet the only true expression of the French "race," songs, he suggested, were uniquely situated to voice the peoples' concerns, fears, and defiance. By rooting songs in centuries of republican performative practices begun by the ancient Greeks and continued by France's Revolutionary partisans and victorious soldiers of the Great War, Laurent drew attention to popular song's ability to serve as aural expressions of democratic France. Calling song the means by which artists and composers "come down from their ivory towers" to "address themselves to the crowds" and the only "direct reflection of the collective heart," his article suggested that songs were a vital mode of communication that could be embraced when other avenues had been foreclosed. Whether he intended to issue a call to musical defiance or not, Laurent provided ample arguments to communicate that regardless of Hitler's cultural policy and active censorship, singing was still a viable method that citizens could use to access the public sphere and express collective sentiment.

This book is the story of how French dissidents read between the lines of Laurent's call for a national embrace of song, seizing popular music as a key mode of political struggle during the Second World War. During the German Occupation of their country from 1940 to 1944, Resistance fighters, Parisian youth, and prisoners of war mined a vast repertoire of symbols and modes of performance from a long national musical tradition and a burgeoning international entertainment industry, embracing music as a rhetorical resource with which to destabilize Nazi ideology and contest collaborationist Vichy propaganda. After the Liberation of 1944, popular music continued to mediate French political life, helping citizens to challenge American hegemony and recuperate their nation's lost international standing. This musical resistance was possible, I argue, through three main genres of popular song—*chanson*, operetta, and jazz—each of which had been linked to various, sometimes competing, notions of national identity. Having been established as the musical expression of the "true" French citizen, *chanson* provided a unique resource for the restoration of a republican national narrative, as its performance was linked to traditional values of liberal individualism.[4] Operetta—a genre of light opera that was well known for its vulgar jokes and political satire—offered a ready-made tool by which the French could deny the power of their captors and recuperate the virility of their fallen nation. Jazz, at once a symbol of racial degeneration and a more "modern," egalitarian France, offered the French a means to undermine the rigid race and gender norms imposed by occupying forces and to contain the threat of Americanization upon war's end. Ultimately, through song, French dissidents rejected Nazi subordination, the politics of *travail, famille, patrie,* and American intervention and insisted upon a return to that trinity of traditional French values, *liberté, égalité, fraternité.*

This study makes a significant contribution to the rhetorical analysis of music, an important area of research whose development has lagged behind the field's expansion in the areas of visual, embodied, and digital discourses. Begun in the 1970s when public address scholars turned their attention to social movements, early rhetorical scholarship set in place a method of analysis that encouraged rhetoricians to examine music just as they approached speeches, looking for the ways that lyrics and music worked together to more "effectively" change attitudes.[5] Despite the promise of these early studies, essays on the rhetoric of music came in disjointed and slow succession, and most continued to treat music as a text whose meanings could be reliably located within lyrical and musical patterns.[6] While these early studies helped to establish music as a legitimate topic of rhetorical study and laid the groundwork for theorizing how sound and text work together, their critical insights were limited by a method of analysis that located the meaning of sonic and textual dimensions on the page. The rhetoric of song could be illuminated, this method suggested, through critical "reading."

Yet, as cultural and performance scholars have shown, treating music as a stable text whose meanings reside within the score is a fool's errand. The first problem with this textual approach is that it fails to account for the polyvalent nature of music, by which I mean the ability of a single song to signify multiple meanings to various audiences. As Lawrence Grossberg has explained in his study of rock-and-roll, "different fans seem to use the music for very different purposes and in very different ways." For some audiences, song lyrics may be extremely important, while others may focus their energies on experiencing sound affectively as cathartic release, vengeful satisfaction, guarded optimism, or something else. Because of this polyvalence, Grossberg urges scholars to stop assuming that music functions primarily "by representing something—meanings, ideas, or cultural experience" and calls us to reconsider the "attempt to define one experience or use of [music] as the only one."[7] The second problem with the textual approach to song is that it elides the historical contexts that have conditioned the meanings of lyrics and music. As Della Pollock explains, texts are "inseparable from the processes by which they are made, understood, and deployed" and continually "evoke their place within a history of tools, uses, and action."[8] By locating all meaning within the musical score, textual readings fail to contextualize music within this broader history of production and use and assume a priori the representational work that lyrics and music perform. Ultimately, as Greg Dimitriadis notes, these critiques of textual approaches to music remind us that we cannot treat a musical score as "internally consistent and entirely self-referential." Contrary to the popular expression, it is not "all on the page so to speak."[9]

Because close textual analysis has been an important hallmark of rhetorical criticism, the critique of a textual approach to music threatened to extinguish the already ailing rhetorical study of music. Yet, recently, a burgeoning interest in sound has reinvigorated efforts to account for the power of musical discourses. As the field of rhetoric has broadened its definition of public address and confronted its privileging of spoken and printed discourse, scholars have turned their attention to aural discourses, seeking to resist the "textocentrism" that has dominated our work.[10] In his analysis of the voices of the victims of the 9/11 attacks, for example, Joshua Gunn calls the discipline to restore its focus "on something singularly human: voice."[11] In his study of recorded sound, Greg Goodale urges rhetoric scholars to develop the ability to understand how "a pause, an intonation, or even a noise can make a forceful argument."[12] A handful of rhetoricians interested in music have taken up this task, focusing on how musicians help oppressed communities to resist domination by promoting alternative collective identities.[13] Through heavily contextualized textual analysis and an at least cursory examination of the paratexts—music videos, liner notes, blog entries—that condition the meaning of this music, these scholars have established music as an instrument of power, while making some methodological progress along the way. Indeed, now sensitive to the problems of a textual approach to music, these scholars have looked beyond the musical score, considering how photographs, previous concert tours, and singer's bodies bear on music's representational power.[14]

This book takes its cue from these recent works, employing an expanded form of textual analysis that reorients our focus from the musical score to the ways people make use of musical works and cultures. Examining how people interacted with musical tools allows me to broaden the object of study beyond the immediate musical work while simultaneously recovering the importance of music's textual appeals. Indeed, taking seriously Christopher Small's reminder that "music is not a thing at all but an activity, something that people do," I look for the ways that people altered and combined the tools provided by popular music in order to craft subject positions that defied new notions of citizenship imposed by Vichy France, Nazi Germany, and the United States.[15] In all cases, the lyrics of the songs that inspired French partisans are vital to the music's rhetorical power, as these words were either originally composed or carefully enacted by those groups themselves. The musical elements of the songs are also important, for these melodies were signifiers of particular, often contradictory, national values. But examining how French people performed musical resistance demands that we also pay attention to the various ways that they appropriated musical culture. Indeed, French citizens' use of music wasn't limited to the act of singing. When groups like the Parisian youth known as the zazous appropriated the culture of jazz, they also borrowed swing fashion and dance to construct a countercultural identity that would disrupt Nazi social norms. Similarly, as French women eagerly accepted invitations to dance parties hosted by American GIs, music critics turned to the pages of *Jazz Hot*, France's popular jazz periodical, to deny American cultural superiority and vie for political power. Thus, while understanding the ways that real people used music helps to recuperate the musical text as a stable signifier, it also opens the object of study beyond the score to consider how embodied, visual, and textual discourses were also key sites of musical enactment.

Looking deeply at how French dissidents used music to resist new social and political norms also allows for a more nuanced understanding of the significance of popular music in the era of the Second World War. Indeed, historians and cultural critics have also analyzed popular music in isolation from the people who listened to it, treating songs as bounded texts operating in historical and performative vacuums.[16] As a result, the literature on popular music in WWII France suffers from two contradictory theoretical presumptions. Overwhelmingly, the scholarship flattens music's significance by treating it either as a means of escape from the realities of everyday life or as a tool of propaganda. The first of these positions, articulated most stridently by André Halimi, denounces those who participated in musical performances as unpatriotic, selfish collaborators. "While other occupied countries conserved a minimum of dignity," he writes, "millions of French people sang during the Occupation."[17] More recent scholarship by authors like Charles Rearick and Keith Reader avoids passing judgment on those who sang during the Occupation, yet still argues that music functioned primarily as a vehicle of escape.[18] Scholarship that does recognize the political potentialities of music during this period has oversimplified its function by reducing it to an instrument of Vichy or Allied forces.[19] While this work certainly helps to reconstruct the milieu in which music operated, it fails to account for the complex ways in which people interacted with music during the war.

Throughout this book, I ground my analysis of the ways in which citizens used music to subvert dominant social norms with theories that emphasize performance as a key tactic of the oppressed. Like Stephen Gencarella and Phaedra Pezzullo, I see performance as "a creative act that occurs in specific times and places, and that promises to repeat, transform, contest, or transgress established cultural patterns."[20] The liberatory potential of these creative acts has been well established by scholars of performance and resistance. Dwight Conquergood, for example, has argued that it is only through their "performative repertoire" that subordinate groups can "skirt patrols, elude supervisors, pilfer the privileged, and make end runs around occupying authorities."[21] Prevented from enacting traditional modes of public speech, these groups must camouflage their "subversive and utopian yearnings" by presenting them in "indirect, nonverbal, and extralinguistic modes of communication."[22] James Scott also has argued for the resistant power of performance, showing how songs, jokes, folktales, and rituals all offer a certain camouflage for resistance and help citizens assemble a "variety of low-profile forms of resistance that dare not speak in their own name."[23] Cheryl Jorgensen-Earp calls this kind of opposition "rhetorical resistance," by which she means the creative "manipulation of discursive or nondiscursive symbols" that allow people to build psychological resistance to regimes that cannot be attacked with physical force.[24]

Living under constant threat of Nazi retaliation, French dissidents eschewed both oratory and pamphleting as means to rally resistance or warn about the dangers of collaboration. Instead of using dangerous and unpragmatic speech acts, they drew from the cultural resources of centuries of French folksinging, operetta, and new, "modern" jazz to compose a potent but subtle rhetoric of resistance that was not immediately recognizable to German occupiers. And while the threat of Nazi retaliation had ended by the fall of 1944, these resources were still useful as the French negotiated incredible power disparities between themselves and the American soldiers who took control of their land from 1944 to 1945. Outright resistance to American requisitions and ordinances was futile and foolhardy, but music provided a safe means to voice opposition to Washington's postwar vision of the world and resituate France in the new geopolitical landscape.

French musical performances did not only work by disguising critique or coding resistance, though these tasks were also certainly accomplished. The rhetorical promise of popular music was that it offered a repository of signifiers, invested with meaning by centuries of civic activism and decades of debate over new musical genres. By mobilizing these signifiers, dissident citizens called forth their collective past in a struggle to resist sweeping changes to French nationalism.[25] John MacAloon notes this dimension of performance, writing that performances are opportunities in which people "reflect upon and define [themselves], dramatize [their] collective myths and history, present [themselves] with alternatives, and eventually change in some ways while remaining the same in others."[26] In other words, performances allow people to draw upon the past in order to become something new in the present.

Theater scholar Elin Diamond's work also helps explain this dimension of performance, noting that the term describes not only a present doing, but also a thing done in the past. Building on Judith Butler's work with performativity—a process of identity formation that relies upon the repeated citation of societal norms—Diamond notes the importance of understanding the performance's location within a preexisting discursive field. Every performance, she writes, "embeds features of previous performances: gender conventions, racial histories, aesthetic traditions— political and cultural pressures that are consciously and unconsciously acknowledged." In other words, despite the unique ways that French citizens performed operettas, Resistance folk songs, and jazz, all of these acts "contain[ed] traces of other now-absent performances, other now-disappeared scenes" that conditioned the process of identity formation.[27] When Resistance fighters sang the melodies that their Revolutionary forebears sang, for example, their performances were always already linked to the project of envisioning and defending a republican France, rooted in the philosophy of liberal individualism. At a time when traditional norms of national belonging were being uprooted, this historicized quality of performance allowed citizens to mobilize a variety of musical acts that were already imbued with nationalistic meaning in order to root their collective identity in a more familiar, more "traditional" sense of Frenchness. Likewise, past performances of *chanson*, operetta, and jazz—and their attendant debates—invested these genres with meanings that citizens deployed in their struggle to envision and enact the nation and their place within it.

In order to account for the ways in which previous performances constrained and enabled French citizens during the Occupation, I draw upon primary sources amassed in French archives and an array of secondary sources to place Resistance singing within the broader history of French political singing, or what I refer to as France's "performative traditions." Coined by James Jasinski, the term "performative traditions" refers to the historical discourses of action that serve as inventional resources for rhetorical action. Accounting for such traditions requires us to place discursive action within a broader historical context of speaking conventions in order to gain a fuller understanding of its meaning.[28] While Jasinksi's notion of performative traditions accounts for discursive forms, Richard Bauman's discussion of "performance traditions" attends to the modes and practices of performance that set precedents and guidelines for future action.[29] Drawing from both these conceptions, my study treats performative traditions broadly to refer to the modes and norms of discursive and nondiscursive practice that conditioned the meaning of music making in WWII France.

My emphasis on the ways that historical modes of practice conditioned performances of musical resistance is not intended to deny the agency of those who lived through Nazi Occupation and Allied Liberation. As Bauman reminds us, past performances "provide precedents and guidelines for the range of alternatives possible"; they do not *determine* the meaning of current events.[30] In order to account for the ways that meaning is constrained/enabled by both historical practice and the rhetors who repurpose it, I turn to Karlyn Kohrs Campbell's helpful conceptualization of agency. For Campbell, subjects are not autonomous originators of power, but "points of articulation" who, through the process of rhetorical invention, cobble together available resources to formulate "*personae*, subject-positions, and collectivities."[31] Indeed, this capacity to imagine oneself differently than occupying or liberating forces intended was the central tactic employed by French dissidents. Enacting a shift in subject position similar to what Kendall Phillips has termed a "rhetorical maneuver," citizens used popular music as a tool to refuse the kind of Frenchness envisioned by Vichy France, Nazi Germany, or the

United States.[32] Yet, as we will see in the case of the French prisoners of war, musical performances sometimes undermined individual intent. As French soldiers being held prisoner in camps donned ladies' clothes to enact convincing representations of women on the camp stage, for example, they inadvertently undermined the very sexual difference they sought to uphold. In all, then, resistant musical performances illustrate the power and limits of human agency, reminding us of Campbell's astute observation that rhetorical acts have agency that is all their own.[33]

To illuminate the ways that French dissidents mobilized musical culture in order to reclaim French national identity, I maintain focus on the performance of music as my central unit of study. This approach requires me to blend an analysis of the music itself (the lyrics, melody, and rhythm) with an examination of the ways citizens enacted the discourse. After all, as Conquergood cautioned, we cannot easily separate "speech and writing, performance and print" because "these channels of communication constantly overlap, penetrate, and mutually produce one another."[34] Through extensive archival research in three French cities, I have uncovered musical texts and descriptions of performances provided in arrest reports, diaries, newspapers, critical reviews, and testimonials. In Paris, I gathered evidence pertaining to musical resistance under the Nazi Occupation held at the Bibliothèque Nationale, Archives Nationales, Institut d'Histoire du Temps Présent, and Préfecture de Police, including newly available documents concerning French prisoners of war. In the departmental archives of Marseille and Le Havre, the port cities through which millions of American GIs passed after France's liberation, I uncovered primary sources that reconstruct music as a site of struggle against the United States' burgeoning global dominance. When examining the musical works that inspired French citizens, I identify the ways discursive and musical tropes work to delimit the boundaries of belonging along the lines of national identity, race, and gender. By reading these musical tropes across the conditions of their performance, I work to account for the ways that embodied and visual dimensions of musical performance, such as vocal timbre, gestures, and fashion, colored the meaning of the musical act.

In order to understand how citizens drew upon their performative traditions to build rhetorical resources of resistance, I begin by placing popular music within the context of wartime France, when jazz's immense popularity began to eclipse that of traditional French *chanson*. Just as jazz fans celebrated what they considered to be a musical representation of freedom from restrictive social boundaries, however, conservative crit-ics decried jazz as a degenerate art form that would ultimately corrupt the French race. These cultural leaders urged the nation to return to its own musical heritage, to embrace *chansonniers* like Edith Piaf and Maurice Chevalier who would protect and promulgate traditional French values. Reconstructing these debates and grounding them in the political upheaval that followed France's defeat in 1940, I show how key sites of production rendered art songs and *chanson* the true paradigm of French musical tradition while relegating jazz and swing to the periphery of civic belonging. As collaborationist politicians and German occupiers at-tempted to uproot long-held notions of French nationalism and promote fascism, these meanings constrained Vichy's efforts and created rich op-portunities for citizens to defy Nazi ideology and invoke their republican heritage.

In chapter 2, I build on the relationship between French republican-ism and *chanson* to examine the folksinging of the Resistance, a practice through which civilians transformed popular music from a tool of po-litical propaganda into a grassroots means of reclaiming control over the boundaries of national identity. As citizens grew increasingly dissatisfied with Vichy's leadership and more sympathetic to the Resistance, they turned to well-known melodies in order to create songs that characterized the authoritarian government as fundamentally "un-French." Based on analysis of nearly 140 songs, resisters' testimonies, and police reports, I argue that singing functioned as a legitimizing practice through which resisters asserted their right to lead the nation by appropriating popular songs promoted by the Vichy regime. Extending a performative tradition of political singing begun during the French Revolution, resisters sang to assert themselves as protagonists in national history while literally prac-ticing the democratic forms they sought to safeguard.

Yet, the act of singing was not the only musical means by which dis-sidents rhetorically reenvisioned their nation, nor was *chanson* the only genre at their disposal. Chapter 3 takes up the second popular musical genre of the era, jazz, to expand the study beyond the act of clandestine singing to the performance of a jazz-based identity on the streets of Paris. Here, I investigate how upper-middle-class Parisian youth, known as "zazous," mobilized jazz music to fashion a subversive identity that expressed their refusal to serve as national scapegoats and their rejection of fascist political ideology. Drawing upon police records and newspaper reports published in the collaborationist press, I argue that the zazous' performance of swing identity undermined the essentialist racial ideology espoused by Vichy and exposed Nazi Germany's "pure" New Europe as a social construct rather than a scientific truth. In the face of existing anxieties over the effects of *nègre* music on French audiences, Parisian youth employed zazou songs and fashion to mark a racialized swing identity on their white, upper-middle-class, Gentile bodies. In so doing, they transgressed appropriate norms of gender and class and symbolized opposition to collaborationist politics. These "degenerate" musical practices presented powerful evidence, visible on the streets of Paris, that what Vichy and Nazi officials presented as the inescapable natural order was really a set of social constructions that were invented and could be contested. The subversive message conveyed by the youths' performance of zazou identity was not lost on Vichy sympathizers and Nazi authorities, who disciplined the zazous by denigrating them in the press and subjecting them to violent street attacks.

In chapter 4, I move outside the boundaries of Occupied France to show the ways in which music served as a rhetorical resource for the reclamation of individual and national dignity among 1.6 million French soldiers held as prisoners of war in German territory.[35] Imprisoned for the duration of the war and thus unable to protect the nation, these men bore the majority of the guilt for France's shocking defeat, a capitulation that was, in part, understood as a loss of national virility. Despite the humiliation of their capture and the austere conditions of camp life, the prisoners established vibrant theaters where they performed hundreds of shows that featured soldiers in the roles of beautiful young women, pining for the emotional and physical pleasures of true love. Through an analysis of three original operettas and countless theatrical reviews, recovered through extensive archival research, I argue that these musical performances enabled not only expressions of homosociality but also, ironically, reassertions of heterosexual prowess through the objectification of "women," or the closest representation of women that could be conjured from resources in the camps. Alienated by Vichy's politics of collaboration and increasingly worried about their wives' fidelity, the prisoners looked to the romances deployed in the operettas as an allegory for their continued national significance. Thus, the operettas performed virile masculinity not only as a tool for surviving prolonged captivity but also for preparing the prisoners to reunite with a nation they feared no longer required their presence.

Chapter 5 pivots away from the politics of collaboration with the Reich to examine the ways that music worked as a site of political struggle between France and the United States in the aftermath of the Liberation. Indeed, as thousands of American GIs poured through the port cities of Le Havre and Marseille, they coaxed French cooperation with American politics not only through chocolate bars, cigarettes, and Coca-Cola, but with scores of new jazz hits. Playing V-discs in their well-appointed camps, blaring the American Forces Network through the radios of their large Jeeps, and hosting festive swing parties for local French women, the GIs confronted an impoverished, starving French population with exciting new sounds, but also evidence of America's material superiority. By examining reactions to American jazz preserved in testimonies and memoirs, I argue that France's enthusiastic reception worked to exacerbate existing fears over the loss of French cultural and political independence. Yet, just as the GIs' jazz put American hegemony on display, France's own history of jazz advocacy provided tools with which the French could resist. French jazz critics, for example, denied American claims to superiority by attacking the United States on cultural grounds. Highlighting the role of French musicians in legitimizing jazz worldwide and denouncing American racism, these critics worked to refute American claims to dominance by casting France as culturally and ethically superior. At once a sign of American opulence and strength and a source of immense French pride, jazz offered an ideal prism through which to refract the struggle over national dominance in the wake of France's liberation from Nazi rule.

In all, centered on French resistance to Nazi control and American intervention, this project recovers the significance of music as a rhetorical means of survival, resistance, subversion, and national identity construction. By combining a carefully contextualized analysis of music and lyrics with a critical reading of performance practices, it offers a nuanced study of the political force of popular music that complicates our understanding of collaboration and resistance in wartime France. While many scholars have analyzed the dialogue between German sympathizers and French dissidents along the axis of organized political resistance, my study illuminates the creative and cunning ways that individual citizens defied the Occupation outside of formal resistance networks and movements. As music scholars have noted, music is not a thing, but an activity that people do, a mode of communication with vast creative potential and significant social force.[36] Shedding light on music's ability to make arguments, symbolize complex identities, and signify national belonging, this book ultimately uncovers and explicates the critical cultural function of music in times of war.

CHAPTER 1

Repertoires of Resistance

Musical Resources for Reimagining the Nation

———•◆•———

Recounting one of the most brazen acts of open defiance during the Occupation, actor Paul Meurisse described an evening at the A.B.C. music hall in Paris during the winter of 1941. Sitting backstage, awaiting her turn to take the spotlight, Edith Piaf listened to murmurs that rose from the French audience. Onstage, singer Marc Hely was finishing his set with a virulent attack on the English government. The German officers snickered, but the French, many of whom still hoped for a British victory, were not laughing. In response to the expressions of displeasure conveyed by her compatriots, Piaf pushed past the stage manager and into the spotlight. "Le Fanion de la Légion!" she yelled to the conductor. Turning to face the balcony of German officers, Piaf sang the tale of thirty French Legion soldiers holed up in a small fort in the Sahara under attack by enemy "bastards" in a fictitious colonial battle. Forcefully pronouncing each French word, she sang the story of Legion soldiers fighting bravely despite the hunger and casualties that

decimated their numbers. The tempo quickened and the instrumenta-
tion crescendoed at the point in the song's narrative when the enemy
seizes the Legion's flag, a tattered but powerful source of inspiration for
the four soldiers who remain inside the fort. Just when it seems that all
hope of victory is lost, Piaf sang, Legion reinforcements arrive to rescue
their comrades, who have replaced the stolen flag with one drawn "on
their stomachs, black with blood." Piaf's inspired performance drew cries
of affirmation from her French listeners, who erupted into shouts and
whistles. The next day, officials summoned Piaf to their headquarters and
informed her that the song was officially blacklisted.[1]

Piaf's performance was one of the most courageous attempts to use
popular music as a medium for dissent and weapon of resistance in German Occupied France between 1940 and 1944. In a climate of aggressive
censorship and political repression, this kind of open defiance was rare.[2]
Indeed, after its swift fall to Germany in the summer of 1940, France
rallied around its new leader, the World War I hero Philippe Pétain, and
acquiesced to his plan of collaboration. On June 17, Pétain announced
to the nation that he had agreed to head the new government, headquartered in the spa town of Vichy, and was asking the Germans for an
armistice. Arguing that sustained fighting would prove militarily and
politically dangerous, the general urged French people to lay down their
arms and accept France's misfortune. Continued warfare, he claimed,
would result in the utter annihilation of the French military and eliminate the possibility of an independent French government. Furthermore,
Pétain insisted that an armistice would guarantee France an honorable,
though subordinate, place in Hitler's new Europe. The suffering France
would endure under the Germans would be brief, he claimed, and would
provide the opportunity for the nation to shed its purported obsession
with individual liberty. Offering himself up "as a gift to attenuate the
country's deep misfortune," Pétain was met with wild public approval.[3]
Across the nation, people lifted him above the stature of modern-day
king, laying gifts of local soil at his feet, raising his portrait behind church
altars, and comparing him to the country's original savior, Joan of Arc.[4]

On June 22, 1940, the French signed the armistice with Germany at
the same forest in Compiègne where Germany had surrendered in 1918.
The agreement divided the nation into an Occupied zone that would be

controlled directly by Germany and an Unoccupied zone that would be administered by Vichy in collaboration with the Reich.[5] The armistice also required France to accept the demobilization of its military and allowed the nation only a small armistice army of 100,000 troops.[6] Existing weaponry was to be handed over to the conqueror or kept under guard. A particularly severe stipulation demanded that France accept Germany's imprisonment of over 1.6 million prisoners of war—the most men taken prisoner in the history of warfare—until a peace treaty would conclude the war.[7] The armistice also required France to pay the costs of its own occupation, a figure that ranged from 400 million to 500 million francs per day because of rapid inflation. By the end of Vichy's reign, these costs reached 65 billion francs, accounting for 60 percent of the national budget.[8] Although the conditions of the armistice were harsh, Vichy lauded the agreement as a safeguard against the full brunt of German repression. Believing that Germany would win the war, Vichy held that a policy of collaboration was the best way to protect France's overseas possessions and domestic interests during the Occupation and to ensure its prosperous future in Hitler's Europe after the war ended.[9]

Yet, by the time Piaf gave her rousing performance of "Le Fanion de la Légion" at the end of 1941, the promise of Pétain's plan was beginning to fade. Plagued by food and clothing shortages and crippling inflation, French citizens started to recognize the material costs of the armistice with Germany. As Paul Simon, an active member of the Resistance and editor of a clandestine newspaper, wrote in his account of Occupied Paris in 1942, the Germans "are interfering with everything." Whereas in 1871 they "occupied only," now "they have installed themselves in the railways, public administration, police forces, banks, insurance companies, press, wireless, films, law and education. They are everywhere, even in the so-called unoccupied zone," he complained.[10] Set against a backdrop of rising discontent during an unusually cold winter, Piaf's performance gave voice to these feelings of resentment and desire for revenge, even though it made no specific call to resist Nazi Occupation. Indeed, the song did not even chronicle the military exploits of the French army, but told the fictitious tale of foreign *légionnaires*. Given the subject of the song, the performance raises important questions about the power of music as a signifier of nationalism under the Occupation. How did a song about the Foreign

Legion—a military branch made up of mostly non-French soldiers—provoke strong patriotic sentiments in a French audience? What vision of the nation did Piaf's performance conjure? How did the act of singing, often presumed to be apolitical entertainment, help Piaf to launch a substantive critique of France's situation under the Occupation and Vichy?

In order to answer these questions and understand how song served as a potent symbol of the French nation during World War II, we must examine the meanings that had been invested in singing before Piaf took the stage. I argue in this chapter that the French audience's reaction to Piaf's performance was not automatic, but contingent upon a unique cultural history that established singing as a significant mode of democratic participation and transformed leading genres of song into representations of competing constructions of French nationhood. This history, I maintain, was vital to the project of resistance because it endowed music with meanings that responded directly to the collaborationist government's attempts to rearticulate French national identity along political and ideological lines. Begun by France's Revolutionary partisans and continued by the soldiers of the Great War, singing had been prefigured as the natural mode of communication for a democratic people who insisted upon voicing their political grievances. Citizens throughout the nineteenth and twentieth centuries considered *chanson*—the term for popular French songs—to be the musical expression of the nation. Yet, by 1940, another musical genre threatened to eclipse *chanson*. Jazz—considered not only as a symbol of cosmopolitanism and freedom but also as American hegemony, racial impurity, and gender confusion—offered citizens new resources out of which to craft an alternative, "modern" vision of the nation. Ultimately, jazz provided tools for the contestation of Vichy's strict gender and racial norms, while *chanson* remained an ideal inventional resource for the rhetorical marking of French republican nationhood.

Republican Repertoires: Singing from the Revolution to the First World War

The logic behind Piaf's decision to use singing as a mode of protest, and the patriotic nature of her audience's reaction come to light when viewed within the context of French political singing. Indeed, her performance was not an isolated moment of politicized music making, but rather was rooted in the nation's long-standing tradition of republican singing. According to historian Laura Mason, singing became a national mode of civic engagement during the Revolutionary period (1789–1799), providing one of the "most commonly used means of communication" for partisans who were often denied access to the public sphere based on their lack of social standing or education.[11] Easily circulated between print and oral cultures, songs provided a common resource through which all people negotiated pressing political and cultural contestations.[12] By the end of the Revolution, Mason contends, the French no longer sang merely to entertain themselves or voice a common complaint. Instead, singing had become a means by which the French participated in civic life, "evok[ing] a concrete political heritage and a set of claims for a more equitable and inclusive polity."[13] Singing demonstrated that the political sphere was not the possession of political elites, but a contested terrain over which many factions of the population struggled.[14] In this way, French political singing was imbued with republican values from the very start.

Revolutionary song culture proliferated among all classes of French society, taking root in the burgeoning theater culture that emerged in Paris at the end of the eighteenth century. At street theaters designated for lower classes, singers made their performances increasingly relevant to political affairs, emphasizing a set of suggestive lyrics or adding a new, highly charged verse. Because the Comédie Française enjoyed a monopoly on the spoken word, songs allowed performers to circumvent the ban on spoken dialogue and comment directly on the political climate.[15] One critic, for example, reported that a frequently performed play had been amended to include "verses about the federation, which were enthusiastically applauded and an encore was demanded."[16] Even the Opéra, the elite institution so thoroughly connected to the monarchy during the old regime, used song to promulgate the nation's new republican principles. Librettists wrote new lyrics that celebrated ancient democracies in Greece and Rome, and composers expanded the role of the chorus to mirror the new commitment to honoring the collective will of the people. By these means, the Opéra transformed itself, as one group of musicians wrote to the Committee of Public Safety, into "a school of patriotism" where "all those generous and republican passions" could be aroused.[17]

After the fall of the monarchy, the new republican government quickly recognized music's value to the project of nation-building. They made songs and anthems a regular feature of the national festivals, the secular celebrations of republicanism that replaced Catholic festivals. Hiring musicians from the Opéra to perform refined pieces, and commissioning composers to write simple songs that the public could learn easily, festival organizers deployed music as a tool to construct the meaning of republicanism for a populace in transition.[18] Not only were songs important for the content that they could transmit, but their sound, leaders hoped, could distill republican ideology in musical form. A uniquely French, republican style of music would communicate the nation's values, strength, and power not just to French people, but to the rest of the world. In a letter to the National Convention, Marie-Joseph Chénier summarized these arguments in the hopes of creating a national conservatory:

> Therefore, if this art [of music] is useful, if it is moral, and moreover if it is necessary to the armies, to the national festivals and, in the broadest sense, to the splendor of the republic, make haste, Representatives, to assure it a safe haven . . . Germany and vainglorious Italy, vanquished in all other arts by France, but long a victor in this genre alone, have at last met a rival.[19]

For Chénier, the government could hardly afford to ignore the musical education of its citizens. Music, he believed, would spur French troops to imperial conquests, build public support for the new republican government, and establish France as a cultural leader on the world stage.

Yet, French citizens were not merely passive recipients of the songs they heard at the theater or local festival. At the Opéra and the street theaters, citizens interacted with the music they heard, interrupting singers to express their views on current affairs with applause, hisses, or demands for encores.[20] During one performance of *Henry IV's Supper*, for example, a group of market women took to the stage in order to join the cast in the celebration of the king. "These ladies sang and drank to the health of the king, whom they kissed in the person of the actor portraying

Henry," reported one witness.[21] A year later, one newspaper reported that audiences on the other end of the political spectrum took over the singing of one "well-known song," transforming the musician on stage into a cantor who "serves only to strike up the song before his voice is covered by that of the entire audience."[22] Individual citizens incorporated songs into their daily lives, singing "La Marseillaise" and "Ça Ira"—even musical versions of the constitution—together at cafés, on the streets, and in their homes.[23] The content varied as widely as the political factions, but the act of communal singing reinforced enthusiasm for the central tenets of republican ideology: liberty, equality, and fraternity. Easy to memorize, songs could travel without leaving a paper trail, empowering people to voice seditious or unpopular opinions in relative safety. Easily composed, inexpensively printed, and easy to learn by ear, they offered even the low bred and illiterate access to the public sphere.[24] Finally, because songs were performed communally, they allowed citizens to enact the concept of fraternity, that "necessary counterweight to republican equality," that protected the common good against unbridled individualism.[25] In sum, singing with one's countrymen allowed French people to enact their commitment to one another, all while affirming their own equal positions as free individuals.

After the Revolution, the French continued to look to singing as a way to participate in public life. As France struggled to stabilize, songs allowed citizens to interpret events around them and make arguments against the policies of their government. In 1850, for example, a locksmith named Demoulin wrote "subversive" songs that he and his fellow workmen sang in taverns until their arrest:

The National Guard
Are a lot of petticoats
They've marched through the mountains
And they've stolen all the grain.[26]

Because most French remained illiterate during the nineteenth century, songs continued to serve as a means by which people could voice discontent. French people adapted well-known melodies to their own purposes, setting new lyrics to popular tunes that could be easily memorized and performed. The ease with which songs could be taught and learned made them an ideal medium for the formation of national identity. Indeed, it was through songs that rural citizens learned what it meant to be "French" and were assimilated into the modern nation.[27] While songs such as "La Marseillaise" encouraged the spread of the national language, others were mobilized as part of a national education campaign designed to teach "a sense of the fatherland, of civilization, and of moral ideals."[28] In this way, the construction of national identity was accompanied by a tradition of singing. Through their songs, French people reflected upon and built their notions of what it meant to be French.

Political critique and song became even more closely associated during the rise of operetta in the mid-nineteenth century. A reaction against the serious, often tragic nature of opéra-comique, a genre of opera that had evolved into a brutally realistic portrayal of everyday life, operetta aimed to bring gaiety and fun back to the stage. The fathers of the new genre, Hervé and Jacques Offenbach, combined heartfelt sentiment with a sense of play, setting humorous lyrics to lively rhythms and soaring melodies. Their finished works were marked by heavy parody and satire, most of which had to be disguised in the plotlines and identities of old folktales and well-known heroes and villains. Nonetheless, the operettas often did not clear the government censors. When Offenbach submitted *La Grande Duchesse* for review, for example, officials banned its production until he softened the operetta's jabs at the French military.[29] The parodies of political life were made even funnier through saucy, bawdy jokes, often camouflaged through clever innuendo. To make the sexual meaning of these jokes clearer, the performances featured all-female choruses, dressed in revealing clothing, their corsets stuffed with newspaper. In one of Hervé's performances, for example, twelve chorus girls hid in the wings on both sides of the stage and thrust their bare legs into the audience's view. By the standards of the mid-nineteenth century, when women were supposed to keep even their ankles covered, such a display of flesh was considered spectacularly titillating.[30] Commenting on the lewd nature of the operetta, composer Camille Saint-Saëns called it "a daughter of Opéra-Comique, a daughter who has turned out badly, but daughters who have turned out badly are not without charm."[31] Because of its saucy humor and political critique, operetta was immensely popular among French people as they navigated a series of significant political changes—between 1848 and 1870, France's government shifted from the Second Republic to the Second Empire, to the Third Republic (in a span of only twenty-two years) and fought the Franco-Prussian War.

The legacy of French political singing was again called upon in World War I, the *guerre totale* that marshaled the collective efforts of civilians and soldiers alike. Aided by the burgeoning commercial music market, song culture became enormously important on the home front and in the trenches. As historian Charles Rearick has demonstrated, songs were one of the primary discursive means through which national leaders rearticulated French national identity, blending the old vision of the French as "leisure-loving, romantic, sentimental, and patriotic" with one that stressed a more militaristic, determined collective identity.[32] A stream of wartime songs emerged in films, music halls, and on the streets, all praising the brave but good-humored soldiers who valiantly defended the Republic.[33] And songs were perfect for the Great War, writes historian Regina Sweeney, as they were "portable, nondiscriminatory (not restricted to the active reader, for example), adaptable, and polyvalent."[34] For those civilians living away from the front, they strengthened morale, gave meaning to seemingly senseless death, and offered an escape from the deprivations of war. For soldiers embroiled in the fighting, songs offered a means by which to critique the government's rosy spin and speak back to the official propaganda that misrepresented their experiences.[35] Across both segments of the population, Sweeney argues, the beauty of singing was that it helped people fulfill their individual requirements and purposes by connecting them with a national repertoire of "trusted cultural icons, such as prewar conventions, traditional language, and symbols."[36] These conventions lent symbolic meaning to songs, making a certain melody a declaration of patriotism, another a villainous act of treason. As soldiers and civilians tried to negotiate their identities amidst a terrifying, alienating political climate, these symbols became vital to their experience with their nation.[37]

Perhaps the best example of the significance of song culture during the Great War is the song "Quand Madelon." Intended for performance in the music halls on the home front, the song first became popular among soldiers in 1916, the year of the bloody Battle of Verdun. Disgusted by the government's exaggerated talk of heroics and fearful about the rise of the independent, "new" woman, the soldiers found the story of the beautiful and old-fashioned barmaid delightfully devoid of propaganda and pleasantly reassuring. As they sang about Madelon's sparkling eyes, eagerness to please, and flirtatious manner, the men of the trenches distracted themselves from the fighting and eased their fears about changing gender norms by conjuring up images of good-natured, subservient Madelon. By 1917, the song had become a staple of the Parisian music hall. Civilians, also concerned about the new, independent class of employed women, relished the nostalgic, comforting tale of Madelon, calling for performances of the tune in theaters and buying tickets to her film adaptation. Madelon's popularity peaked, though, during the arrival of American soldiers to French soil. "In juxtaposition to the new music from America," as Rearick explains, "'Madelon' was more old-fashioned than ever, continuing an old tradition of French guardsmen's songs about a sweet maidservant and a young soldier."[38] As a representation of a traditional, conservative France, the song helped citizens to maintain control over their national identity in the face of social change, horrific violence, and increasing exposure to American culture.

Having facilitated the rise of French nationalism and sustained citizens over centuries of political turmoil, singing offered a logical mode of communication for those who found themselves suddenly under Nazi repression.[39] Germany defeated France within just six weeks, stupefying a nation that had won the Great War twenty-one years earlier.[40] Like the citizens who risked the guillotine for running afoul of the status quo during the Revolution, French citizens living under Nazi control suddenly saw their civil rights severely curtailed as German administrators began censoring the press, deporting foreigners, and blacklisting Jewish workers and artists. As historian H. R. Kedward has noted, the French slowly realized that they were not "facing a strictly military presence with defined powers and limited intentions but an all-pervading authority which was steadily enlarging its capacity to influence, infiltrate, and control."[41] The Germans intervened at nearly every level of daily life, imposing curfews, cutting electricity, censoring newspapers and radio stations, and forcing cinemas to play reel upon reel of Nazi propaganda.

As Nazi Germany moved to restrict freedom of speech, the tradition of political singing provided a safer means to voice defiance. Decisively beaten and subjected to interferences at all levels of daily life, the French became acutely aware of the Reich's power and their own subordination. Most responded with an attitude of *attentisme* (wait-and-see), attempting to quietly fly under the occupiers' radar until the war's outcome could become clearer. Writer Jean Paulhan described the atmosphere in a letter to a friend: "Have I told you that in the little bistro where I drink a coffee every morning in the company of five or six working men and women from the *quartier* [neighborhood], never the same ones, in all their thousands of complaints over three months I have never heard a single mention of the Germans. It's a matter of prudence, dignity, fear, perhaps a mixture of all three!" In a 1942 letter to his colleague Lucien Febvre, historian Marc Bloch also described the silence of his compatriots: "One of the things that strikes me most today is how impossible it is for any of us to know what his closest neighbor is thinking and doing."[42] These testimonies reveal the pressure on French citizens to fall in line with the Nazi Occupation and avoid any indication of dissatisfaction with the Reich's policies. Singing—an oral mode of communication not dependent on the written word—offered dissident citizens a means to defy the Occupation without leaving an incriminating paper trail.

In addition to being practical, singing was particularly well suited to recovering French national identity in the wake of the Reich's devastating requisition of French industrial and agricultural products.[43] For the French, who took great pride in the nation's renowned cuisine, the seizure of food stood as an assault on national belonging. By the end of the Occupation, the Germans had taken 2.4 million metric tons of wheat, 891,000 metric tons of meat, and 1.4 million hectoliters of milk. The rationing program did little to alleviate hunger. In the winter of 1942–1943, for example, official rations fell to 1,200 calories per day. Even with the help of the black market, the French consumed only an average of 1,500 calories per day.[44] To make matters worse, Germany's interference in the French economy resulted in a severe gap between prices for goods and wages. The Reich's economic controls failed to contain inflation or curtail shortages, so prices rose an average 17 percent each year, for a total of 90 percent over the course of the Occupation. These same economic policies were very successful, however, at keeping wages low. According to historian Lynne Taylor, by the end of the Occupation, two-thirds of

French citizens were unable to purchase the minimum food ration, let alone afford the cost of housing, clothing, and transportation.[45] German data corroborates this figure. In a 1942 study, the Reich noted that prices had increased by 70 percent in France, while wages had only gone up by 30 percent.[46]

Not only did the performative tradition of singing arm French citizens against Nazi Germany's assaults on their national identity, it also offered a resource to defend Frenchness against Vichy's attempts to radically redefine national belonging. Hoping to prepare citizens for their future role in the Reich's Europe, French leaders voted by an overwhelming majority (569 to 80) to abolish the Third Republic (the government in place at the time of France's fall) and allow Pétain to draft a new constitution for a National Revolution.[47] An ideological campaign designed to regenerate the country, the National Revolution held that rebirth depended upon the eradication of liberal individualism, the guiding political philosophy in France since the French Revolution. According to Pétain, democracy had corrupted France, promoting an obsession with individual liberty that made citizens unwilling to sacrifice for the nation's needs.[48] In an article published in the January 1, 1941, edition of the *Revue Universelle*, Pétain railed against individualism, arguing that it destroyed the family by "breaking and loosening attachments," damaged work by "promoting rights to the end of laziness," and endangered the fatherland by "shaking cohesions when it does not totally dissolve unity."[49] For him, individualism was a "parasite" that would prevent any national progress as long as it remained France's dominant political philosophy.[50] In order to return France to its pre-Revolutionary greatness and recover a national emphasis on duty, Pétain held that citizens needed a return to the organic, local communities of family, workplace, and region. To this end, he penned Vichy's 1941 "Principles of the Community," a set of obligations that were to replace the Declaration of Rights of 1789.[51] With this new constitution, Pétain hoped to eradicate France's Revolutionary republican trinity of *liberté, égalité, fraternité*, and replace it with a new order of *travail, famille, patrie* (work, family, fatherland).[52]

Even Nazi and Vichy authorities recognized the link between French national identity and the nation's musical traditions, intervening into French culture in order to reorient the nation's artistic and aesthetic practices toward their own, sometimes competing ideological ends. Indeed, while the Germans had brought France to its knees, crushing its military and decimating its economy, Hitler still felt threatened by France's reputation for cultural superiority. Despite the titans of classical music that Germanic culture had produced, "it was Paris," writes journalist Alan Riding, "not London, not Rome, not Vienna, and certainly not Berlin—that defined style and taste for the region."[53] The problem for German propaganda officials was that French culture enjoyed broad influence outside the boundaries of the nation. In a 1940 report, Fritz Werner, a propaganda official tasked with promoting German classical music, summed up this anxiety. "Over recent centuries," he wrote, "the French have become masters in the art of penetrating other peoples with their cultural policy." The task of German officials, he continued, should be to dismantle French culture, which he compared to a wall dividing Germany and France and impeding entente.[54] To contain French music, the Reich tasked three administrative bodies with overseeing musical policy. The Propaganda Staffel, divided across fifty offices in Paris, controlled six sections of French cultural life, including the radio, cinema, music, theater, fine arts, music hall, and cabaret. The German Embassy and Institut Allemand (German Institute) also held offices in Paris and exercised control over music, promoting the performance of German music composed by Germans instead of Frenchmen. Ultimately, as Fritz Piersig wrote in his 1942 memo for the Propaganda Staffel, the Reich saw musical domination as a way to convince French citizens that "the new Germany is also reclaiming cultural domination in Europe and that it is in the process of proving the justification for this reclamation through its presentations."[55]

French music was also of great concern to the Vichy government, which hoped that a vibrant French musical culture would sustain morale and help demonstrate the nation's vitality. "France was not defeated on the battlefield of the arts," wrote Louis Hautecœur, university professor and director of the Administration of Fine Arts, in a report to the minister of national education. "Our architecture, our painting, our sculpture, [and] our music continue to inspire admiration."[56] In Vichy's eyes, music was a particularly important cultural treasure. Musicologist Leslie Sprout has shown that, while government intervention into the arts was not new under Vichy, the regime did more than other governments to support music specifically. "The allocation for music in the budget of the Administration of Fine Arts increased sharply during the four years of occupation, even as the administration's total budget decreased," she notes. By 1944, funding for music accounted for over a third of the total arts budget.[57]

In the interest of placating the defeated nation, German propaganda officials had to balance requests for more French music with their own cultural objectives. Captain Lucht, chief of the Propaganda office in France, wrote that any concessions made to the French "must be offset by advantages for German cultural propaganda on such a scale that will indisputably substantiate Germany's claims to cultural leadership."[58] In other words, if the Germans allowed the performance of one piece by a French composer, they should require the performance of two German pieces. To ensure proper German representation, officials even regulated the nationality of audience members. The Propaganda office claimed 20 percent of all seats in the theaters—at Vichy's expense—and arranged for tickets to be sold to German military officials at half price. According to Sprout, half the audience was German at the Opéra throughout the Occupation.[59]

Yet, as Piaf demonstrated, singing was a nimble resource that could also be exploited by everyday citizens. One could, as she did, use song to whip an entire auditorium of French citizens into patriotic fervor and walk out of the Nazi cultural offices with only a slapped wrist. This is because France's performative traditions allowed Piaf, and others, to deploy a mode of communication already linked to a republican, democratic tradition. Like her forebears who sang in order to access the public sphere during the nation's most politically contentious times, Piaf presumed a republican right to political discussion—a right that had been prohibited by the Nazi Occupation. As she sang, she deployed her nation's tradition of political singing to argue for a vision of the country that did not square with the politics of collaboration. In choosing the story of soldiers engaged in valiant battle against a seemingly unconquerable foe, Piaf suggested to her listeners that France had not yet been defeated, that the nation, injured as it was, still held hope for a free future. During one of the coldest winters of the Occupation, she invited hungry and exploited French audience members to understand themselves as an extension of those defiant Legion soldiers who crafted makeshift flags out of their own blood, and aligned German officers with the Saharan "bastards" who trespassed on Legion territory. Mobilizing her own working-class ethos, rooted in her meager beginnings as a street singer on the unsavory Rue Pigalle, Piaf sounded determination and rallied her compatriots to believe in France's eventual freedom. Like the heroes of the song, French citizens would endure their suffering under the Occupation while maintaining resolute allegiance to the nation. German authorities, Piaf asserted, were unlawful usurpers who would eventually be overthrown.

Two Genres, Two Frances: Chanson and Jazz versus Vichy's New France

Piaf's defiance at the A.B.C. music hall did not just rely on the performative traditions that imbued singing with republican, nationalistic meaning. In addition to inheriting a mode of communication from her Revolutionary forebears, Piaf was also heir to a genre of French popular song known as *chanson*. Centuries of cultural debates had established *chanson* as the country's truest music, the only authentic expression of French national identity. Historian Jules Michelet, for example, wrote *chanson* into the narrative of the nation, linking the birth of popular song to the healthy French citizen. According to Michelet, the regular rhythmic meter of *chanson* came from the strong heartbeats of the ancient French weavers who first performed it. "The rhythm of the shuttle," he explained, "pushed forth and pulled back at equal intervals, patterned itself to the rhythm of the heart, and by evening it often happened that in addition to the cloth, a hymn or ballad had been woven."[60] Not only did the regular meter of *chanson* suggest a seemingly natural relationship to the French citizens, but its emphasis on diction served to highlight the beauty of the French language. Many singers sang their verses in a recitative delivery, a mixture between speech and song that facilitated the telling of their often complicated stories. Indeed, as American composer Ned Rorem has observed, *chanson* was always as much a "verbal form as a musical form." Indeed, famous *chansonniers* like Piaf were remembered "more as *litterateuse* than as *musicienne*."[61]

The purported musical expression of the fit French body, *chanson* maintained its association with the everyman throughout the nineteenth century. Performed in informal venues known as *café-concerts*, *chansons* maintained their simple melodic structures while evolving into commentaries on the comedic and tragic events of quotidian life. They were easy to learn and provided working men and women with a way to unwind after a long day's work, purge painful emotions, and commiserate over social injustice. Consider the words of one nineteenth-century patron, who described *café-concert* audiences as "intoxicated by the nauseating atmosphere of tobacco and refreshments," and delighted by the ability to "join in the singing of an idiot chorus that the singer bawls out." Most importantly, he wrote, one did not have to abide by traditional modes of decorum while enjoying a *tour de chanson* (round of singing). A person could "keep one's hat on and smoke while drinking a beer," he explained.[62] This boisterous, informal atmosphere propelled *café-concerts* to great popularity. Between 1848 and 1914, there were at least two hundred of these cafés in Paris. By contrast, the number of theaters averaged only forty.[63] Thus, performed in informal spaces designed for and devoted to the themes of economic difficulty and unrequited love, *chanson* maintained its position as the appropriate musical expression of the French body politic.

While new musical genres threatened the popularity of *chanson* in the early twentieth century, it reemerged in the 1930s as an inherently nationalistic genre of music, devoted to celebrating the beauty of Paris and the expansion of the French empire. The economic collapse of 1929 renewed interest in French *chanson* as the old themes of hardship and despair suddenly became germane for citizens coping with unemployment, reduced wages, and inflation. The economy also meant tough times for the luxurious music halls that staged elaborate variety shows, as these venues lost significant audiences. In 1929, for example, France hosted 1,910,000 foreigners, many of whom were wealthy patrons of Parisian entertainment venues. Yet, by 1935, that number had been reduced to only 390,000.[64] As unemployment rose, nationalist concern for French workers resulted in lost jobs for many foreign jazz musicians. The French, as historian Charles Rearick has argued, were "turning inward culturally," showing "new enthusiasm for songs and films about the French people— in French."[65] The market, relieved of the financial burden of employing large orchestras, chorus lines, and dance troupes, pumped out new songs about old France. Themes were nostalgic, celebrating long walks along the Seine with one's lover, or a stolen kiss in front of the Eiffel Tower. In an attempt to revive confidence in France's future, songs also celebrated the nation's imperial history. Perhaps inspired by the 1931 Exposition Coloniale Internationale, an exhibit designed to give citizens the experience of traveling to the Casbah in Algiers or a palace in Morocco, songs took listeners on a musical journey beyond the hexagon. The Foreign Legion drew particular interest, as the nation romanticized the adventures of its imperialist soldiers. In 1936, Marie Dubas recorded "Le Fanion de la Légion," the song that Piaf would choose for her defiant performance at A.B.C. music hall in 1941.

Having emerged as the "natural" expression of true French citizens, *chanson* offered an ideal rhetorical resource for the subversion of Vichy's new vision of France. While Vichy's National Revolution failed to resonate strongly with many French people (for whom France's legacy of republicanism was central to their vision of the nation), Pétain was met with widespread support. The shock and pain of military loss, coupled with the Third Republic's unpopularity, helped the former general assume the role of redemptive savior.[66] His own illustrious war career offered compelling evidence of his ability to lead France through the Occupation. Having proven his patriotism and courage on the battlefields of the Great War, Pétain presented himself as the noble and wise grandfather of the nation, a benign patriarch who would guide his children to prosperity. Official Vichy propaganda strengthened his political authority by combining this image with claims of Pétain's essential Frenchness. Not only was he a tested military leader, this propaganda claimed, but he was the physical embodiment of French culture and values. Consider this widely circulated poster in which a stately portrait of Pétain appears atop a pointed caption (figure 1). "Are you more French than he is?" the poster asks. The obvious answer was "no." Pétain, the propaganda confidently asserted, was the most authentic embodiment of French ethnicity and French values and, therefore, the only legitimate head of state. Armed with the ethos of an infallible leader, Pétain remained popular throughout the war, especially during its first two years. Even those who disagreed with the armistice trusted him, believing that he was secretly playing a double

Figure 1. Vichy propaganda poster.

game with Germany, biding his time until the moment when he would deliver a fatal blow to the occupiers.[67]

In the context of Vichy's attempts to radically refashion French national identity, *chanson* stood as a powerful tool with which French citizens could express continued devotion to the traditional order. Even though Piaf's performance of "Le Fanion de la Légion" made no explicit reference to the old trinity of *liberté, égalité, fraternité*, it sounded traditional Frenchness. Indeed, when Piaf took to the stage, she not only mobilized a performative tradition that was already aligned with France's republican values, but she sang in the tradition of those French workers whose healthy heartbeats allegedly gave rise to the nation's popular songs. Singing in a genre that had evolved as a cathartic response to the collective hard times of *le peuple*, Piaf vented French frustration through the allegory of the Foreign Legion soldiers, men who accepted their apparent demise with a sense of fatalism and patriotic dignity. A *chanteuse* par excellence, she emphasized the

French text, using recitative delivery to articulate each word with impeccable diction in order to evoke a proud, defiant spirit. Most importantly, as she sang in the musical vernacular of the French nation, she identified herself as a true patriot and contested the national belonging of those who would accept the politics of collaboration. By asserting herself as a true French citizen, Piaf cast doubt on Pétain's Frenchness and rejected the authenticity of his claims to political legitimacy.

While *chanson* stood as a marker of traditional Frenchness, citizens also had jazz at their disposal, a musical marker of a more modern and cosmopolitan France. Indeed, despite its popularity throughout the nineteenth century and reemergence in the 1930s, *chanson* lost audiences during the early twentieth century when African American soldiers brought jazz to Europe during the Great War. Jazz music soared in popularity in 1920s France, quickly replacing *chanson* as the nation's most beloved genre of popular music. According to Matthew Jordan, jazz was so pervasive that as early as 1925, it was common to hear the music streaming out of open apartment windows while strolling down the streets of Paris.[68] Indeed, the rising availability of radios, whose sales increased from 3,200,000 in 1936 to 4,700,000 at the end of 1939, helped jazz find new audiences.[69] The burgeoning film industry, whose profits increased by 45 percent between 1934 and 1938, also featured elaborate musical routines.[70] And French people purchased sheet music and recordings to enjoy at home. The 1936 hit song "Au Lycée Papillon," for example, sold over 100,000 copies of sheet music, and 12,000 records sold in less than three months. More than 200,000 copies of the song sold in 1937.[71] Performed by black American musicians and disseminated through improved technologies, jazz represented the kind of cosmopolitanism that was possible in a postwar world. And while this vision of universal fraternity was certainly not in line with the Nazi platform, France's love of jazz was so widespread that even the Reich did not attempt to forbid it when they conquered the nation in 1940. Despite the ban on American jazz after the United States entered the war, French jazz proliferated throughout the Occupation, flourishing in the absence of competition from across the Atlantic.[72]

For many of the beleaguered, war-weary French, jazz's syncopated rhythms and upbeat tempo also signaled opportunities for societal transformation. Praised even by French cultural critics, jazz shook old, aristocratic notions of beauty, suggesting that artistic boundaries were more porous than previously thought. Whereas critics of high art music had previously embraced strict rules relating to musical composition, jazz music illustrated that classical technique was not the only path to musical excellence. Jean Cocteau, for example, argued that jazz could not be measured by traditional standards. Based on simplicity, instead of "numbers and geometry," the new American music was a soothing balm to "the fatigue of our ears."[73] Indeed, for critics, jazz's syncopated rhythms and improvisation conveyed a sense of freedom and liberation from traditional rules of harmony and voice leading. Film and music critic Emile Vuillermoz hailed jazz as a democratic departure from the old, stuffy music, that "secret and confidential language of an aristocracy particularly proud of its privileges."[74] Jazz, these critics agreed, should be "felt" instead of critically appraised and evaluated.[75] In short, jazz demonstrated that the norms of French cultural excellence were not absolute and challenged classical musicians' monopoly on good music.

Jazz's close association with black Americans led cultural critics to link the genre to racialized tropes of primitivism. For audiences scarred by "civilized" warfare, they argued, jazz offered a welcome return to nature. Indeed, early after its appearance in France, critics and enthusiasts alike began to link jazz to the black body, arguing that only black musicians possessed the unique physiology to play it authentically. For conductor Ernst-Alexandre Ansermet, "the Negro . . . discovers a whole series of effects produced by the lips alone, which make it a new instrument. There is a Negro way of playing the violin, a Negro way of singing."[76] Even the French language conveyed a physiological connection between blacks and jazz. According to the *Littré* dictionary, the term *syncope* first emerged to describe the medical condition of an irregular, sickly heartbeat. Unlike the strong heartbeats that marked Jules Michelet's industrious ancient weavers, *syncope* occurred in the "primitive" black body, not the healthy French body.[77] Robust French citizens, possessing regular heartbeats, would naturally express themselves in the regular rhythm of *chanson*, he held. These linguistic connotations prefigured discussions of jazz as a uniquely black music, paving the way for critics like musicologist Blaise Pesquinne to describe it as the "artistic manifestation of a race that is different from our own."[78]

Of course, not all French people celebrated jazz's association with modernism and black culture. Traditionalists who hoped to preserve class hierarchy and strict gender norms feared that jazz would destabilize French society. Not only did the democratic structure of improvisation and the loosening of standards of artistic beauty threaten social order, but even the experience of attending a jazz performance led to the erosion of class difference. Indeed, new, elaborate music halls deliberately sought to equalize the economic standing of their patrons, offering tickets at affordable prices and arranging patrons in visually identical seating sections. The ideal music hall, according to drama critic Legrand Chabrier, should treat patrons "as equally as possible, this is to say that the series of seats should be as little distinct as possible, not formed into separate groups."[79] Moreover, the jazz concert was also criticized as a destroyer of proper gender identity. In a column for the newspaper *La Revue de Paris*, Albert Flament expressed his inability to identify the genders of the bodies he saw dancing at the music hall, asking, "Is this the bust of a woman which glides, under this ghastly head of a young man, jawbone drubbed with ashes? Is this the body of a man, under the mask of this alert sexagenarian, coifed with a green Tyrolean hat?"[80] Columnist Gustave Fréjaville also criticized jazz concerts for their alleged destabilization of the natural order, writing that "the most precious joy for the music hall fan is, in effect, to dream while awake, to see impossible things realized." Jazz enthusiasts, he charged, took pleasure in imagining "that the sky and trees are yellow," that women's "lips are too red, their eyes too black or blue."[81] In short, jazz led to a dangerous blurring of a priori distinctions between rich and poor, man and woman.

Linked to African American culture and representative of modernism, jazz was also deemed a foreign threat to French culture. Concerned for the future of the "race," conservative critics rushed to the defense of the *chanson* genre, lamenting the decline of music sung for French everymen in the French language. In a 1926 column for the cultural weekly *Comoedia*, one man complained that only two out of ten songs performed on the music hall stage were sung in French, a trend that represented the "slow, sure death of French song."[82] Fréjaville urged French singers to reprise the performance of the traditional *tour de chant*, so that the audience could experience the collectivity of their "hearts beat[ing] to a single rhythm and respond[ing] to each intonation by the singer."[83] By contrast, jazz, an "uncivilized" and "racially degenerate" musical genre, would allegedly slowly change French temperament and behavior, leading to the death of the nation. In an article for a conservative newspaper, Yvonne Moustiers predicted that "the death of [French] song would be to an extent the death of the French spirit."[84]

As a symbol of modernity, cosmopolitanism, and transgressive social norms, jazz offered enterprising citizens another musical tool to level against the new conservative social order imposed by Vichy. In the attempt to reverse the "disastrous" effects of modernity, Vichy paired its rearticulation of French political philosophy with the aggressive promotion of traditional values. Specifically, Vichy decried the erosion of strictly defined gender identities that had occurred in the interwar period and called upon citizens to recognize innate sexual difference.[85] Only by rejecting the current "civilization without sexes"—to borrow Mary Louise Roberts's term—could French people return to traditional family values and learn to respect church and state authority.[86] Citizens were to honor and obey the Catholic Church, women were to stay at home and devote themselves to raising children, and men were to assume their rightful place at the helm of their families and local communities. To facilitate a return to these social norms, Vichy passed legislation that promoted conservative religious teaching in French schools. For example, in November 1940, a law passed that allowed lessons on "duties to God" to be added to the public curriculum. In January 1940, local governments were required to subsidize Catholic schools. In January 1941, Catholic instruction was made available as an elective in public schools.[87] Vichy also used its legislative powers to limit women's civil rights. An October 11, 1940, law, for example, mandated that married women whose husbands could support them be fired from their public sector jobs.[88] In April 1942, another law made divorce more difficult to obtain.[89] Accompanied by propaganda attacks on contraception and abortion, both of which had already been restricted or prohibited during the interwar period, these laws were powerful instruments by which Vichy worked to reintroduce "traditional" French values among its purportedly "modern" citizens.[90] "The script was familiar," writes historian Miranda Pollard, "taken from the stock repertoire of right-wing ideology."[91]

One of the most popular propaganda posters for the National Revolution expresses Vichy's objectives in clear visual imagery, representing old and new France as two different houses (figure 2). On the left, the artist depicts Republican France as a crumbling shack, ill-supported by a weak foundation of Laziness, Demagogy, and Internationalism. The house crashes down in a billow of red smoke, an allusion to both the communist forces that were allegedly eroding French stability and the internal bleeding suffered by the nation. A Jewish Star hangs over the collapsing house, aligning France's demise with its Jewish population and capitalistic greed. On the right, the artist depicts Vichy's New France as a paradigm of order and stability. The image recalls the biblical instruction to build one's life on the rock, or the sturdy and timeless teachings of Jesus Christ, rather than on sand, or the fleeting and superficial values of nonbelievers.[92] Like the biblical wise man who built his house on the rock, the poster asserted, Vichy had anchored France upon the solid foundation of Work, Family, and Fatherland, supported by the pillars of school, artisanry, peasantry, and the Legion. Marshal Pétain, symbolized by the six stars of his insignia, watches over the stable French house, kept in good order by the woman who emerges from the shutters, presumably letting fresh air into her clean and tidy home. As Pollard notes, this new representation of Vichy France is, above all, inward-looking, constructed in opposition to what Vichy considered an overly cosmopolitan and modern Republic.[93]

Ultimately, as a symbol of modernity and more liberal norms of race and gender, jazz was uniquely positioned to argue against Vichy's vision of a pre-Revolutionary, Catholic France. As the collaborationist government embraced the radical racism of fascist Germany, called citizens to honor religious teachings, and urged women to return to domesticity, jazz stood in direct contrast to the aims of the National Revolution. Trading Louis Armstrong records, organizing clandestine dance parties, and reading tracts about the liberatory potential of improvisational music, jazz lovers rejected Vichy's construction of the nation and chose, instead, a new, cosmopolitan France where black and white musicians could at least perform together, even if they could not stand on an equal social footing, and where women could at least dream of a life beyond the home, even if substantial barriers impeded their professional success.

Figure 2. Poster for the National Revolution by R. Vachet.

Conclusion

In sum, this history shows that French citizens living under the German Occupation had at their disposal a performative tradition of republican singing and two distinct genres of popular music. *Chanson*, the nation's oldest popular genre, remained a marker of nationalism, reemerging as the economic recession of the 1930s renewed its relevance to struggling citizens. Imbued with meaning by both fans and critics, jazz stood as a potent symbol of modernism, cosmopolitanism, freedom, racial impurity, and foreignness. As well-known representatives of the nation's values, these genres offered inventional resources out of which dissident citizens could build political identities and critiques. Indeed, when Piaf took the stage to protest the mockery of the British government and to rally her audience to patriotic defiance of the German Occupation, she appropriated not only a song about proud French Legionnaires, but the *chanson* genre and its attendant meanings. Singing the simple music of able-bodied French workers, she bolstered her position as a French national and claimed the right to speak. Popular music was not just the tool of professional singers, but was performed by everyday citizens who strove to fashion resistance to both German occupiers and American liberators. Indeed, as Piaf left her meeting with the German censor, French Resistance fighters were combing the repertoire of French folk song, appropriating the beloved and well-known melodies of *chanson* to write their own critiques of Vichy's politics. Characterized as out-of-touch and misguided young boys, France's Resistance fighters wove musical culture into the fabric of their everyday lives, mining the realm of popular music for tools with which to delegitimize Vichy's leadership and imagine themselves as France's true guardians.

CHAPTER 2

La France en Chantant

The Rhetorical Construction of French Identity in Songs of the Resistance Movement

———•◆•———

On November 11, 1940, more than three thousand Parisian high school and college students gathered around the Arc de Triomphe to stage the first public protest of the German occupation of France.[1] At 8:30 a.m., they began marching down the Champs Elysées, where five months earlier the Germans had paraded in triumph. As they marched, the students yelled subversively, "Long live de Gaulle!," "Long live France!"[2] Reflecting the patriotic character of the protest, some young people wore tricolor rosettes on the lapels of their jackets and nearly all sang "La Marseillaise," the French national anthem, which had recently been banned by the Nazis.[3] In the early evening, German soldiers arrested the protesters and transported them to Paris police headquarters for sentencing.[4] Upon being questioned by police, high school student Robert Monnerary told the authorities that he did not know why he had been arrested because he "didn't sing or shout." Similarly, René Chuzeville told the police that he was simply walking through the streets with friends from his school and had not sung "La Marseillaise" or "protested in any way."[5] The facts that the arrested students consistently denied engaging in the act of singing the French national anthem, that the protesters joined in singing the anthem as an act of resistance, and that Nazis had outlawed the song in the first place all betray the multitudinous ways in which the performance of "La Marseillaise" exerted rhetorical power in Occupied France.

Despite the country's swift defeat and the harsh terms of the armistice, the students mobilized the principal musical representation of national strength and determination in order to give voice to their hopes of a free France. Originally written as a rallying cry for French Revolutionaries, "La Marseillaise" evoked the memory of the struggle that had come to define France's national character, and called citizens to honor the legacy of its fallen patriots. Indeed, as they sang, the students likened the German occupiers to those eighteenth-century Austrian and Prussian "tyrants" who would dictate France's future, and imagined themselves as the faithful partisans who would eventually carry the nation to "triumph and glory." In this way, the French national anthem served as a powerful and widely used cultural tool in the psychological fight against German Occupation; yet it was just one of the hundreds of songs sung and circulated by members of the French Resistance during the country's *années noires* (dark years). Whistled over the clanking of tools while sabotaging trains, sung in secrecy while hiding in caves, hummed to fight despair while interred in German prison camps, French folk songs sustained Resistance fighters throughout their struggle against the Nazis and their collaborators.

Folk songs, I shall demonstrate, served as a key form of cultural resistance that ideologized, inspired, and emboldened Resistance fighters in France's war against Hitler. As resisters sang, they reprised a performative tradition of French political singing begun during the French Revolution. By extending this performative tradition of political singing, resisters asserted themselves as protagonists in national history while literally practicing the democratic forms they sought to safeguard. The discursive features of the songs strengthened resisters' claims to national identity. Deploying traditional national narratives, appeals to soldierly masculinity, and parody, Resistance songs, I maintain, defined the individuals who opposed German Occupation as members of a transhistorical community of French heroes. In this way, the songs sought to represent resisters as the guardians of true "Frenchness," an identity that excluded the Vichy regime from the national community and robbed it of its political legitimacy. Under the threat of fascism and the material constraints of war, the performance of Resistance songs allowed partisans a means to assert political power and maintain influence in the public sphere when other forms of communication were unavailable.

These conclusions are based on an analysis of 137 folk songs, most of which were sung—and in this way, circulated—throughout France from 1940 to 1944. Because being caught with subversive printed materials could lead to execution, resisters rarely committed songs to paper, creating a challenge for the researcher intent on finding primary sources.[6] Despite the ephemeral nature of Resistance singing during the war, my archival efforts in the Bibliothèque Nationale and the Institut d'Histoire du Temps Présent have uncovered the lyrics and melodies of thirty songs sung by Resistance fighters from 1940 to 1944, including an unpublished collection compiled by Jean Maurin, a Resistance fighter in the Val d'Allier region.[7] These newfound texts significantly expand upon existing collections of Resistance songs, most of which are contained in two anthologies, *La Résistance en chantant* and *Paroles et musique: Les chansons et la Deuxième Guerre mondiale*.[8] The texts that I have recovered and those available in the anthologies circulated through a variety of media and in multiple contexts. Some songs gained national popularity while others remained regional, their circulation documented in personal memoirs.[9] Some were heard over the radio while others were composed and distributed orally between factions of the Resistance. By examining both the songs written by members of the Resistance and those broadcast over the BBC, my analysis draws upon songs that circulated regionally as well as nationally.

Despite the importance of folk songs to the success of the Resistance movement, no scholar has analyzed how they functioned rhetorically.[10] This chapter treats seriously the voices of Resistance singers, showing the ways the act of singing constructed them as guardians of a traditional French republicanism at a time when national identity was in flux. By situating the songs within the sociopolitical context of WWII France, I uncover the ways that resisters used a longstanding mode of political singing to connect resisters to an idealized, historical French community. The performance of Resistance songs, I maintain, defined members of the Resistance as the guardians of traditional French values and descendants of France's heroes while excluding Vichy from the nation and subverting the government's claim to political authority.

Fallen France: Vichy, the Resistance, and Public Opinion

While Pétain's National Revolution failed to resonate strongly with many French people for whom France's legacy of republicanism was a central tenet of French nationhood, the Vichy regime installed itself quite easily due to the unpopularity of the Third Republic. The shock and pain of defeat turned the Republic into a handy scapegoat, while Pétain settled into his role as redemptive savior.[11] Seeking to ease the transition to an entirely new political ideology, Pétain's supporters capitalized on his image as France's truest patriot, grounding the legitimacy of his political authority in his "Frenchness."

As a result of Pétain's popularity, few people actively resisted Vichy's collaboration with Germany during the first two years of the Occupation.[12] Even those who disagreed with the decision to sign the armistice were unlikely to oppose Vichy and Germany due to their confidence in Pétain, uncertainty about the war's outcome, and fear of German retaliation. In 1942, French essayist Jean Guéhenno documented the anxiety that paralyzed many, calling France a country that was "nothing but a frightened protoplasm." Even as Allied victory became more certain, many French people were haunted by "the same fear, the same rot" that accompanied the beginning of the war. "The people are terrified," Guéhenno complained in 1944. "They are wary of everything, the Germans, the English, the Russians; all they can think about is 'getting through' without coming to any harm." "It is as if," he wrote, "to the great mass of this country, nothing matters except survival, at any price."[13] Certainly, most French people's response to the war was to try to live as normally as possible. Trusting in Pétain's alleged plan to throw off Germany, many kept beneath the radar for the entire Occupation.

Despite overwhelming support for collaboration with the Nazis, a tiny segment of the French population did rebel against Vichy's policy. During the first two years of the Occupation, resistance was initiated by small groups of like-minded friends and family, most of whom knew nothing of each other's existence or of Charles de Gaulle's efforts to coordinate an organized Resistance in London. Slowly, these localized, small groups of resisters formed larger groups that eventually became the well-known movements and networks of the French Resistance. In the Occupied zone, the movements were smaller and more self-conscious due to the German presence. Their main goal was to change attitudes among the population, an objective pursued primarily through clandestine newspapers and pamphlets that encouraged citizens to *narguer* (irritate) the Germans by any means possible.[14] Far more secretive, the networks had specific military objectives such as collecting intelligence, executing sabotage, and organizing escape routes. They were eventually linked to Allied intelligence groups, including the Free French in London, the British intelligence service, and the Special Operations Executive, Britain's program to undermine Germany in occupied Europe with specially trained agents. In addition to the movements and networks, Resistance groups also formed more militant units called *maquis*, the French word for "a group of dense shrubs or bush," which reflected their practice of hiding in the countryside in order to resist German Occupation through acts of sabotage and violence. These units began appearing in 1942 and were first composed of Jews fleeing Vichy authorities, deserters from Vichy work camps, and young men trying to escape mandatory work service in Germany.[15]

While public memory has romantically swelled the numbers involved in the various resistance groups known collectively as the French Resistance, historians agree that membership was actually quite small. Throughout the Occupation, joining the active Resistance was a difficult choice to make. In the beginning, the public's trust resided so fully with Pétain's leadership and with Germany's imminent victory that the few French who refused to accept German Occupation were often considered to be absurd, idealistic rebels. Claude Bourdet, a leader of the "Combat" movement, suggested that resisters were those eccentrics who had already "broken with their social and professional milieu." Jean Cassou, another resister, claimed that they were those "without possessions, without inheritance or title, with no fixed home, no social status, no real profession."[16] So great were the risks associated with resistance that those who chose it needed to have nothing to lose. Even in relationships where political ideologies did not clash, joining the Resistance required a break with friends and family. Because continued communication put resisters and their loved ones in danger, many stopped speaking to their friends and family. Social isolation was particularly burdensome among members of the *maquis* who had to remain physically removed from their homes in order to escape deportation to German work camps. Thus, for a variety of resisters, Resistance activity was often a lonely endeavor.[17]

Despite Pétain's popularity, the events of 1942–1943 caused public support to shift against Vichy's policy of collaboration. As hundreds of thousands of French men and women were rounded up for tours of forced labor in Germany, increasing food shortages left entire regions without bread and meat, and German soldiers pushed past the demarcation line to occupy the free zone, Vichy's policy of collaboration began to lose its appeal. Now under the full brunt of German Occupation, French citizens grew hostile to Vichy's policies. The entrance of the United States into the war at the end of 1941 and mounting Allied victories, both of which began to forecast the defeat of Germany, strengthened this opposition and made public opinion more sympathetic to Resistance efforts.[18]

Yet, even this change in popular opinion did not make joining the Resistance a popular choice. Indeed, just when the public became suspicious of Vichy's policies, the government increased its efforts to stamp out partisan activities, setting action against the Resistance as the new gauge of collaboration with the Reich. Indeed, by 1942, Vichy had deported so many of France's Jews and foreigners that the government no longer had sufficient leverage at Germany's bargaining table. Faced with the threat of losing authority in the Unoccupied zone, Vichy targeted the Resistance, offering police action against its members as evidence of cooperation with the Third Reich.[19] As a result, many resisters were arrested, tortured, and executed. Those who escaped could not rejoin their units, as their colleagues feared that they would lead police to the group. In addition to strengthening police action against the Resistance, Vichy launched a propaganda campaign, conducted through the medium of the radio. Led by collaborationist politician Philippe Henriot, Vichy's radio broadcasts simultaneously characterized Resistance fighters as naive, misguided adolescents and dangerous outlaws from whom the French needed protection. One broadcast, for example, called the *maquis* "a bunch of bandits and thieves and also, alas, some sincere young boys, abused by the fallacious propaganda from London." These foolish youngsters, the announcer predicted, "will soon realize the enormous material superiority of Germany, and they will be condemned to stay in their camouflage in their forest, in their cavern, and in their den, waiting for a landing that will never come."[20] Thus, Vichy's vicious police and propaganda attacks tempered the popularity of the Resistance. While some citizens may have supported the cause of the Resistance, many were simply too afraid to join. Others continued to trust Pétain's portrayal of resisters as dangerous ideologues who were best avoided.

Despite subsequent romanticizations of the French Resistance, those who participated were the object of the public's scorn and Vichy's disdain. In the early years of the Occupation, popular opinion rested overwhelmingly with Pétain. Trusting in their Christ-like figure to protect them from the full force of German repression, the French focused their efforts on resuming life as usual. Those who chose to resist often were ostracized from their communities and families. Some were characterized as maladjusted outsiders; others lost contact with their friends and family to try and protect them from the Germans. Just as public opinion began to change in favor of the Resistance, Resistance fighters found themselves the target of an aggressive French police hunt and maligning propaganda campaign. In the face of these hardships, how was the Resistance to establish any sort of political legitimacy? How were the emerging Resistance fighters to imagine themselves as France's rightful political leaders when public support favored the collaborationist Pétain? How were they to craft a positive collective identity for themselves and the French people in the face of Vichy's slanderous propaganda? How were they to sustain morale in the face of the torture and execution of their comrades? A crucial means employed by the French Resistance to overcome these challenges was the singing of folk songs. Through the performance of these songs, resisters recited and disseminated a legitimizing discourse that allowed them to imagine themselves, and to be imagined by their fellow citizens, as the true arbiters of French culture and values.

Resistance Singing: A Historically Situated Performance Practice

In order to understand the rhetorical function of Resistance singing, we must first reconnect music with its performance. As musicologist Christopher Small wrote in his influential book *Musicking*, "music is not a thing at all but an activity, something that people do."[21] Small's stress on the act of making music reminds us that songs are not simply composed of lyrics and melodies, but instead make up a complex medium of communication that combines textual elements with embodied, contextualized performance. Indeed, more than simply constructing a repertoire of songs, Resistance musical culture extended the historical practice of political singing begun by France's Revolutionary ancestors and continued by the victorious soldiers of the Great War. These historical practices of French singing established the performance of songs as a means by which French citizens could participate in democratic life and in the construction of French republicanism. By 1940, national singing was not a form of entertainment, but a mode of action directly linked to the preservation of national identity. This performative tradition is vital to understanding singing in the French Resistance, as the behavioral structures and patterns of political singing that resisters inherited from their forebears worked alongside the songs' explicit textual appeals to construct the rebels as guardians of French republicanism. Indeed, it was this combination of mutually reinforcing performance practices and textual appeals that made the singing of Resistance songs so powerful in the battle for political legitimacy, and so threatening in the eyes of the occupying forces.

At one level, the songs functioned in a manner not unlike print culture in constituting nation-states in the nineteenth century. As Benedict Anderson notes, nothing played a greater role in the development of the modern nation-state than "print-capitalism, which made it possible for rapidly growing numbers of people to think about themselves, and to relate themselves to others."[22] Songs, like national languages, newspapers, and speeches, were among the symbols through which people identified themselves as members of the nation. At another level, however, singing—unlike print media or even public address—could not be as easily mobilized by the hierarchical structures of the nation-state because of its participatory nature. Unlike Robespierre's speeches at the National Assembly in which one rhetor addressed an audience, the performance of these songs collapsed the divide between speaker and audience. The peasants and aspiring politicians who sang Revolutionary songs participated in the creation of the rhetorical message; they were not merely recipients of it. And while Robespierre's speeches were delivered once, songs were sung repeatedly, serving new and different purposes at each performance. Therefore, singing was a radically democratic performance practice that allowed individual participants to simultaneously contribute to the meaning of the rhetorical act and derive their own unique interpretations of it.

By appropriating this historical performance mode, Resistance singers practiced the very republicanism they sought to embody. The act of patriotic, nonhierarchical singing violated the Vichy regime's emphasis on obedience and service and marked singers as republican citizens, struggling to restore the tenets of liberal individualism. Whether or not they were aware of the rhetorical function of their performances, evidence from the personal memoirs of Resistance fighters demonstrates that they intended to safeguard republican traditions. For example, Alban Vistel wrote that his decision to participate in the Resistance had been a "reaction of individual honor" and "a victorious refusal of any historical determinism."[23] Many articulated their adherence to natural rights in opposition to the anti-Semitism embraced by Vichy and Germany. Like Jules-Geraud Saliège, the archbishop of Toulouse, these resisters believed that people were governed by "human morality which imposes duties and recognizes rights. These duties and rights are derived from the nature of man . . . it is in the power of no mortal to suppress them."[24] Engaging the widely held conception of France as a historic champion of human liberty, these resisters combined patriotism with reverence for individualism. Resisters had a "common patrimony" that bequeathed to them a "profound feeling for human dignity," as the mayor of Toulouse stated in 1944.[25] Because political singing had developed in France as a decentralized mode of action tied to the preservation of republican ideals, it offered resisters a perfect inventional resource for the reclamation of a traditional national identity.

Fragmentary evidence of singing in the French Resistance gathered from police reports and resisters' testimonies attests to the capacity of singing to mark French people as uncompromising opponents of collaboration. As the story of the protest on November 11, 1940, reveals, the singing of the French national anthem, "La Marseillaise," constituted a diverse group of high school and college students as unyielding French patriots who would never submit to German rule. These reports and others repeatedly demonstrate that the act of singing allowed police and citizens to identify resisters. A police report on August 17, 1941, documents the attempted arrest of 150 young people who sang the national anthem at Paris's Place du Chateau Rouge.[26] On August 20, 1941, authorities were alerted that four French people had been heard singing the national anthem behind the backs of three German soldiers at Place d'Italie, one of Paris's largest squares. The accused singers ran off before an arrest could be made.[27]

Perhaps the most moving testament to the power of singing to mark citizens as guardians of a republican France can be found in the records of singing in German prisons and concentration camps. Roger Tabar, a prisoner of war from Paris, composed songs of resistance for his fellow Frenchmen. Even within the prison walls, Tabar argued that resistance was possible through singing. "All the prisoners weren't admirers of Pétain," he said, "nor were they collaborators like many who lived in Paris." Tabar's songs allowed these prisoners to enact their resistance, to "demoralize the Germans" and mark themselves as members of the Resistance.[28] Tabar's testimony is only one of many that emphasize the role of singing in linking prisoners to a larger community of resisters. For example, two women who were prisoners at the Ravensbrück concentration camp remember singing the Resistance anthem "Le Chant des Partisans" to "feel at home even in the heart of Germany" and "to reinforce our solidarity, despite our political, religious, and social differences."[29] Other prisoners sang "Le Chant des Partisans" before being killed. Maurice Druon, one of the song's lyricists, recalls that a group of prisoners sang the anthem before being executed by a firing squad.[30] Composer Anna Marly remembers that two prisoners sang it while they dug their own grave before being shot by the German guards.[31] A musical symbol of French resolve and revolutionary spirit, "Le Chant des Partisans" offered a final means by which to defy German authority and express loyalty to France. Thus, while singing held myriad meanings in these moments, one of its powers was to symbolically connect prisoners to an idealized French nation in moments of deep despair, loneliness, and mortal danger.

A form of rhetoric available to all classes of people, singing provided French citizens with a participatory, profoundly democratic form of communication that mirrored their republican values. As all singers participated in performance, the hierarchical divide between rhetor and audience collapsed, allowing them to enact republican ideals. If, however, the performance of songs was to be an effective strategy for seizing of political authority, resisters needed additional means by which to claim national identity for themselves and exclude Vichy from the nation's fold. Thus, the discursive and musical tropes discussed in the next section were vital to the rhetoric of Resistance singing as they worked to construct resisters as ideal French citizens. The use of lyrics and music grounded in the musical tradition of France transformed the radically decentralized and democratic practice of communal singing into a means of marking resisters as the only true French and denying the Frenchness of Vichy. Ultimately, singing allowed resisters to negotiate two seemingly conflicting goals: the inclusive act of embodying brotherly republicanism and the exclusive act of rejecting those they considered foreign to the nation.

La France en Chantant: *The Discursive Construction of "Frenchness"*

In the winter of 1942, Anna Marly, a French composer of Russian origins, wrote the music and Russian lyrics to what would become the most famous anthem of the French Resistance. Though Marly had lived in her adopted country since childhood, reports of the bloodshed awakened her "Slavic soul" and inspired her to write a piece in her native language that would evoke the "iconography" and "enchanting music" of France.[32] In the spring of 1943, the song was set to French text and chosen as the theme of the BBC's *Honneur et Patrie*, a program aimed at encouraging those in Occupied France to continue the struggle against the Germans. To the first-time listener or reader, "Le Chant des Partisans" functions most obviously as a call to action, urging Resistance fighters to "come up from the mines" and "down from the hills" in order to take up arms against the German occupiers. Embedded in this overt call to action, however, is a national narrative, evoked through appeals to traditional French values of *liberté, égalité,* and *fraternité.* By exploiting these tropes, the song calls forth the memory of France's past and connects Resistance fighters with the nation's historical heroes and patriots.

Like other Resistance songs, "Le Chant des Partisans" deploys a national narrative through both lyrics and music. The constitutive power of narratives to communicate experiences of national belonging has received considerable attention in the field of rhetoric. Scholars like Michael McGee, Maurice Charland, Karlyn Kohrs Campbell, and Kathleen Hall Jamieson have underscored the ways in which stories about a nation's history work to construct a sense of a collective "people."[33] While these critics have focused on narratives deployed through discursive means, others have illuminated music's potential to tell national stories. For example, James Irvine and Walter Kirkpatrick show that melodies and rhythms work by evoking listeners' "experiential capacity," or the collections of personal experiences that imbue a set of symbols with meaning.[34] Alberto Gonzalez and John Makay echo this argument, demonstrating that music functions through a process of ascription whereby listeners assign meaning to certain musical patterns and then recall those meanings each time the familiar music plays.[35] Yet, music does not merely call forth the history of the nation but also sounds the emotions that attend the remembrance of the past. As Deanna and Timothy Sellnow write, "music sounds the way feelings feel."[36] Thus, in order to see the ways in which singing constituted resisters as traditionally French, we must probe the songs' discursive and nondiscursive elements for the evocation of a traditional, idealized national narrative. By examining the tales of France's national heroes, appeals to its legacy of individual liberalism, and the sounding of its national rhythms and melodies, we can see how invoking the memory of a perfected France works to constitute resisters as the true sons and daughters of that nation.

Like many other songs of the Resistance, "Le Chant des Partisans" uses appeals to the great Revolutionary triumvirate of *liberté, égalité, fraternité* to subvert the platform of Vichy's National Revolution and identify Resistance fighters as members of a collective subject that has long been dedicated to the protection of traditional French ideals. Its lyrics exploit the trope of *liberté* through an emphasis on individual rights. By identifying Resistance fighters as free agents who control their own destinies, the song emphasizes each person's agency. As the song proclaims, in the *maquis* "each man knows / What he wants, what he's doing." This belief in the individual's control over his/her own choices marks a significant departure from Vichy's emphasis on communal living and evokes the Revolutionary doctrine of individual liberalism. By appealing to liberalism's main tenet—individual rights—the lyrics of "Le Chant des Partisans" serve to ideologically connect Resistance fighters to French Revolutionaries. As the song continues, appeals to individual liberty grow even more evident as the lyrics encourage illegal acts of resistance in the struggle for freedom. For example, Resistance fighters may take up arms against their enemies ("Remove from the straw / The rifles, machine gun / And grenades!"), or they may disobey the law by freeing members of their movement from prison ("We are the ones who break / The prison bars / For our brothers").[37] As these lyrics suggest, the fighters are encouraged to battle tyranny through any means necessary; liberty demands and legitimizes any form of resistance. The song ends with a final appeal as the last stanza characterizes Resistance fighters as the champions of liberty, encouraging other members to "whistle . . . in the night," so that freedom may hear them. Here, a personified liberty draws close to the Resistance fighters in order to guide and protect them throughout their struggle, just as she did with their Revolutionary forebears.

Like "Le Chant des Partisans," many songs of the Resistance call upon the trope of liberty in order to link the resisters to a transhistorical national community and legitimize their vigilante acts. Made in opposition to the Vichy government, which, in the words of one song, "puts France in the service of the Nazis" for "the pleasure of strangling the Republic," the appeals ground themselves in an allegiance to French Revolutionary republicanism.[38] Whereas Vichy would happily let the country limp along in servitude, the Resistance proclaims the pursuit of liberty to be the guiding principle under which they fight:

Liberté! Cette grande espérance	Liberty! This great hope
Qui brillait tout au fond de nos coeurs,	That has been shining deep in our hearts
Liberté! Pour nous et pour la France	Liberty! For us and for France
Nous ne voulions pas d'autre bonheur.[39]	We wouldn't want any other happiness.

Here, Resistance fighters claim to be driven by a singular desire to restore freedom in France, the same hope that spurred the Republic's very founding. By continuing their forebears' struggle for *liberté*, the singers align themselves with these historical heroes. Other songs make this connection even more explicit by setting France's Revolutionary soldiers as the guides to freedom. As the song "Pas de Kollaboration" states, the example set by France's ancestors will lead them to reclaim the nation's freedom:

Nous ne voulons pas vivre en esclavage	We don't want to live in slavery
De nos aïeux retrouvant la fierté	From our ancestors, finding pride again
Nous saurons défendre l'heritage	We know how to defend our heritage
Des droits et de la liberté![40]	Our rights and our liberty!

Indeed, the appeal to liberty derives its rhetorical power from its status as a culturally salient trope. Appeals to *liberté* carry particular connotations and associations, most obviously evoking France's unique and character-defining battle against the tyranny of King Louis XVI. By exploiting this trope, the Resistance fighters identify themselves as the "defenders of liberty," the descendants of those who have fought for France's freedom.[41]

"Le Chant des Partisans" also gives voice to the second Revolutionary ideal of equality by emphasizing the equal status held by members of the Resistance. Because all "march . . . kill . . . [and] die like dogs," no member is valued above another—all are equal in rank and status. This sentiment is echoed in the fourteenth stanza where the lyrics remind Resistance fighters that no person is more integral to the fight for French independence than another. When one man dies, another "emerges from the shadows / To take [his] place." While these lyrics may seem callous in their rejection of individual worth, they serve to emphasize the equality among Resistance fighters. While status, wealth, and success may matter in the external world, these things are irrelevant to the fight against Germany. Indeed, many of the songs emphasize this equality among Resistance fighters. One attests that the *maquis* is made up of "children of the common people and of the bourgeoisie"; another asserts that the movement makes no distinction between those who are "rich or without fortune."[42] Despite socioeconomic status, these "soldiers of equality" "are all the sons of our France."[43]

Not only are men equal in the eyes of the Resistance, but all are bound together in pursuit of their goal. The unofficial Resistance hymn makes explicit appeals to brotherhood, or *fraternité*, as the resisters sing of their attachment to one another. The lyrics address fellow Resistance fighters repeatedly as "friend," "brother," "comrade," and "companion." These words work to constitute the Resistance fighters as an intimate group. In reality, the Resistance was made up of a variety of networks and movements that worked separately and secretly to overthrow German forces. By addressing fellow Resistance fighters as "friends" and "brothers," however, resisters created a discursive means by which to overcome the diffuse nature of their movement's organization and conceive of themselves as members of a larger, more significant community. Indeed, an overwhelming majority of the songs exploit the trope of brotherhood, claiming that resisters are "united like brothers by the same noble ideal," and "march together for happiness and justice."[44] The songs portray a fierce devotion among members of the Resistance, even pledging not to leave captured members behind: "We are the ones who break / the prison bars / for our brothers."[45] By evoking the ideal of fraternity, the lyrics not only constitute Resistance fighters as a group unto themselves, but implicate them in a broader collective subject. The guardians of *fraternité*, they become a part of France's Revolutionary past.

The music of "Le Chant des Partisans" also functions to align Resistance fighters with their republican forebears. The song opens with a militaristic cadence played on a single snare drum. Somber and fatalistic, the cadence calls to mind the image of soldiers resolutely marching toward the battlefield in order to cast resisters as state-sanctioned warriors. The song maintains this militaristic sound by deploying march-like rhythms reminiscent of "La Marseillaise," the song that became popular during the French Revolution and was later chosen as France's national anthem. Emphasizing beats one and three, the beats on which a soldier's steps would fall, the song evokes a strong sense of forward motion. To lend a sense of exigency to this momentum, "Le Chant des Partisans" begins each musical phrase with a pickup, or a beat before the downbeat of the measure in which the phrase sounds. By beginning the phrase before the actual start of the measure, the song evokes the same urgent call to action found in the opening lines of the national anthem. Appropriating march-like rhythmic devices from "La Marseillaise," the melody of "Le Chant des Partisans" enhances the song's lyrical appeals to Revolutionary values by grounding them in a musical representation of the Revolution. As they sing, Resistance fighters identify themselves as soldiers in the same Revolutionary tradition, fighting to protect France's traditional values.

Yet, while "Le Chant des Partisans" seeks to align resisters with the soldiers of the French Revolution, its sound makes a clear distinction between the romanticized and mythologized overthrow of the monarchy and the unpopular, arduous work of the Resistance. Indeed, in timbre, or color, and melody, the song sounds of somber determination and perseverance. For example, the singer's voice is rich and dark, much like the sound we would expect to come from the lips of the muscular and fearless Marianne, the allegorical symbol of republican France. Singing in her lower register, the soloist enunciates in a deliberate manner as if each word is a conscious and defiant act of resistance. By deploying glottal stops and articulating the consonants in clear precision, the singer establishes herself as a free agent, resolute in her decision to overthrow the Nazis. As she sings, a chorus of men and women double her in unison, softly humming to convey the solidarity and fraternity to which the lyrics appeal. Unlike "La Marseillaise," this melody is confined to a narrow range of pitches. Rather than soaring in idealistic expressions of optimism and hope, it remains grounded to the tonic, or the central pitch of the key, as if painfully cognizant of the consequences of defying the Nazis. Shortly, an accordion enters the musical fabric, playing ascending melodic flourishes and sustained chords that call attention to its unique and unmistakable sound. The traditional musical instrument of France, the accordion bestows a sense of tradition and patriotism upon the resisters, reinforcing their status as the nation's true patriots and protectors. By sounding the feelings of patriotic determination and fatalistic acceptance, the song constitutes Resistance fighters as modern-day soldiers, bravely and stoically facing the dangerous task of resisting the Germans despite the uncertainty of the war's outcome.

While "Le Chant des Partisans" appropriates rhythmic features of "La Marseillaise" in order to identify Resistance fighters as members of a national community, other songs borrow entire Revolutionary melodies to make this connection. For example, "La Marseillaise du Maquis" appropriates the melody of "La Marseillaise" for its lyrics:

Amis, voici la Résistance;	Friends, here is the Resistance
Les vaillants soldats du maquis!	Valiant soldiers of the *maquis*!
Debout pour sauver notre France	Ready to save our France
Forces françaises du pays!	The French forces of the nation!
Ils descendent de nos montagnes	They are coming down from our mountains,
Comme nos ancêtres guerriers	Like our warrior ancestors,
Et viennent en vrais chevaliers	And come like true knights
Protéger villes et campagnes.[46]	To protect our cities and towns.

Here again, the melody and lyrics work together to connect Resistance fighters to the "ancestral warriors" of France's past. Because the song takes the melody of "La Marseillaise," the listener or singer cannot help but associate the Resistance members with Revolutionary soldiers who sang the hymn while storming the Bastille.

This same connection occurs in "Le Chant du Maquis," a Resistance song set to the tune of the Revolutionary War song "Le Chant du Départ."[47]

Originally a rallying cry among Revolutionaries, the song became popular again as soldiers and civilians mobilized for World War I.[48] Having developed as a national symbol spanning at least two of France's main wars, the melody existed as a trope of traditional French patriotism. By setting new words to the same melody, the Resistance song seeks to evoke the same legacy of individual liberalism. This melody lends added meaning to the lyrics, which also contain appeals to traditional French values. Together, the lyrics and the melody offer a potent appeal to France's Revolutionary values. By evoking the Revolution through existing musical and discursive tropes, the Resistance song seeks to integrate Resistance members into the Revolutionary tradition.

"Le Chant du Départ"	"Le Chant du Maquis"
Victory singing	Do you hear over there
Opens the gates for us	The hordes of invaders
Liberty guides our steps	On the faraway path?
And from the North to the South	Listen as the sound of the chains
The war trumpet	That the oppressors hold for our arms approaches
Signals the hour of the fight	Rather than become slaves
Tremble, enemies of France	And serve our enemies
Kings drunk on blood and pride	The time has come,
The sovereign People come forth	Come along brave soldiers
Tyrants go down to your graves	We must leave for the *maquis*
The Republic is calling us	Let's march boys, because hope
Let us prevail or let us perish	Flowers again along our path
A Frenchman must live for her	We will keep the soul of France
For her a Frenchman must die.	We will be her soldiers tomorrow.

Like "Le Chant du Maquis," other Resistance songs also appropriate the melodies of popular and historic national hymns. Among the most popular melodies chosen are those of "L'Internationale," "La Carmagnole," "Régiment de Sambre et Meuse," and "Alsace-Lorraine," all of which originated during the Revolution and were remobilized for France's effort in World War I.[49] As symbols of national identity, these melodies provided

Resistance members with a powerful resource in the construction of their own collective identity as the only true French.

The act of singing reinforced these discursive tropes, offering resisters a means to enact their solidarity and resolve. Testimonies from former Resistance fighters reveal that singing was an everyday part of life, a communal act that helped them to feel close to one another while giving voice to their shared ideals. For example, recounting his time in the French Resistance more than forty years earlier, François Musard described one Saturday night on the outskirts of Les Glières, a mountain town near the Swiss border. The men had finished their suppers and were playing cards to pass the time. To combat boredom, their sergeant suggested a singing tour, where each man would perform a song of his choosing. "Almost all of the group contributed," Musard remembered. "Some sang well-known tunes, while others, whose voices weren't as good, spoke monologues or recited bits of poetry." The men sang many different songs, from military marches to love ballads, but the most memorable was one soldier's original composition, written on behalf of their unit. As Musard recalled, the song's "first verses and refrain stayed in the ears of our comrades for a long time."[50] Julien Helfgott, another member of the *maquis*, also remembered the bonds forged through singing: "Stuck together, we dreamed, brothers bound by the same oath, united by a common ideal that we expressed in our songs, our words, and our laughter."[51] As both of these testimonies demonstrate, singing was a powerful constitutive practice because it gathered resisters together to enact their ideals of brotherhood and voice their commitment to the reestablishment of a republican France.

Thus far, my analysis has emphasized the ways in which the songs of the Resistance exploited existing discursive and musical tropes in order to connect its members to a legacy of French republicanism. While appeals to national identity allowed resisters to gain political authority by identifying themselves as members of a pure French citizenry, these appeals also enabled them to represent themselves as mature, manly soldiers. As Vichy tried to downplay the legitimacy of the movement by representing resisters as well-intentioned but misguided "boys" and "bandits," the songs used appeals to national identity in order to characterize them as tough, steadfast national defenders. Take, for example, the last stanza of

"Haut les Coeurs," a song written in 1944 to "glorify the Resistance" and "provide the brave boys of the *maquis* with a march."[52] While the author calls the subject of his praise "boys," his lyrics certainly do not represent immature, inconsequential youngsters. Instead, the song claims that the Resistance fighters are the descendants of France's historic heroes. "Firm and stoic," the boys follow in the footsteps of their forebears to save France:

Nos martyrs, dignes de l'antique,	Our martyrs, dignified with age
Ont bravé leur bourreaux,	Faced their executioners
Sans faiblir, fermes et stoïques	Without weakening, firm and stoic
Ils sont morts en vrais héros,	They died true heroes
Leur exemple nous entraîne	Their example leads us
Dans le noble et dur effort	In our noble and difficult effort
Pour une France souveraine	For a sovereign France,
Libre et fière dans son essor.[53]	Blossoming, free and proud.

Not only do these lyrics characterize the resisters as noble martyrs by associating them with France's past heroes, but they also help to build a sort of military masculinity among the resisters through a more implicit argument about the nature of the battle. In order for the Resistance to be constituted as a legitimate movement, the songs must illustrate the significance of their struggle. By comparing the resisters to France's past heroes, the songs make an implicit comparison between the situation faced by France's mythic soldiers and the battle facing Resistance fighters. The link between these struggles is particularly explicit in the song "Les Libérateurs, Marche des FFI." Here, resisters evoke the memory of France's loss in the Franco-Prussian War (which cost France the territory of Alsace-Lorraine, an area they recovered after World War I) to add weight to the Resistance's fight against the Germans:

Au chant de La Marseillaise	Singing the Marseillaise
Les jeunes, imitant leurs anciens,	The young, imitating their elders,
Se jettent dans la fournaise	Throw themselves into the fire
Furieux Paris tue le Prussian.[54]	Furious Paris kills the Prussian

By comparing the battle against the German Reich and Vichy to other historic military conquests, such as World War I, the resisters imagine themselves as the next generation of resolute national defenders.

Perhaps one of the fullest examples of the attempt to reassert resisters' masculinity through appeals to national identity is the song "Maquisards." Written in 1944 "for the glory of the *maquisards*," the song alludes to both the French Revolution and to World War I in order to represent the resisters as a group of mature soldiers, fighting together for a sacred goal. The refrain begins by likening the struggle of 1940–1944 to that of the French Revolution. The first line alludes to 1793, the year that a poverty-stricken French citizenry brought Louis XVI to the guillotine. In case the audience/singer misses this reference to the Revolution, the author adds a second allusion to the Revolution by referencing its anthem, "La Marseillaise."

Du sol français,	From French soil,
comme en quatre-vingt-treize,	like in ninety-three,
Surgit soudain un peuple de soldats	A people of soldiers suddenly appeared
Qui sur l'aile de La Marseillaise,	Who on the wings of La Marseillaise
Vint prendre sa place au combat	Came to take their place in combat.
Pendant quatre ans, la haine les enflame,	For four years, hatred has inflamed them,
Sauter, enfin, aux gorges des pillards.	Jumping, finally, at the throats of the looters.
C'est pourquoi tout l'univers acclame	That's why the whole universe acclaims
Et salue nos vaillants maquisards.[55]	And salutes our valiant *maquisards*.

While this allusion to the French Revolution serves the previously mentioned goals of connecting the Resistance to a transhistorical French community, it also constitutes members as a legitimate, solidified group of soldiers. The lyrics call upon the image of Revolutionary France—where lower-class citizens mobilized to overthrow a corrupt government—in order to represent the Resistance fighters as a "peuple de soldats." Indeed, the phrase a "people of soldiers" makes a great deal of sense in regard to both the Revolution and the Resistance, as both movements mobilized the citizenry to effect change. Neither battle was fought by a national military, but by the people themselves. Regardless of their civilian statuses, French Revolutionaries are considered France's truest and bravest heroes. By evoking the history of this army of citizens, the song transfers the validity and respect given to Revolutionaries onto the Resistance fighters.

The act of singing lent credence to these kinds of discursive attempts to construct resisters as manly soldiers, engaged in a fight to the death for the liberation of France. Anecdotes from former members reveal that Resistance groups often sang to boost morale and renew dedication to the cause after traumatic events, such as the capture or death of fellow comrades. On March 1, 1944, for example, the *maquis* unit in Les Glières received word that one of their comrades, Michel Fournier, had been caught in a police roundup while trying to procure medicine for his unit. Upon hearing the news of Fournier's capture, one of the *maquisards* grabbed his guitar and played the first measures of "L'Hymne des Glières," the group's official anthem. As one comrade remembered, "a few people raised their voices, humming the first verses; the choir became more vigorous at the refrain."

En avant bataillon des Glières	At the ready, battalion of Glières
Décidés à vaincre ou à mourir	Determined to win or die
Pour chasser l'ennemi sanguinaire	In order to chase the bloodthirsty enemy
Nous vaincrons, bataillon, nous vaincrons.[56]	We shall overcome, battalion, we shall overcome.

In a moment of despair and anger, the performance of this hymn gave voice to the group's frustration while enacting their status as a battalion of soldiers, resolutely fighting against the Germans to free France. Indeed, the singing of the Les Glières' Resistance anthem offered a means of reasserting the gravity of the struggle against the Germans, and the resisters' status as resolute and self-sacrificing patriots.

Yet, like all constitutive rhetoric, Resistance singing could only effectively construct collective identity if it also excluded certain citizens from the resisters' community of national heroes. Indeed, as the songs aligned resisters with the republican warriors of the past, they also attempted to dismantle the Vichy government's political legitimacy by barring it from the nation's fold. Many of the songs accomplish this goal by combining national narratives with appropriations of Vichy's songs. Setting their own lyrics to Vichy's melodies, the Resistance parodies the government's discourse and illustrates the hypocrisy of its claims to national identity. English scholar Linda Hutcheon has theorized parody as imitation that points out difference through critical distance and irony.[57] Hutcheon rejects a definition of parody as necessarily satirical, recovering its original meaning as a neutral form of ironic repetition that "can be playful as well as belittling," "critically constructive as well as destructive."[58] Through an ironic appropriation of the form of the original text, parody allows rhetors to demonstrate points of separation and contrast and invite alternative interpretations for consideration. As Bakhtin writes, it shows that one meaning is "incapable of exhausting the subject" and "forces us to experience those sides of the object that are not otherwise included in a given genre."[59] By setting new lyrics to Vichy's own melodies, Resistance parodies pointed to the discrepancy between Vichy's optimism and the harsh reality of life under the Occupation. The songs offered resisters the opportunity to open Pétain's discourse for collective reflection and to revise the public's understanding of the regime. The goal was to subvert Vichy's own claim to national identity, to portray the regime as corrupt and manipulative outsiders while representing Resistance fighters as the true guardians of French values and culture.

In order to deny the Frenchness of Vichy, the Resistance chose one of the most popular hymns to Vichy leader Marshal Philippe Pétain, "Maréchal, Nous Voilà!" Written in 1941, the song lauds Philippe Pétain as France's "savior" and pledges service in Vichy's National Revolution:

Une flamme sacré	A sacred flame
Monte du sol natal	Comes up from native soil

Et la France enivré	And an intoxicated France
Te salue Maréchal!	Salutes you, Marshal
Tous tes enfants qui t'aiment	All your children who love you
Et vénèrent tes ans	And venerate your years
A ton appel suprême	To your supreme call
Ont répondu: "Présent"	Responded: "Present"
Maréchal, nous voilà!	Marshal, here we are
Devant toi, le sauveur de la France	Before you, the savior of France
Nous jurons, nous tes gars	We pledge, we, your guys
De server et de suivre tes pas	To serve you and follow your steps
Maréchal, nous voilà!	Marshal, here we are
Tu nous as redonné l'espérance.	You have given us back our hope
La patrie renaîtra	The fatherland will be reborn
Maréchal, Maréchal, nous voilà![60]	Marshal, Marshal, here we are!

To accompany this optimistic pledge, the Vichy song employs a jubilant march, full of pickups and dotted rhythms similar to those found in "La Marseillaise." Full orchestration, including a regal brass section, lends additional pomp and confidence to the jaunty march. Recorded by French singer André Dassary and the Ray Ventura Orchestra in 1941, the song opens with an eight-measure trumpet fanfare that deploys the brass's imperial tones in order to call French citizens to attention as they "venerate" their authoritarian leader. The trumpet section continues to blast triplet figures as the soloist sings, marking Dassary's praise of Pétain with the regal sound of a coronation ceremony. During each refrain, a men's chorus echoes Dassary's operatic tenor, lending a sense of strength and virility to the song's pledge to national service. At the end of the recording, the men join Dassary in a final, climactic refrain. The men sing at full volume, combining their voices to bestow a sense of tough manhood to the song's call to service. Leading the nation's rebirth is not a slight task, the men's voices suggest, but a struggle that demands physical and mental fortitude. Through the combination of these strong, manly voices, the imperial brass flourishes, and the march-like rhythms, the song characterizes Pétain as a king-like leader whose majesty compels the eager obedience of a tough and muscular citizenry. Vichy attempted to use this melody to ascribe a sense of military honor to the act of serving Vichy and its National Revolution.

However, given the conditions of the armistice (whereby Vichy agreed to the reduction of the French army to 100,000 men, the disarmament of the navy and air force, and the surrender of all French weapons) and Vichy's failure to shield French citizens from the horrors of the Occupation, such a confident, glorious military march seems inappropriate for Vichy's call to service. Indeed, in light of the harsh living conditions for most French, Marshal Pétain hardly qualified as the "savior of France." The Resistance points to the ludicrousness of Vichy's claims of national defense and protection by pointing to the truth about the Vichy regime, setting their lyrics to the collaborationist government's own melody:

Ayant trahi la France	Having betrayed France,
Les hommes de Vichy	The men of Vichy
Ont fait une alliance	made an alliance
Avec nos ennemis	with our enemies
Ils prêchent la défaite	They preach defeat
Et la resignation	and resignation
Mais ils paieront leur dette	But they will pay their debt
A toute la nation.[61]	to all the nation.

Indeed, not only do the Resistance songs blame Vichy for the German Occupation, but they argue that France can only be saved without Vichy's interference:

Nous gars d' la Résistance	We, the men of the Resistance
Qui n'avons pas peur de rien,	Who aren't afraid of anything
Nous sauverons la France	We will save France
Sans ce triste Pétain.[62]	Without this sad Pétain

While these examples put forth compelling and explicit arguments about the hypocritical and treasonous nature of the Vichy government, what is most interesting about the Resistance's use of parody is the way in which the songs deploy the same national tropes I described previously in order to integrate the Resistance into the nation's fold while excluding

Vichy from the nationhood. By setting discursive appeals to the nation's history to the music of the Vichy regime, the songs point out the falsity of Vichy's claims to national identity and assert that the Resistance fighters are the only true guardians of France.

Perhaps the best example of the rhetorical strategy of parody employed in the songs of the Resistance is "Les Voilà, Nos Soldats."[63] The song opens with the same lines as the Vichy song, but deviates from the original by the end of the first verse. While "Maréchal, Nous Voilà" begins by describing Marshal Pétain as the subject who calls the people to action, "Les Voilà, Nos Soldats" identifies France as the issuer of the call:

"Maréchal, Nous Voilà!"	"Les Voila, Nos Soldats"
A sacred flame	A sacred flame
Comes up from native soil	Comes up from native soil
And an exhilarated France	And a bereaved France
Salutes you, Marshal	Comes back to life at its signal
All your children who love you	All of the Empire who love France
And venerate your years	And call themselves her child
To your supreme call	To her supreme call
Responded: Present	Responded: Present

By identifying France as the source of the call to action, the Resistance song transfers political authority from Pétain and Vichy to a mythic French community. Marshal Pétain does not issue the alarm, but France herself beckons her citizens to arms. While this shift may seem subtle, it has three major implications for the Resistance movement. First, this shift takes away Pétain's right to lead and designates France herself as leader of the nation. Because the Resistance serves an abstract France and not a concrete Pétain, its members need an indication of what France would have them do. The only place to look for such guidance is within France's own history. Second, this shift distinguishes Vichy as separate from France. The Resistance song indicates that serving France is not the same as serving Vichy. By separating the French government from the idea of the nation itself, the Resistance song excludes Vichy from the national narrative. Third, the shift transfers agency from the Vichy leaders to the French people. The original song casts Pétain as the main agent in France's fight and asserts that the people's role is merely to follow him. However, because the Resistance song identifies France as the issuer of the call to action, the people are led by history's example instead of a human agent. In the absence of a human leader, the people must become agents in the fight against Germany. They cannot look to a politician or a soldier to restore France to her sovereign state, but must take individual action in order to overcome the enemy.

Having identified France as the source of the people's call to action, the song then constructs an idealized vision of the nation. In the refrain, the song evokes a narrative of France that features the nation's most revered military heroes.

Jeanne d'Arc, les voilà,	Joan of Arc, here they are
Nos soldats, les sauveurs de la France.	Our soldiers, the saviors of France
Les voilà, nos soldats.	Here they are, our soldiers
Ceux de Clovis, de Turenne et de Foch.	The ones of Clovis, of Turenne and of Foch.
A nouveau de l'ennemi,	Once again from the enemy,
Ils ont refoulé la fureur boche	They drove back German fury
Debout, la France est là,	Standing tall, France is here,
Et la gloire couronne ses soldats.	And glory crowns her soldiers.

This refrain names Joan of Arc, the young martyr who returned the area of Orléans to France in the fifteenth century; Clovis, the king who united the Frankish tribes in 481 C.E.; Turenne, the general who saved Alsace from German annexation in 1675; and Foch, the French general who planned the final offensive against Germany in World War I, as the main figures in the narrative of France's glorious past. Taken together, these soldiers represent France's most celebrated military conquests. While the original song identifies Pétain as the "savior of France," this new refrain undermines his credibility and authority by ascribing French heroism to other figures. In other words, the Resistance song denies Pétain's hero status by omitting his name from the list of France's true heroes. Not only does this omission challenge the sincerity of Pétain's intentions and the strength of his abilities, it also serves to separate him from the national community that makes up France's past.

While the refrain excludes Pétain from the national community, it includes the Resistance fighters as members of this transhistorical group. After all, the Resistance fighters are the "soldiers of Clovis, of Turenne, and of Foch." By representing members of the Resistance as the descendants of a lineage of French heroes, the song fully integrates Resistance fighters into the national narrative. Constructed as true French citizens, the Resistance fighters then secure ultimate political and moral authority. They may disobey Vichy's laws, sabotage German operations, harbor Jews, and so forth because they are members of France's national community. Thus, national identity legitimizes their vigilante approach, transforming a group of rebels into a band of national heroes.

By setting these lyrics to Vichy's own melody, the Resistance song exposes the absurdity of Vichy's appeal to allegiance and demonstrates that such a glorious military march is only appropriate for France's true soldiers, the Resistance fighters. Only when the melody is used to call upon citizens to oppose German occupiers can its confident, militant sound be genuine. While Resistance singers obviously could not replicate the elaborate and dramatic sound of the original song in their camps, they still associated the military pomp and fanfare of "Maréchal, Nous Voilà" with their version of the song. By mimicking the original melody, the Resistance song denies Vichy's claim to military honor and transfers such honor to the Resistance fight. Indeed, such a grandiose sound proves quite appropriate for the heroic band of French heroes that the Resistance fighters join.

Conclusion

Written by French citizens and disseminated orally across the nation, the songs of the French Resistance played a vital role in the legitimization of the movement. Suffering from a lack of broad public support and targeted for denunciation in an aggressive propaganda campaign waged by Vichy to mollify Germany, the Resistance remained unpopular until the Liberation in the summer of 1944. Yet, Resistance fighters challenged Vichy's negative representations through the performance of songs. By reprising a performative tradition of political singing rooted in republican patriotism, Resistance fighters mobilized a beloved popular-culture form to define themselves as genuinely French. Through the singing of the songs, they aligned themselves with a transhistorical community of patriotic French citizens, using discursive and musical tropes to delineate the boundaries of membership. In this way, the performance of folk songs allowed resisters to remain squarely within France's revered republican tradition while excluding Vichy and its supporters from the nation. Not only did these performances bolster resisters' claims to political leadership, they also helped to combat Vichy's infantilizing propaganda. Finally, the songs of the Resistance used parody to subvert Vichy's political authority. While the government's propaganda aimed to persuade the French that no one was more French that Philippe Pétain, the Resistance used songs in order to demonstrate Vichy's betrayal of the French people and to cast collaborators outside the nation's fold. Setting their own national appeals to Vichy's melodies, they illustrated the ludicrousness of Vichy's alleged patriotism and asserted themselves as the only true French.

While *chanson* was uniquely suited to the project of stripping Vichy of its political authority, it was not the only musical genre available to dissident citizens. Indeed, as resisters settled in for rounds of singing in their makeshift camps, French teenagers known as "zazous" were causing a scene in Parisian cafés, humming the tunes of "degenerate" jazz refrains while wearing the ostentatious clothing of American zoot-suiters.

CHAPTER 3

Zazous in Zoot Suits

Race Play in Occupied Paris

———•◆•———

O n the evening of June 8, 1942, Ginette Orien, a seventeen-year-old Catholic from Paris's wealthy seventh *arrondissement*, was arrested near Place de la République. Just one day after implementation of the Eighth Ordinance, the law that forced Jews to identify themselves by attaching the government-issued yellow star to their clothing, Orien was caught wearing her own homemade star. Made from yellow construction paper across which was written "Swing 135%," Orien's star marked her as member of the zazous, a countercultural group inspired by their love of jazz, or swing, music.[1] The star, an imitation of the star that Jewish citizens were forced to wear, deployed representations of "degenerate" jazz to mark a new, racialized swing identity on Orien's white, Gentile body.[2] Indeed, when writing his report of the young teen's actions, Orien's arresting officer wrote that her star took on the "same dimension as the racial insignia" (*de même dimension de l'insigne racial*) and poked fun at the very serious threat that Jews posed to France's future.[3]

Across Paris, Orien's fellow zazous were engaging in the same protest. Carefully crafting their own yellow stars to match the style and size of those French Jews were forced to wear, and emblazoning them with the words "jazz," "swing," and "zazou," these youth mocked fascist France's anti-Semitism by transforming a symbol designed for oppression and control into a symbol of their subversive jazz identity. For participating in this act of defiance, at least eleven zazous were arrested, many of whom were sent to the labor camps at Drancy and Tourelles.[4] To this day, their faded yellow stars hang in the headquarters of Paris's Préfecture de Police.

While the Yellow Star campaign serves as a powerful example of the ways in which jazz music and culture offered a resource for resistance in Occupied France, it is but one example of the zazous' subversive tactics. Blamed for the decadent behavior that had allegedly caused France's defeat, and charged with the task of leading the nation's rebirth, these youth struggled to free themselves from Vichy's oppressive rhetoric and policies throughout the Occupation. The promise of jazz culture, I shall show, was that it held tools out of which the creative zazous could fashion a subversive identity that symbolized their refusal to serve as national scapegoats and their rejection of fascist political ideology. Specifically, I argue that the zazous' performance of swing identity undermined the essentialist racial ideology espoused by Vichy and exposed Nazi Germany's "pure" New Europe as a social construct rather than a scientific truth. In the face of existing anxieties over the effects of *nègre* music on French audiences, zazou songs and fashion helped the swing kids to mark a racialized swing identity on their white, upper-middle-class, Gentile bodies that violated appropriate norms of gender and class and symbolized opposition to collaborationist politics. The subversive message conveyed by the youths' performance of zazou identity was not lost on Vichy sympathizers and Nazi authorities, who sought to discipline the zazous by denigrating them in the press and subjecting them to violent street attacks. Ironically, the harsh reaction of Vichy France and Nazi Germany to contain the zazous worked to amplify their transgression, as it confirmed the cultural intelligibility of the zazous' subversive, racialized identity.

Despite the zazous' open defiance of the social order imposed by Nazi and Vichy authorities, these youth did not leave any personal records detailing their motivations or experiences. Because of the absence of such sources, many scholars have looked to the state's criticisms of the zazous in order to understand the group's political meaning and significance. These scholars have recovered key source material and have demonstrated the ways that the collaborationist press portrayed the zazous as nonsensical teenage rebels. For example, historian Patrice Bollon has argued that zazous were problematic because they were perceived to lack a clear and consistent ideology. The zazous, he writes, "seem almost possessed by a desire to be unclassifiable . . . one even has the impression that they take pleasure in the status of objects that are almost indifferent, neutral, mute."[5] According to Bollon, the zazous rejected a coherent set of motives and goals; their dress and behavior were subversive by virtue of being incomprehensible and meaningless. Jon Savage echoes this interpretation in his study of youth culture, suggesting that the zazous "cultivated a blank façade" that mirrored the nebulous nature of life under the Occupation. By "turning adolescent obnoxiousness into street theater," he writes, "they offered a symbolic resistance to the Occupation's 'ambient, abstract horror' that also mirrored its ultimate vacancy."[6] These scholars' efforts at recovering the state's representations of the zazous as empty and meaningless have provided a vital foundation for future studies of the countercultural group. Indeed, they encourage us to take up the question of why, if the zazous were "blank," "meaningless," and "incomprehensible," their behavior provoked such virulent condemnation in the collaborationist press.

Other scholars have complicated the understanding of zazous as devoid of meaning by uncovering additional institutional sources that point to the zazous as a legitimate countercultural group. In the most recent study of the zazous, for example, historian Sophie Roberts analyzes arrest records to argue that the zazous participated in a rejection of the Vichy regime and should be understood as positioned somewhere between organized resistance and collaboration, in a category she calls "dissidence."[7] Similarly, in her exhaustive analysis of newspaper coverage of the zazous, Emmanuelle Rioux concludes that Vichy saw the zazous as stubborn republicans, holding onto the individualistic, decadent behavior that brought about France's defeat.[8] Cultural-studies scholar Matthew Jordan's insightful analysis of debates about the acceptability of jazz and the formation of French national identity reveals the ways in which they

served as a screen onto which Vichy projected its anxieties about reforming national belonging.[9] While Jordan notes the racial dimension of the
zazous' public performance, his study examines Vichy's attempts to delegitimize the zazous as "degenerate" Jews, and leaves room for an examination of the swings' own performances of racial identity. Noting that the
Vichy regime pointed to the racial impurity of jazz in order to "denounce
the useless snobs who performed the very public swing persona instead of
their proper racial identity," Jordan invites us to consider *how* the zazous
transgressed the lines of appropriate whiteness.[10]

Given the absence of any records of the zazous' philosophy or beliefs,
it is hardly surprising that past scholars have based their conclusions on
available institutional sources. Nonetheless, expanding our understanding of the zazous necessitates an examination of the group on their own
terms. Although a dearth of primary accounts of the zazous' activities
presents challenges to reconstructing their subversive performances, the
task is not impossible. Indeed, we can recover zazou "voices" by reading the music and fashion that structured their identity. Just as orators'
organization, syntax, and arguments reveal insights about their ethos, the
cultural products that these teenagers embraced tell us a great deal about
the people they endeavored to become.[11] Borrowing cultural critic John
Storey's observation that popular music often supplies the resources out
of which countercultures constitute themselves, I consider jazz music
and fashion to be the tools by which the zazou community discovered
and reproduced itself.[12] I view the lyrical tropes, rhythms, and dress that
were popular among swing kids as the foundations of swing culture. My
approach, then, is to probe jazz music and culture for clues by which to
decode the subversive meaning of zazou identity. I ask, for example, how
did popular swing songs draw the lines of zazou belonging? In what ways
did their eccentric dress reify or alter the collective identity articulated
in jazz music and lyrics? What do these appropriations of jazz culture tell
us about the zazous' opinions of fascist ideology? In sum, what kind of
collective identity did the zazous build from the jazz cultural products
available to them?

Answering these questions requires us to understand the historical
context in which the zazous enacted their resistance, particularly Vichy's
attempts to reform the nation's youth, a demographic it charged with the

crucial task of national renewal. Against this backdrop, the rhetorical significance of the cultural products that the zazous mobilized to construct their swing identity emerges. Such products include *Mademoiselle Swing* (1942), the musical film that was immensely popular among the zazous, and four of the most popular French swing songs of the era.[13] The first of these songs, Johnny Hess's "Je Suis Swing" (1938), gave rise to the youth movement by coining the term "zazou." The second, Loulou Gasté's "Elle Était Swing" (1941), offers helpful insights into the formation of swing identity, as it was released prior to the press's reactionary attack in the summer of 1942. The last two songs, Henri Martinet and Raymon Vincy's "Y'a des Zazous" (1942) and Johnny Hess's "Ils Sont Zazous" (1943), were recorded at the height of the zazou movement, before the threat of forced labor in Germany encouraged zazous to go underground or join the *maquis*.[14] A close reading of the symbolic appeals invoked in these products recovers the significance of zazou fashion—documented in a photograph and described in personal memoirs and the noncollaborationist press—as a material effort to remark the young Parisian body. Given the coherence of this new and fully embodied zazou identity, it is no wonder that Nazi and Vichy authorities mobilized to stamp it out. Launching an attack through the collaborationist press, they worked to bring these youth back under the control of fascist society, but ultimately contributed to the swings' cultural-political critique. In their failure to discipline the zazous, these insults merely echoed the zazous' subversion, providing the youth with a mouthpiece for their resistance.

Youth in the Occupied Zone

Vichy's plans to revitalize France focused on the nation's youth, a demographic that they simultaneously blamed for the defeat and held accountable for a prosperous future.[15] Brought up under the influence of capitalistic, liberal republicans, French youth, authorities held, had become soft, leisure-loving, and lazy, characteristics seen as responsible for the 1940 military loss to Germany.[16] As one politician wrote in the Catholic newspaper *La Croix*, young people needed to give up their obsession with "being witty, light, libertine, mocking, skeptical, and whimsical" and focus on "God, nature, work, marriage, love, children—all that is serious, very serious, and looms ahead of [them]."[17] Not only had young people inherited a skewed set of priorities, Vichy officials argued, but they had become weak-willed and resigned. In a pamphlet circulated among the Compagnons de France, one of Vichy's youth movements, minister of foreign affairs Paul Baudouin summed up the problems that plagued French adolescents, decrying the ways in which "youth lived without ardour, discouraged before it acted." Because this generation of French youth "was refused its chance" under the previous government, "it no longer even cherished the desire to demand one" but "fled from risk and shrank from effort. It was sad and paralyzed."[18] Yet, in spite of these alleged shortcomings, many believed that the youth were uniquely poised to reinvigorate the nation. In one edition of *L'Illustration*, a popular middle-class magazine, columnist Henri Joubrel argued for the need to "excite" the youth, because "the majority of adults are too impregnated by the ideas that had run in the old government to see their errors." Unhardened by the passing of time, the youth were still malleable enough, Joubrel held, that even their "hearts" could be changed.[19]

In order to eradicate the evils of the past and make youth into future disciples of the National Revolution, Vichy targeted France's public school system. Since the law required children between the ages of six and fourteen to attend school, young people offered Vichy a captive audience of impressionable citizens on whom they could attempt to impose the new social order. While government leaders vacillated over the ideal educational model throughout the war (Pétain went through three different ministers of education in one six-month period), most agreed that education should stress traditional morality, militaristic obedience and discipline, a return to the Catholic faith, and allegiance to Pétain.[20] When Abel Bonnard took over the Ministry of Education in 1942, these principles were joined by an effort to eliminate class difference. As Bonnard wrote, "the reign of the French bourgeoisie is over."[21] To promote efficient labor, whether performed in the nation's homes or factories, young girls and boys were taught separately in "traditional" domains. Vichy made *enseignement ménager*, the French equivalent to home economics, for example, a compulsory subject for female students. In a pamphlet distributed to teachers, the Commissariat Général à la Famille (General Agency to the Family) argued that "it is very useful to make young girls like all these feminine tasks for which they are particularly gifted and that secretly correspond to their desires."[22] Young men, on the other hand, were to be taught "force, steadfastness, courage, and other virile qualities" that would aid them in their future workplaces.[23] These reforms were accompanied by the teaching of essentialist racial constructs. Officials replaced educational textbooks that were considered to be anti-German with new anti-Semitic books and encouraged instructors, in the words of political activist and journalist Maurice-Yvan Sicard, to bring French youth back "to the elementary forces which make up our country: land, blood, and race."[24]

While 5 to 7 percent of French youth did continue their schooling beyond the age of fourteen (notably the children of the middle and upper-middle classes), most could not afford the cost of secondary education and consequently sought employment. In Paris, where Vichy's official youth movements were banned, collaborationist youth organizations formed, all promising to train unemployed youth for the hard work and moral fervor necessitated by the National Revolution. According to Halls, these organizations were not widely popular, attracting only one out of six French youths.[25] Nonetheless, because these groups were widely discussed and promoted in the fascist press, their influence extended beyond actual members.

The discourse of two of the most influential of the collaborationist youth movements, the Jeunesses Nationales Populaires (JNP) and the Jeunes Populaires Français (JPF), reveal the kinds of ideological pressures operating on Parisian youth during the war. The former was the youth section of the socialist Marcel Déat's collaborationist party, Rassemblement National Populaire. This organization envisioned a state that would be neither capitalist nor communist, where socioeconomic class would not depend upon wealth or family heritage. The JPF was created in 1942 as the youth wing of politician Jacques Doriot's fascist party, Parti Populaire Français, and held a doctrine similar to that of the JNP. Anti-Semitic, anti-capitalist, anti-communist, the movement claimed to be the only revolutionary organization in France. Indeed, so radical were its leaders that in May 1942 they called for a series of racial and hereditary investigations before members could marry.[26] The JPF believed that Vichy's National Revolution was not stringent enough to combat the ills of young people, and, in the words of Halls, "rejected what they considered the milk and water pabulum served up as 'moral renewal.'"[27] Leader Daniel Vauquelin urged his members to adopt a violent machismo in their campaign, encouraging youth to "know how to strike" and reminding them that "it matters little if we are hated."[28] Young women were called to reject work outside the home and to dedicate themselves to continuing the French bloodline and upholding the nation's spirit.[29] Vauquelin also placed great emphasis on the physical appearance of his followers, claiming dress to be "the sign of the race" and warning that France's fate depended upon "whether you hold yourself well or poorly."[30] While not all of the collaborationist youth movements were officially affiliated with the fascist party, they adhered to fascist ideology in their emphasis on moral, disciplined living; suspicion of foreigners and Jews; and hatred of capitalism and communism.

Given Vichy's attempts to remake French youth into obedient disciples of the National Revolution, and the collaborationist youth movements' more radical calls to embrace Nazi ideology, French youth were under considerable pressure to dutifully take their place at the helm of national revitalization. Yet, in the spring of 1941, the Parisian press began reporting inappropriate behavior practiced by wealthy "petits swings" (little swings) in the capital's cafés. Dressed in oversized suit jackets and cropped pants, the self-proclaimed "zazous" were allegedly shirking their civic responsibilities and mocking the nation's defeat by dancing to the latest jazz and swing hits. The word "zazou" was nonsensical, first appearing in a scat from American jazzman Cab Calloway's 1933 "Zaz Zuh Zaz" before being immortalized in French singer Johnny Hess's 1938 hit song "Je Suis Swing." As Parisian teenagers appropriated the word for the title of their countercultural movement, other French musicians featured it in their songs, celebrating the adoption of zazou identity. Most zazous were between the ages of seventeen and eighteen years old, although arrest records show that some zazous were as old as twenty.[31] As their access to restricted clothing and frequent patronage of expensive Parisian cafés reveal, many of them were the sons and daughters of middle- to upper-middle-class Parisians.

The teenagers had eclectic taste in music, listening to a range of jazz and swing. Philippe du Peuty, a contemporary of the zazous, remembered that they "listened indiscriminately to Armstrong, Django, Jacques Pills, Irène de Trebert, Raymond Legrand."[32] They seem to have used the terms "jazz" and "swing" interchangeably, a habit that infuriated jazz critic Charles Delaunay. "Jazz, Jazz-hot, Jazz Swing, Swing, Swing, Swing, Swing . . . this word blares out our ears," he fumed in May 1941. "No one can say exactly what swing is and what it's not. And the most embarrassed will be without a doubt the clever '*pommades*' that frequent the fashionable bars and rush with enthusiasm to jazz concerts and stamp their feet with pleasure" at the drum and trumpet solos.[33] From Delaunay's perspective, the zazous' "abusive" use of the term "swing" threatened to undermine jazz's status as a new art form. He feared that the craze surrounding swing—a form of jazz intended to accompany dancing and closely associated with white big bands—threatened to shift attention away from the "hot" jazz played by black musicians that he sought to promote. For the zazous, though, such issues of musical authenticity were not paramount. Whether listening to Armstrong or Glenn Miller, they simply wanted to dance.

"Je Suis Zazou": Articulating the Zazou Race

Despite the fact that the zazous left no personal writings, we can reconstruct their performance of collective identity by examining the cultural products that inspired their community. The zazous built their identity on jazz music, a genre whose popularity grew immensely during the Occupation. Radio-Paris, the capital's publicly broadcast network, went from playing nearly four hours of jazz music per week in September 1940 to playing twenty-four hours a week in December 1941. By April 1941, the station featured more than thirty-five hours of jazz per week.[34] One of the earliest of the swing hits was French singer Johnny Hess's 1938 single "Je Suis Swing" (I Am Swing), a celebration of jazz music that would coin the nonsensical term "zazou." The song begins by marking a generational shift in musical preferences, declaring "negro music and hot jazz [to be] old things" and that "now, being in style requires swing" (*Maintenant pour être dans la note, il faut du swing*). As the song continues, Hess makes an ontological claim about "being swing" that asserts a deep connection between musical tastes and the body:

Afin d'chanter un opéra j'allais	In order to sing in the opera, I went
voir le directeur	to see the conductor
J'voulais chanter la Traviata en	I wanted to sing La Traviata in
Ré Majeur	D Major
Il m'a d'abord interrogé	First, he asked me
Est-ce que vous êtes ténor léger	If I was a light tenor
Basse chantante ou baryton	Lyric bass or baritone
J'ai répondu "Ah mais non"	I responded, "Oh no"
Je suis swing	I am swing

In these lyrics, Hess deploys the flexibility of the French verb être (to be) to herald a transformation in fans' relationship to their favorite music. In French, "I am" is used to denote ontological meaning, but also to convey tastes and preferences. For example, one could say "je suis professeur" (I am a professor) or "je suis sushi" (I like sushi). Exploiting this linguistic slippage, Hess invites listeners to "be swing" instead of "like swing." Hess supports his assertion that one *is* the music one loves with an argument rooted in physiology. Indeed, when the conductor of *La Traviata* asks Hess what his voice type is, he replies that he is not a tenor or bass, but a swing. This new voice type evokes physical difference to separate Hess from his forebears and to explain his obsession with jazz music. Instead of possessing a voice suited to the stereotypically stodgy, stiff operatic arias of the aged and uncool, Hess has the voice of a young, hip swing singer and must, therefore, sing jazz. The claim of these lyrics is that there is a chicken-and-egg relationship between the body and one's musical preferences. While the song does not reveal whether biology causes a love of swing, or a love of swing alters one's biology, it does represent jazz as a state of being that is rooted in and marked through the (young) body.

The notion that Parisian swing fans had a physiological connection to jazz music was highly problematic in Occupied France, because it resonated with long-standing denunciations of jazz as racially "degenerate." Throughout the 1920s and 1930s, French music critics consistently defined jazz as the product of American blacks and argued that its pulsating rhythms would have disastrous effects on the morality of white audiences. For example, in his 1923 pamphlet "Danseront-elles" (Will They

Dance?), José Germain cautioned audiences against the effects of *nègre* music, calling jazz an external influence that eats away at French nationhood and triggers a dangerous "change of mentality."[35] Performances such as Josephine Baker's 1925 *La Revue Nègre*, an erotic dance set to jazz music, confirmed conservative critics' convictions that jazz was "the triumph of lustfulness, the return of the morals of the first ages."[36] These anxieties grew even more intransigent in the 1930s as the rise of fascism encouraged xenophobic reactions to foreign cultural products. According to Gustave Fréjaville, a critic for the cultural weekly *Comoedia*, jazz required the French to hide "the characteristics of our race and national temperament."[37] Another critic warned that jazz "makes us degenerate, like certain human races that appear to have lost their ancestral history."[38] As the "expression of an un-French ethnos like the *nègres d'Amerique*," they maintained that jazz would inevitably have a weakening effect on French audiences.[39]

Johnny Hess's "Je Suis Swing" confirmed these fears as it claimed that young jazz fans were, in fact, racially different from their parents' generation and their teenage contemporaries. By representing the love of jazz music—a genre that had already been maligned as "degenerate"—as marked on and through the body, the song suggested that the zazous shared a physical connection to American and African blacks. This kind of symbolic *métissage* muddied the white waters of French national identity, exacerbating preexisting fears over a nation in decline. Indeed, set against the backdrop of Nazi and Vichy's sweeping reforms to France's sociopolitical landscape and the absence of nearly two million French men in German prisoner-of-war camps, the presence of the young zazous intensified fears over the loss of both French customs and French bodies. After all, a physiological disposition for jazz could be passed genetically to future generations. The protagonist of Hess's song, for example, goes from having three children by two different women, to producing another "four children in one shot" with yet another mistress. Thus, zazous were not only proof of jazz's demoralizing effects on "national temperament," but also evidence of the decline of the Catholic family. Instead of reproducing the French race through sanctioned, traditional sex and gender norms, young jazz fans, their music asserted, would submit to the lascivious impulses awakened by primitive rhythms and produce another generation of weak, immoral citizens. Thus by being "swing," the zazous were spreading un-French genetics and cultural practices, placing the future of the nation at even greater risk.

"Je Suis Swing's" representation of "zazouness" as a racial category, however, pointed to a deeper problem with the Parisian youth. Not only did their performance of swing identity threaten Vichy's notion of a "pure" French race, but it compromised the integrity of the Nazis' entire racial hierarchy. On one level, the fact that the zazous were aligning themselves with blacks undermined Hitler's "scientific" race theory, as it demonstrated symbolically that race was a flexible category whose lines could be redrawn according to a person's tastes. If the zazous' love of jazz music and fashion made them racially different from their French counterparts, then the potential for self-determined racial identity seemed limitless. Pitted against infinite possibilities for newly created racial identities, Hitler's essentialist "truths" about the inherently inferior qualities of other races could not hold.

Yet, the song's construction of swing identity was particularly threatening because it challenged the dominant position of whiteness within Nazi race hierarchy. Indeed, by claiming zazou identity, young Parisians demonstrated the possibility for racial "play" on the white body. As they listened to Hess describe "swing" as a physical state and danced to his "nègre" jazz rhythms, zazous stepped outside the appropriate boundaries of whiteness and experimented with alternative racial markers, an act that, ironically, was made possible by their own racial privilege. As race scholars have recently argued, whiteness derives its power by presenting itself as an invisible, universal identity.[40] In the words of film scholar Richard Dyer, white is perceived as "not anything really, not an identity, not a particularizing quality." It appears as "no colour because it is all colours."[41] This status as a universal allows whiteness to stand at the locus of racial organization, serving as the standard by which all other races can be measured and subordinated.[42] When the zazous embodied the swing race, they relied on the "invisibility" of their whiteness in order to perform a new racial identity, but also undermined whiteness's position as the center of racial organization by suggesting that permutation was possible within the allegedly universal category of white.[43] As young white swings adopted the notion of zazou as a racial construct, they particularized their racial identities. This kind of race play dislodged whiteness from its place at the center of racial organization, thus calling alleged truths about the inferiority of "undesirable" races into question.

Johnny Hess's appeal to a fundamental link between biology and the love of jazz was echoed in many of the French swing songs of the early 1940s. When Vichy grew more aggressive in its anti-Semitism in 1942, popular swing songs became even more explicit in their assertions that "zazou" was a racial identity. One of the clearest examples of this is Henri Martinet and Raymond Vincy's 1942 hit "Y'a des Zazous." The song begins by heralding the arrival of a new zazou race:

Jusqu'ici sur terre	Until now on earth,
un homme pouvait être	a man could be
Blanc ou noir ou jaune ou rouge	White or black or yellow or red
et puis c'est tout	and then that was it
Mais une autre race est en train	But another race is appearing
d'apparaître	
C'est les zazous	It's the zazous

After announcing the appearance of the zazou race, the singer describes the group's physical characteristics. In a playful nod to the fascist understanding of race as rooted in shared physical characteristics, the song states that one can identify a zazou by looking for those who wear a "fake collar that comes up to the tonsils" and sport "hair cut up to the backbone." The lyrics grow more subversive, poking fun at fascist notions of racial contagion by characterizing "zazouness" as a sickness that can spread outside of genetic transfer. Indeed, "the zazou, it's contagious"; the singer himself is already "half of one." The theme of contagion appears in many swing songs of the era, notably in Johnny Hess's 1943 "Ils Sont Zazous." Here, Hess sings of swing as "the sickness that took his daughter, his wife, his priest, his doggie" and that "in the end the whole family, the whole world became zazou." The symptoms of "zazouness" are again visible on the body:

Les ch'veux tout frisottés	Hair all curly
Le col haut de dix-huit pieds	The collar eighteen feet high

Aaah, ils sont zazous	Ah, they are zazous
Le doigt comme ça en l'air	The finger like that in the air
L'veston qui traine traine par terre	The jacket that drags, drags on the ground
Aaah, ils sont zazous	Ah, they are zazous

By describing the unique physical characteristics and habits that are then passed down biologically to future generations or through a process of contagion, the lyrics of this song again represent "zazouness" as a racial category. The introduction of this new race worked to symbolically destabilize existing social hierarchies by demonstrating the potential for racial play. By asserting that zazou identity was rooted in the white body of swing fans, these songs called into question a social hierarchy that relied on a universal whiteness at its center. With no universal white identity left to serve as the standard of measurement, essentialist assumptions about other races suddenly appeared arbitrary and ill-founded.

Yet, the swing songs that were popular among zazous did not merely assign physical features to the swing race, but fleshed out the category to include descriptions of zazou behavioral norms. Perhaps influenced by Nazi/Vichy stereotypes about oversexed blacks, the songs portrayed zazous as insatiable lovers. Take, for example, Loulou Gasté's 1941 hit single "Elle Était Swing," a silly chronicle of a young man's love life. After his zazou girlfriend leaves him, the singer runs off to the countryside to marry another woman who, "blonde and skinny," has all the "proper allures." After they marry, he discovers, to his delight, that the woman he thought to be such a prude is actually zazou. While she "wasn't beautiful" and even "slobbered lightly," she had one physical thing going for her—"something very surprising":

Elle était swing, swing, swing, swing	She was swing, swing, swing
Oh terriblement swing, swing, swing	Oh terribly swing, swing, swing
Je la trouvais divine	I found her divine
Je devins son amant en deux temps trois mouvements	I became her lover in two times three movements

Elle était swing, swing, swing	She was swing, swing, swing
Oh terriblement swing, swing, swing	Oh terribly swing, swing, swing
Et sa lèvre mutine	And her mischievous mouth
Me plaisait follement sans savoir ni pourquoi ni comment	Drove me crazy without knowing how or why

Here, again, the song reasserts "zazou" as a racial identity by character-izing swing as something that one *is*, not something one likes. On the heels of the description of this unpleasant-looking girl, the portrayal of her as physically "swing" evokes the notion of jazz as a bodily marker. After all, it was by *looking* at the girl that the singer could tell that she was not beauti-ful, slobbered a bit, and was swing. However, this physical feature was not revealed to the singer until after his marriage, implying that "swingness" is somehow rooted in sexuality. As the song progresses, the singer reveals more about the race-specific sexual desires that his girlfriend exhibits: "she was a little bizarre, during the day she slept / but what noise what racket when the night fell." These details about the nocturnal passions of his new wife evoke stereotypes about the sexuality of black jazz to represent the zazous as animalistic and sex-crazed. The singer completes this move to make "zazou" into a racial marker at the end of the song, announcing that he and his wife "you guessed it / had a lot of children who sing and dance all the time." Here, the implication is that zazous have voracious sexual appetites that result in many swing children.

Perhaps the best example of the sexual dimensions of zazou identity can be seen in Richard Pottier's 1942 film *Mademoiselle Swing*. Premiering at the height of the zazou phenomenon in June 1942, the film tells the story of Irène, a young girl from the small provincial city of Angoulême, who defies traditional gender norms to become a famous swing singer and dancer.[44] Irène's journey begins one fortuitous night when her swing club hosts a performance by a traveling Parisian band. After the concert, she sneaks out of her uncle's house and goes to the train station to give the handsome bandleader, Pierre, a copy of her own swing composition. Just as she places the song into Pierre's luggage, Irène gets trapped in the cattle compartment of the train and taken to Paris. In the capital city, she adopts an alter ego, Mademoiselle Swing, and captivates Parisian audiences with her hit song and tap-dancing routine. A celebration of the self-made woman, the film offers a model of femininity that transgressed Vichy's emphasis on the domesticated and dutiful Catholic wife. Indeed, while the regime sought to convince women to dedicate their lives to their husbands and children, *Mademoiselle Swing* gave zazous an example of freethinking femininity in the figure of the autonomous and successful Irène.

The film consistently deploys swing music as a symbol of the professionally and sexually liberated woman. In the film's central jazz scene, for example, the Parisian band begins its set by playing a medley of folk songs from a variety of French provinces. As the musicians play, dressed in regional costumes, the camera focuses on a percussionist mocking traditional life. Disguised as a provincial bride, the drummer rejects the flowers offered by his fellow bandmate and only agrees to the pretend marriage when given a goose. The refusal of the flowers suggests that the provincial bride does not want or need to be seduced by romantic gestures. Rather than silly, frivolous flowers, she prefers practical gifts better suited to traditional life. The actors' silly grins and bad costumes make clear the fact that this exchange is intended to poke fun at the ridiculousness of outdated dating customs and conceptions of female desire. The audience responds in kind, laughing at the old-fashioned model of a woman so devoted to her role as a homemaker that she would reject flowers but accept a goose as an appropriate sign of affection. Suddenly, the music changes as the swing band takes up the folk melody, discarding its stiff rhythms for swing syncopations. As the band blasts their catchy riff on traditional songs, the percussionist takes off his disguise and the traditional musicians exit the stage. The sudden musical shift suggests that the world has moved beyond archaic regional courting rituals and parochial notions of domestic femininity. Jazz, the scene argues, operates as a force against the foolish and oppressive ideals of the past.

As the scene continues, swing music deploys an even more overt critique of traditional gender norms. When the bandleader asks if there are any swing enthusiasts in the crowd who would like to perform with the band, the camera pans across the audience for several seconds, searching for someone brave enough to take the stage. Since Pierre's entire band, like most jazz bands of the era, is composed of men, viewers expect a male volunteer. But Pierre's invitation is eventually answered by a group of twelve young women. As the women hurry to the stage, the viewer reflects upon the absence of a courageous male performer. Given Vichy and Nazi Germany's emphasis on strong, tough men and demure, prim women, it seems odd that women would be the ones to take the limelight. The scene's subversive message becomes clearer as the women begin to sing the children's song "Mon Père m'a Donné un Mari" (My Father Gave Me a Husband). At first, the young women sing the song unaccompanied, in straight 4/4 meter. After one verse, the band enters, swinging the rhythm in a jazz style. The women begin to dance, smiling mischievously as they sing about the small size of their husbands:

Mon père m'a donné un mari,	My father gave me a husband,
Mon Dieu, quel homme, quel petit homme!	My God, what a man, what a small man!
Mon père m'a donné un mari,	My father gave me a husband,
Mon Dieu, quel homme, qu'il est petit!	My God, what a man, how little he is!

In this moment, the women issue an even clearer challenge to Vichy and Nazi Germany's emphasis on muscular and tough manhood. Indeed, while prevailing notions of masculinity emphasized physical fitness and strength, the song decries a Frenchman so small that his suit is made from a leaf (*d'une feuille on fit son habit*). By the third verse, the song takes on undeniable sexual overtones as the women continue, lamenting the difficulties of having a small husband in the bedroom:

Dans mon grand lit je le perdis,	In my big bed I lost him
Mon Dieu, quel homme, quel petit homme!	My God, what a man, what a small man!
Dans mon grand lit je le perdis,	In my big bed I lost him,
Mon Dieu, quel homme, qu'il est petit!	My God, what a man, how little he is!

In this verse, the women invite viewers to imagine the sexual failings of such a tiny man. After all, if this husband is so small that his suit is made from a leaf, we can envision the intimate scenarios during which his presence might be underwhelming. Thus, what began as the performance of a familiar, child-like song ends as a statement about the rejection of patriarchy and the recognition of female sexuality. By volunteering to sing a song about the small stature of their husbands, the women point to the failings of the men that governing authorities held responsible for reasserting the nation's virility. The repeated complaints about the husband's small size—particularly the size of his reproductive organs—mark women as sexed beings with desires outside the realm of motherhood. For the zazous, this liberated femininity stood as another component of swing identity.

Just as the lyrics of swing songs proclaimed the advent of the new, sexualized zazou race, to fans, the music sounded the possibilities of identity play. In one of the zazous' most revered treatises on the promise of swing, *De la vie et du jazz*, famous music critic Charles Delaunay wrote that the most important aspect of jazz music was its liberatory swing rhythm.[45] According to Delaunay, swing seemed to defy linear time by displacing the beats from where they would logically fall in a rational progression of time. Without swing, he wrote, "the note, the musical phrase, even the general atmosphere, doesn't appear to detach from the rhythm on which it falls regularly, automatically, mechanically, like the ticktock of a pendulum."[46] Swing's power to give notes a "sort of rhythmic mobility" made it a powerful symbol of freedom from reason, a divisive quality that Delaunay charged with having "separated man into compartments, classes, parties, and races" and led to the First World War.[47] Thus, for the zazous, swing songs were even more powerful tools for the symbolic construction of an alternate identity. Listened to as musical representations of freedom, the rhythms of the songs seemed to mirror the promise of a more open social system that allowed for alternative performances of race and gender. Furthermore, the opinion among jazz fans that swing was a unifying music seems to indicate a degree of intent among the zazous. While we cannot know if they were conscious of the subversive effects of their presence, their reading of Delaunay's book suggests that they would have been in support of the disruption of France's essentialist and divisive racial hierarchy.

Despite the subversive nature of swing lyrics and music, these jazz hits were immensely popular among French audiences. Indeed, given the ban on American jazz, French musicians, who were permitted to record and perform jazz, achieved enormous fame. Thus, we cannot explain the reasons why the zazous were perceived as such threats to French society through an analysis of their music alone. The problem clearly was not jazz music itself; it was jazz music sung on the lips of upper-middle-class white students, dressed in the extravagant and outlandish clothing of American zoot-suiters. As testimonies and newspapers attest, wild combinations of dress and hairstyles accompanied the subversive lyrics of swing songs. The zazou race was taking material form.

Zazous in Zoot Suits: Fashion
as the Embodiment of the Zazou Race

The zazous' appearance was perhaps the most vital component in their subversion of racial hierarchy, as it offered physical evidence of a transgressive, particularized French identity. Their fashion and haircuts often mimicked the descriptions of zazous contained in songs by celebrities like Johnny Hess, Henri Martinet, and Raymond Vincy, suggesting that the zazous existed in real life, not just in the commercial music industry's imagination. Dressed in long, oversized jackets and cropped pants, zazou men adopted a version of the American zoot suit, a style they likely first saw on the bodies of American jazz performers during their prewar concert tours in Europe. Young swing men complemented these suits by wearing their hair long, greased, and often curled.[48] Women zazous wore short skirts, high heels, and heavy makeup. Both genders often embellished their outfits with an umbrella draped over the crook of an arm, an accessory that recalled Neville Chamberlain's habit of carrying an umbrella during public appearances. Poking fun at the fascist notion that race is rooted in and displayed through common physical characteristics, these outfits created the features that would mark the young swings as "zazou." From the perspective of Nazi and Vichy authorities, the zazous' clothes and hair disrupted dominant gender norms by marking swing men as effete and swing women as oversexed, promiscuous jezebels. Drawn from American and British fashion and purchased at exorbitant rates on the black market, these outfits also signified a rejection of Vichy's National

Revolution and allegiance with the Allies. An overt form of resistance, swing fashion elevated the threat posed by the zazous beyond teenage rebellion to the ranks of national betrayal.

In the case of the swing youth, dress offered a powerful method for the construction of racial identity because it allowed zazous to alter the appearance of their bodies. The zoot suit was particularly useful as a marker of zazou identity because it distorted the proportions of the body, causing the arms to look abnormally long, the chest too wide, and the legs bizarrely short. The suit's ability to alter the look of the body is well documented in fictional accounts of the jazz era. In his novel about a young black man's quest for self-discovery, author Ralph Ellison describes his first encounter with black zoot suiters through the voice of his protagonist. "It was as though I'd never seen their like before," he recalls. Amazed at the zoots' physical difference, the hero marvels at how their legs swung "from their hips in trousers that ballooned upward from cuffs fitting snug about their ankles" and how their coats hung "long and hip-tight with shoulders far too broad to be those of natural western men."[49] Struggling to make sense of these altered bodies, he compares them to "those African sculptures, distorted in the interest of design."[50] As Ellison describes, the zoot suit was ideal for changing the appearance of the human body. This feature made it a powerful tool by which zazou men could mark themselves as racially different from their French counterparts. While women zazous did not wear the zoot suit, their makeup, high heels, and short skirts functioned similarly to change the body's proportions and coloring. According to the March 1942 edition of the widely read bourgeois magazine *L'Illustration*, women zazous chose fashions that would alter their bodies, creating outfits out of "bum-freezer jackets with boxy shoulders," "short and pleated skirts" that revealed their legs, and flat shoes with soles stacked as "large as ships."[51] When the zazous complemented these outfits with their own versions of the Jewish yellow star, they provided even more evidence that "zazou" was a racial identity.[52]

Through their fashion, the swing youth deployed the same performance of open sexuality that was described in their songs, particularly for "loose" jazz women. Trading the knee-length skirts and tasteful makeup of the day for "scarlet lips and nails" and "short pleated skirts," these women embodied the sexual freedom that had already been associated with jazz since the 1920s. That their dress was interpreted in this way was obvious to zazou women, who heard complaints and condemnation from their families and from mainstream popular culture. The women's magazine *Pour Elle*, for example, urged women to resist being "swing" so that men would not "think they are something they are not." Arguing that showing so much skin was a mark of "bad taste," the magazine urged women to "love swing in the concerts and not to make it a rule of existence."[53] "Ultra short skirts," the magazine held, were wholly inappropriate for wholesome French women. For the zazous, the same skirts signaled that they weren't that type of girl.

While no photographs exist of zazou women, the costume of the protagonist in the film *Mademoiselle Swing* helps demonstrate the ways that jazz fashion emphasized female sexuality. Before young Irène becomes the fiery and mysterious Mademoiselle Swing, she wears a conservative dress that covers her chest with a high neckline and conceals her shoulders with short sleeves. The waist of the dress is fitted and falls to a feminine and youthful knee-length, full skirt. Yet, when Irène sneaks out to give her first performance on the Parisian stage, she leaves her modest, everyday dress at home. In a frantic search for her runaway niece, Irène's aunt finds the discarded dress and asks in horror, "Did she leave naked?" As the camera shifts to the music hall, we see that Irène did not leave the house nude, but in an elaborate and revealing swing costume. Composed of a strapless black-sequined bodice and matching wide-legged pants, the new outfit marks a significant departure from Irène's gamine-like dress. By exposing her bare chest and shoulders and featuring pants instead of a skirt, the swing outfit portrays Irène as a modern, sexualized woman. Colored by her aunt's suggestion of Irène's potential nudity, the sequined swing ensemble stands as a symbol of promiscuous swing femininity.

For men, the carefully styled appearance of the zazou ran counter to dominant images of appropriate youthful masculinity, projected mainly by the muscular bodies and militaristic dress and haircuts of men in the collaborationist youth movements. Take, for example, one description of swing men from the March 1942 edition of *L'Illustration*:

They wore long checked jackets riddled with pockets and belts. Their shirts had high collars, with long sleeves covering manicured, beringed hands. They were often decorated with woolen and string ties. The trousers were straight, the socks of bright primary colors. The whole effect was topped off with huge crepe-soled shoes and hair, 'oiled like salad,' that hung over their collar. As a final, dandyish touch, they fixed handkerchiefs in their buttonholes.[54]

Within the context of WWII France, the preponderance of complicated accessories like pockets, belts, woolen ties, and handkerchiefs, mixed with the maintenance of "manicured, beringed hands" marked zazou men as effeminate consumers of jazz culture. Indeed, since the 1920s, music critics had portrayed jazz consumerism as a feminine preoccupation, extolling the virtues of face powder and hair-styling cream for women who wanted to stay beautiful as they danced.[55] The long, carefully coifed hairstyles of zazou men recalled this gendered consumption and helped to solidify the notion that male zazous were effeminate and soft. The French adaptation of American zoot suits contributed to this perception by making swing men appear shorter than they really were. A rare photograph of a zazou man demonstrates the ways that the cropped, high-waisted pants shortened the length of the legs and torso and made the male body appear slight (figure 3). The photo underscores the notion of effeminate swing masculinity by capturing the swing in the middle of a swing dance routine. Grinning broadly as he points one finger in the air, the small zazou hardly seems concerned with reasserting the strength and vitality of the nation.

Not only did outlandish clothes and hairstyles position zazous as disruptive men and women, but they also revealed a troubling political dimension of "zazouness." First, the American and British fashions that inspired swing style suggested that the youth sought to align themselves with France's new enemies. Simone de Beauvoir notes this connection in her memoir *The Prime of Life*, recalling that "their Anglophile and anarchic attitude did stand for a kind of opposition to the regime. We saw some of them in the [Café de] Flore, and despite their affected airs, we rather liked them."[56] Wearing versions of American zoot suits and carrying Neville Chamberlain umbrellas, the zazous identified with the two most powerful Allied nations at a time when national survival had been staked upon collaboration with Germany. While the severity of this political

© Albert Harlingue/Roger-Viollet/The Image Works.

Figure 3. Photo of zazou.

betrayal remained obscure—did the clothes mean that the zazous merely liked English music and culture, or did they signify outright support of the Allies?—swing outfits revealed a refusal to view the United States and England as dangerous national enemies. This attitude struck authorities as an unpatriotic national treachery.[57]

More than communicating disloyalty to France, zazou fashion also implicated the swings in a political critique of Vichy's economic policies. As the regime moved to eradicate capitalism and collapse class difference, the zazous stubbornly embraced the economic privilege made possible under the nation's previous government by wearing exorbitantly expensive and complicated swing clothing. Indeed, as historian Dominique Veillon has shown in her study of fashion during the Occupation, the clothing required to embody zazou identity was extremely difficult to procure. While a majority of French textiles were requisitioned by Germany, the remaining cloth and leather was difficult to transport across the boundaries of France's new zones. Additionally, the absence of 1.6 million men held as prisoners of war meant that factories could not maintain normal rates of production.[58] By January 1941, one could only procure leather shoes through a voucher program that constrained citizens to one resoling and one new pair of shoes per year. To conserve materials, the thickness of the sole and the shape of the uppers were regulated. By 1942, no leather shoes were available at all, leading citizens to perfect wooden soles.[59] Clothing was also in short supply. February 14, 1941, marked the last day that department stores could freely sell their merchandise before the implementation of a voucher program. Two months later, citizens would have to comply with the additional burden of donating two items of used clothing for each new item purchased. Women's magazines began featuring articles that advised women how to lengthen their children's shoes, mimic the look of silk stockings with the judicious application of leg dye, and make purses from scraps of leather.[60]

Given such severe shortages of cloth and leather, the zazous' ornate and complicated outfits signaled upper-class belonging, a class performance that ran counter to the economic aims of Vichy's National Revolution. Indeed, the necessary colored socks, oversized jackets, short skirts, large shoulder bags, and sunglasses could only be acquired on the black market, a system that was notorious for price-gouging, charging as much as 200 percent more than prewar costs.[61] Being a zazou was therefore a sign of wealth, for it required access to nonessential materials in a time when most people worried about replacing a worn winter coat or stretching meager food rations through the end of the week. This display of material privilege symbolized the zazous' rejection of the alleged sins of a capitalistic, republican government and demonstrated the young swings' refusal to submit to the authoritarian controls of Vichy's government. These wealthy students, who spent their afternoons in the cafés of Paris's most fashionable neighborhoods, threatened occupying forces because they drew attention to class difference, using their privilege to symbolically embrace the capitalistic system of prewar France. In all, the zazous' fashion combined a demonstration of gender and political difference that did not square with the German and Vichy authorities' emphasis on racial purity or communal living.

Strange Bedfellows: Zazous
and the Collaborationist Press

By early 1942, collaborationists had observed the racial dimension of zazou identity and were releasing a series of articles and cartoons that would underscore the threat presented by the swings' racial play. One of the earliest cartoons to comment on this hazard was "Éclipse de Race: Les Swings" (Racial Eclipse: The Swings), a front-page drawing that ran in the January 29, 1942, edition of the fascist newspaper *Au Pilori* (figure 4). The cartoon depicts a group of Parisians, some seated at a sidewalk café, others walking and talking in the street. The men wear standard zazou clothing; their pants are slightly too short, their coats are made from ostentatious checkered fabric, and their hands grasp long umbrellas. The women are also dressed like zazous, sporting short skirts, teased hair, and platform heels. The headline, "Racial Eclipse," reveals that these outlandish clothes had produced the zazous' desired effect, standing here as physiological markers of racialized zazou identity. The young men and women who wore this clothing, the cartoon suggests, were literally obscuring the French race from view.

"Éclipse de Race" was not the only cartoon whose attempt to denounce the swings worked instead to amplify their critique of the social order in Occupied France. As the zazous perfected their swing outfits and complicated their political and social critiques, the press published myriad columns and cartoons that highlighted their transgression of social norms, reifying the very identity it sought to eradicate. Portraying the swings as impure, queer snobs, the press continually criticized them from within the social order that they rejected. This strategy failed to discipline the zazous because it depended upon the assertion of the very norms that the zazous had already abandoned. In other words, in the process of denouncing the zazous, the press succeeded in exposing the totality of their subversion. Dick Hebdige has observed this phenomenon in his seminal study of subculture and style, noting that countercultures often seek to expose the "false obviousness of everyday practice" by embracing a total departure from the mainstream culture.[62] In a strategy that he calls "revolting style," countercultural groups revere objects that are disdained by society in order to communicate significant difference from the society

Figure 4. *Au Pilori* (January 29, 1942).

they hold to be false.[63] For the zazous, this strategy was particularly effective because it rendered Vichy France and Nazi Germany powerless to control and discipline them. As the flustered press continued its efforts to malign the zazous, it merely drew attention to the their total rejection of fascist values. By the summer of 1942, the press had worsened the threat of zazous by providing inspiration for their resistance. Paradoxically, then, the collaborationist press's efforts to delegitimize the zazous actually worked in their favor. With each cartoon and column, the press affirmed their purposeful transgression of race and gender norms and inspired new methods by which they could critique pro-Nazi France.

Perhaps the most recurring critique of the zazous centered upon their performance of wealth. Pierre Ducrocq, a columnist for the right-wing paper *La Gerbe*, was an especially vocal detractor, using his regular column, "Swing Qui Peut" (Swing Who Can), to denounce the swings as opportunistic consumers. Yet, as I have shown, the zazous' critique relied upon their status as privileged bourgeois citizens and required the defiance of Vichy's economic policies. Thus, when Ducrocq lamented the presence of the snobby zazous in the June 4, 1942, edition of *La Gerbe*, his attack confirmed the success of the zazous' performance of upper-class identity, even as it denounced the youth as greedy and materialistic. According to Ducrocq, "At a time when we must above all count on the youth, they betray our hope." Instead of following Pétain's plan for a society based on community and work, they "dream of a bourgeois 'rascaltocracy' [*voyoucratie*]."[64] Later in June 1942, he explained the primary conditions of becoming a zazou—having money but "not having anything to do."[65] For Ducrocq, the zazous' eccentric fashion was the ultimate proof of their wealth. Criticizing the "blind parents" who financed the "bourgeois" and "expensive" tastes of their swing children, he exclaimed that "Swing is bourgeois! Swing is expensive!"[66] Other columnists echoed Ducrocq's assessment of the zazous' financial ease, lamenting the arrival of "zazou snobbism," and encouraging an attitude of disdain for those "daddy's boys" who don't "stand for anything but themselves and the gains of the black market."[67] For the wealthy zazous whose expensive fashion worked to symbolize their refusal to take ownership of the nation's alleged sins, such a critique was powerless. Instead of shaming them into submission, Ducrocq's insults drew attention to the teenagers' refusal to play by Vichy's new class rules.

The press also remarked on the zazous' failure to adhere to traditional codes of gender and sexuality. According to the September 16, 1943, edition of *Au Pilori*, the zazous augmented the nation's shame by putting on exhibitionist shows of passion in front of German soldiers. Recounting a particularly steamy scene between a zazou couple on the metro, the anonymous author describes the inappropriate way that the young swings behave. Cuddled tenderly together, the "'male' whispers confidences in the ear of the 'female'" who "as if in a state of ecstasy swoons, giving the performance of a physical tension at the last stage, the one that precedes the great launch" (*comme en état d'extase, se pâme en offrant le spectacle d'une tension physique au dernier stade, celle qui précède le grand départ*). The author's recounting of such inappropriate public sexual activity and use of quotation marks around the words "male" and "female" reveal that he perceives zazou youth as lying outside the boundaries of respectable masculinity and femininity. Yet, for the zazou women who had celebrated the success of the sexually liberated protagonist of the film *Mademoiselle Swing* and danced to the syncopated rhythms of a song about the sexual shortcomings of their lovers, this public display of female sexuality was hardly cause for alarm. Instead, the *Au Pilori* author's condemnation of the zazous' "parade of love" worked as validation that the swings' gender transgression was culturally intelligible.[68] Pitted against the swings' continued defiance of gender norms, the article demonstrated the zazous' complete rejection of fascist notions of respectable femininity.

Due to the American influences on their musical and fashion tastes, the zazous were also portrayed as lovers of Anglo-Saxon culture and supporters of the Allied Forces. According to an article in *Au Pilori*, the zazous incorporated English into their everyday speech, greeting each other with a hearty "A l'eau! A l'eau!" (Hello! Hello!) and departing with a "Baille, baille" (Bye-bye).[69] Pierre Ducrocq warned of their dancing habits, casting doubt on the zazous' national fitness because of their affinity for an "epileptic, Anglo-Saxon dance."[70] These cultural preferences allegedly signaled betrayal of France and support for Great Britain in the war effort. One columnist in *Au Pilori* wrote that "the zazou-zazou is . . . of gaullist sentiments."[71] Another columnist, writing before the summer vacation of 1942, wished his readers a happy vacation in spite of the pesky zazous who had reportedly appeared in the western region of France. "They're going," he said, "probably to testify in their own way to the high regard in which they hold the ineffable Neville Chamberlain."[72] For the zazous who appropriated the zoot suits of American jazzmen and accessorized them with umbrellas like those carried by Neville Chamberlain, the critiques of zazous as pro-Allied were hardly devastating. Rather than exposing some horrible secret about the zazous' wayward politics, these insults merely emphasized the zazous' alignment with the Allies. In the end, the press's critiques demonstrated that the zazous had so fully rejected the social codes of fascist France that they could no longer be disciplined through symbolic means.

By the summer of 1942, the collaborationist press had proven to be such a constructive force for publicizing the zazous' subversive identities that the young swings began drawing inspiration from its criticisms. In their most significant effort to malign the zazous, editors at the fascist newspaper *Au Pilori* published a series of cartoons that aimed to deny the existence of a unique zazou race by depicting the swings as Jews. If they could represent zazous as Jews instead of wayward white teens, *Au Pilori*'s editors hoped, they could deny the possibility of race play and rehabilitate an essentialized racial hierarchy. Portraying zazous as Jews was a promising strategy for collaborationists, as the connection resonated with fascists' earlier efforts to establish jazz as the product of both black and Jewish musicians. As musicologist Michael Kater has shown, earlier race "scientists" had already documented that these groups shared common blood, despite Jews' allegedly superior mental powers. Black blood coupled with sly cunning, according to the Nazis, accounted for Jews' special talent as jazz performers and their success as commercial music managers.[73] Moreover, as the smarter, genetic cousins of blacks, Jews were portrayed as especially fearsome sexual predators. Indeed, while blacks allegedly had no control over their sexuality, Jews, the Nazis held, were purposefully plotting to seduce Aryan men and women.[74] To sell these beliefs, fascist music critics and concert organizers blended symbols of black and Jewish identity in order to align the two groups. The poster for Dusseldorf's 1938 exposition of "degenerate" music, for example, featured a monkey-like black, wearing a Star of David and playing the saxophone.[75]

Rooting their cartoons in these past attempts to portray jazz as black and Jewish music, *Au Pilori* emphasized the alleged similarities between the zazous and Jews in order to deny the existence of a unique swing race. A cartoon from the May 28, 1942, edition of *Au Pilori* shows two Jewish women preparing for an evening out (figure 5). The blonde woman is dressed in typical zazou fashion, wearing a loud, polka-dotted dress and a hat adorned with the Croix de Lorraine, the symbol of Charles de Gaulle's Free French Forces. The dark-haired woman, drawn with a stereotypically large Jewish nose and a Star of David on her dress, offers her opinion on her friend's new hat: "I think it's charming, but is it not a bit too original?" The blonde replies, "You mean to say that it's the most zazou of all of my swing hats!" The dialogue emphasizes three alleged similarities—political disloyalty, greediness, and promiscuity—between Jewish and zazou consumer practices to align the two groups. While there is no record of zazous actually wearing the Croix de Lorraine, the cartoon deploys the Gaullist symbol to allude to the zazous' alleged support of the Allies. To compare zazou and Jewish consumption practices, the cartoonist underscores the fact that the ridiculous Croix de Lorraine hat accounts for just one of the blonde's collection of ostentatious swing hats. Finally, the cartoonist depicts the blonde in a tight, low-cut dress and heavily applied makeup to assert zazou and Jewish women as oversexed vixens, well outside the boundaries of Vichy's model of domestic femininity. Like

— Je le trouve charmant, mais n'est-il pas un peu trop original?
— Vous voulez dire que c'est le plus zazou de tous mes chapeaux swing!

Figure 5. *Au Pilori* (May 28, 1942).

the pro-Allied, greedy, immoral Jews, the zazous, the cartoon asserts, are unpatriotic, loose, and capitalistic detriments to society.

Other cartoons were more explicit in drawing the link between the capitalistic, immoral Jews and the zazous. For example, on June 6, 1942, the ominously titled fascist newspaper *Je Suis Partout* (I Am Everywhere) published another cartoon featuring a hypothetical version of France, governed by Charles de Gaulle, personified as a Jewish, zazou woman. The woman dances scandalously for the rest of the European nations, all depicted as leering, wealthy Jewish men (see figure 6). The caption reads, "For a Swing France in a Zazou Europe." The claim of the cartoon is

Figure 6. *Je Suis Partout* (June 6, 1942).

that the zazous, like the Jews, would ruin France by refusing to abandon their corrupt attachment to capitalism. Instead of returning to the land and relying on their local communities, de Gaulle and his zazous would make France vulnerable to the trends of the world market. The cartoonist symbolizes this economic "selling out" of the nation through a veiled reference to prostitution. Standing atop a bar, dancing with her legs open, Zazou, Jewish, Gaullist France seems willing to let any nation defile her for the right price. In both of these cartoons, the artist mixes the physical markings of zazous and Jews to insinuate that both groups present the same menace to French society. By subsuming zazous into the category of Jews, the cartoon attempts to discipline the zazous by denying the existence of a unique "swing" race.

Yet, rather than being silenced by the press's attacks, the zazous simply appropriated them into their subversive repertoire. In June 1942, weeks after *Au Pilori* printed their first Jewish/zazou cartoons, young swings like Ginette Orien seized the connection between themselves and the Jews as inspiration for their Yellow Star campaign. Historian Sophie Roberts has noted the direct link between the press's cartoons and the zazous' Yellow Star campaign, arguing that these caricatures motivated the zazous' protest by setting them far enough outside the boundaries of society that they could embrace overt political resistance.[76] My analysis invites us to reconsider their resistance within the context of an ongoing constructive relationship between the press and the zazous. As I have shown, the zazous had removed themselves from Vichy/Nazi society long before *Au Pilori* published its cartoons. By pinning homemade "zazou" yellow stars to their clothing, the zazous acknowledged and exploited their purported similarity to the nation's most "undesirable" group to insist upon their status as a racial community. As they played along with this connection, the youth argued for their own *unique* swing identity. Inscribing their stars with the words "swing," "jazz," and "zazou," the youth refused to accept a collapse of Jewish/zazou identity and alerted authorities to the fact that there were at least two impure "races" threatening the nation. Therefore, the campaign should be understood as another act of subversion, another moment in which the zazous transformed collaborationist insults into a means of thumbing their noses at fascist social and political ideology.

By the end of June 1942, the zazous' subversive ideology proved to be too far outside fascist social order to combat through symbolic means. Ultimately, collaborationists would resort to violence to subdue the unruly teenagers. In an article published in the June 11, 1942, edition of *Au Pilori* entitled "What Is a Zazou-Zazou?," author Ferdinand encouraged readers to damage the zazous' clothing and shave their hair. "The most practical remedy for getting rid of a zazou," he wrote, "consists of either cutting his jacket or overcoat with scissors, or with removing his hair with clippers." These solutions, Ferdinand continued, avoided the risk of making the zazou into a martyr while "demoralizing" him and "depriving him of all his means of action."[77] One week later, another columnist noted that the "zazou hunt . . . is already open."[78]

Figure 7. *Le Cri du Peuple* (June 23, 1942).

Responding to these articles, members of the Jeunesses Populaires Françaises organized to execute attacks on the zazous they saw in the streets, reprising a familiar strategy for the correction of disloyal female sexuality (figure 7). As Fabrice Virgili has documented in his study of women accused of "horizontal collaboration," the shearing of hair has long been a method of punishment for female sexual betrayal, existing in France during the thirteenth and fourteenth centuries before being reprised during the Liberation in 1944.[79] The JPF tackled the zazous to the ground and tore their clothes and shaved their heads, no doubt recalling their leader's admonition that "you will be hard, you will be strong,

you will be violent, but you will be correctly dressed."[80] Given the fact
that zazou men purposefully dressed themselves in ways that violated
Vichy's codes of virile masculinity, we can read the shaving of their heads
as an effort to rid the zazou of his sexual and class identity and remark
his body as a sign of appropriate French manhood. The discourse that
accompanied the press coverage of these attacks corroborates this explanation. Full of sexual innuendo, the caption at the bottom of a June 23,
1942, cartoon from fascist newspaper *Le Cri du Peuple* asks the trampled
zazou if "he wouldn't like a little rubdown" (*friction*). Even the cartoon
evokes the sexual dimension of the attacks. In a posture that recalls the
act of rape, the JPF member straddles the zazou from behind to shave his
hair, unmarking his swing identity and bringing his body back under the
control of dominant codes of race and gender.

Conclusion

Far from empty or meaningless teenage rebellion, the zazous' swing
identity was deeply disturbing to occupying authorities because it destabilized the social order espoused by Nazi and Vichy authorities. Jazz
music, a cultural product considered to be an inferior, "Negro" art form,
provided the symbolic means by which Parisian youth could mobilize
their white privilege and invent a new racial category that troubled the
essentialized social norms of the era. By adopting the clothing described
in the songs they sang, these young people embodied their "zazouness,"
marking themselves as transgressive men and women and individualistic
capitalists who threatened the rebirth of a pro-German France. Even the
collaborationist press's efforts to malign them contributed to their countercultural identity. Repeatedly portraying the zazous in terms of their
own swing identity, the press merely demonstrated society's inability to
bring them back under the control of fascist ideology.

By the end of 1942, the press's campaign against the zazous had
subsided. While the young swings may have been cowed by the JPF's attacks, it is more likely that the implementation of forced labor for French
youth in German munitions factories led many of the swings to trade
their zoot suits for less conspicuous clothing. Indeed, as Vichy agreed

to supply Germany with increasingly large numbers of young workers in 1942 and 1943, dressing as a zazou became too risky for those who hoped to fly under the authorities' radar and remain in France. Yet, just as the zazous were hanging up their short skirts and umbrellas, across the Rhine river, more than 1.6 million of their compatriots were busily forming jazz ensembles, staging variety shows, and writing original operettas. France's prisoners of war, emasculated by the nation's defeat, also turned to musical culture to survive the *années noires*, mining the genres of *chanson* and operetta for tools with which to survive their long captivity.

CHAPTER 4

From Prisoners to Men

Operettas on the POW Camp Stage

———•◆•———

D uring their five-year captivity in Oflag XVII A, a German prisoner-of-war camp in northeastern Austria, a group of French soldiers surreptitiously filmed a documentary entitled *Sous le Manteau* (On the Sly). Hiding the film in the soles of their shoes and camouflaging the camera inside a hollowed-out dictionary, the prisoners recorded rare images from inside the camp, including scenes from its vibrant theater culture. The documentary begins by taking the viewer into the middle of the performance of a play in which a married couple pushes their baby stroller across a pretend boulevard. Garbed in a floral dress and white gloves, the beautiful, feminine wife pauses to comb her fingers through her shoulder-length blonde hair as her husband admires her. Suddenly, footage of the play ends and the film shows another, more raucous performance. Instead of a prim and modest housewife, we see a beautiful dark-haired woman, swishing her skirt to expose her bare legs as she performs a cancan routine. The camera then moves to the audience, showing the soldiers seated in the front row leaning forward to get a closer look. They exchange glances, jabbing each other in the ribs to see if their friends are equally appreciative of the dancer's charms. As the cancan routine comes to a close, the prisoners' faces change from prurient admiration to amusement. Remembering that the beautiful starlet is really just a costumed male prisoner, they laugh and applaud vigorously. Underscoring the falseness of the female impersonation, the camera moves to behind the stage where the "actresses" remove their skirts and put on their fatigues. The film's narrator closes the montage by explaining the unmarking of female identity as a process of shoring up manhood. "The [male] sex takes back its rights" (*le sexe reprend ses droits*), he observes.

The footage of theatrical performances given in Oflag XVII A offers a unique glimpse into the rhetorical function of culture for more than 1.6 million French prisoners of war held in captivity from 1940 to 1945. These soldiers were imprisoned for the duration of the war and bore the majority of the guilt for France's shocking defeat, a capitulation that was largely understood as a loss of national virility. Despite the humiliation of their capture and the stark conditions of camp life, the prisoners established vibrant theaters where they performed hundreds of variety shows, dramas, and original operettas, most of which told tales of beautiful young women pining for the emotional and physical pleasures of true love. As the narrator of *Sous le Manteau* reveals, these performances were not mere entertainment, void of political import. Indeed, the power of these performances, I argue, was that they invited prisoners to "take back the rights" of their sex, to reclaim their manly dignity and national pride. As male prisoners watched the compelling performances of their comrades, dressed in tailored skirts and well-styled wigs, they objectified and subordinated the female body, a process by which they could measure their sexual dominance and reclaim a sense of virile masculinity. While the most commonly displayed body was that of the European woman, operettas also featured representations of women indigenous to France's colonies. These embodied representations, I argue, played a particularly important role in consolidating French manliness, as they directed the expression of heterosexual desire through the prism of colonial domination to cast the men as powerful, civilized agents.

Yet, despite their convincing nature, the female impersonations were an imperfect means of securing the prisoners' positions as virile men. Indeed, as actors adopted the mannerisms and dress of women, they also pointed to the performative nature of gender, demonstrating that even an unkempt man could transform his body into that of a beautiful, elegant starlet. Ultimately, then, the female impersonators threatened the notion of essential manhood that the prisoners were trying to recuperate. Wrestling with the ambiguity of gender, the men reacted to the staged performances by producing additional discourse that reminded them of the female impersonators' true identities. I argue that these reminders, found in the cartoons and theatrical reviews of the camp press, worked simultaneously to guard against the homoeroticism inherent to cross-dressing while upholding the authenticity of the "women" that grounded the notion of essential manliness. Together, the performances and the printed responses reveal that the POW operettas walked a discursive tightrope between believable but transparent female impersonations.

But POW operettas did not just remind the men of their desire for women. Through the representation of a hypersexualized femininity, these performances also reminded them of women's desire for men. Indeed, as male actors disguised as beautiful young heroines yearned for the pleasures of heterosexual intercourse, they invited prisoners to see themselves as the only beings capable of satisfying women's physical needs. While the nation's defeat had stripped the men of their status as talented and heroic soldiers, operettas offered another foundation on which to build manly self-worth—sexual prowess and dominance. This self-image, already grounded in French national identity, proved particularly useful as the men struggled to accept a seemingly interminable captivity that jeopardized their national relevance. Distraught by their lack of political influence and anxious about the continued fidelity of their wives, prisoners assuaged their fears, I argue, by staging allegorical operettas that deployed heterosexual love as a metaphor for their relationship to fallen France. These tales worked in tandem with appeals to manly sexual prowess to assure the prisoners that the nation was pining for their return.

While the recurring phenomenon of prisoner-of-war theater has been documented across a variety of historical and national contexts and publicized in films like Renoir's *La Grande Illusion*, scholars have been slow to analyze the critical function of French prisoners' theatrical and musical performances during World War II.[1] Although two seminal studies, Pierre Gascar's *Histoire de la captivité des Français en Allemagne: 1939–1945* and Yves Durand's *Prisonniers de guerre dans les Stalags, les Oflags et les Kommandos, 1939–1945,* document the importance of cultural life within the camps, neither work attempts to reconstruct and explicate the performances themselves as tools of survival. Nonetheless, these scholars have paved the way for future analysis by excavating vital primary sources that document the theater's ability to provide a creative outlet and a means of temporary escape.[2] Marshaling evidence from prisoner testimonials, letters, and diary entries, these works shed light on the theater as a refuge from the loneliness and depression suffered in captivity, and lay the groundwork for critical analysis of the performances themselves.

More recently, scholars have begun interrogating the ways in which cultural life inside German prison camps, or the prisoners' performances of plays, operettas, orchestral concerts, and variety shows, served as a site of resistance. Andreas Kusternig, for example, has documented the protest of a cabaret group called "Les Bigophones" that performed in the cabaret at Oflag XVII. Using similar sources as Durand and Gascar, Kusternig demonstrates that the theater provided prisoners with a variety of props that could camouflage the construction of escape tunnels.[3] While Kusternig's work helps to establish the theater as a political space of resistance and dissent, it does not consider how the performances themselves gave voice to partisan attitudes or fostered subversion. How, for example, did theatrical storylines and music provide the symbolic means through which prisoners could assuage the guilt and humiliation of their defeat? How did staged performances provide rhetorical opportunities for French prisoners to recover a sense of agency in a camp where their every move was dictated and controlled by the Reich? How did the theater offer inventional resources through which the prisoners could rehabilitate a damaged relationship with their home country, a nation that many felt had abandoned them?

I approach the analysis of POW theater as a reflective space where prisoners could recast and resolve their unique social struggles. Borrowing from Victor Turner's theory of the theater as a set of magic mirrors that magnify, distort, or diminish the faces that peer into them, I view the POWs' staged performances as opportunities for POWs to combat their feelings of emasculation and shame by creating images of themselves that emphasized their virility and strength.[4] After all, to borrow Turner's words, "no one likes to see himself as ugly, ungainly, or dwarfish"—or, in the case of the prisoners, untough, undesirable, or unmanly.[5] The prisoners' own writings underscore the constitutive function of the stage. Indeed, actors and spectators urged fellow prisoners to submit original scripts and audition for roles so that the theater could be "better suited to their wishes."[6] Paul Juif, a former captive in Stalag VII A, compared the role of the prisoners' theater to that of the ancient Greeks, urging his comrades to treat the stage as a vehicle for expressing their patriotism and building their manhood. "The theatre," he wrote, not only offered a "powerful agent for the diffusion of Hellenism" and "all the ideas and feelings that attach" to Greek nationalism, but it also "helped in the emancipation of man," the development of the freethinking "modern man."[7] Others encouraged their fellow men to use the theater as a means of defying German oppression. In a pamphlet entitled "To Understand the Prisoners," for example, Joseph Folliet remembers that under "the eye of the victor," dramatic and musical performances proved that, although defeated, "we are not broken."[8] The writings of prisoners like Juif and Folliet demonstrate that the theater was more than a tool for escape or an avenue for creativity. The stage offered a rhetorical venue where they could throw off the humiliation of defeat and reclaim their positions as proud Frenchmen, beloved by country and family.[9]

Throughout my analysis, I strive to maintain emphasis on the performed nature of POW operetta. Like music critic Simon Frith, I treat these songs not as literary objects to be "analyzed entirely separately from music," but as "speech acts, words to be analyzed in performance."[10] While the prisoners staged productions of all sorts of theatrical events—including drama and dance—their musicals provided a particularly rich rhetorical opportunity as most of the melodies were taken from the genres of *chanson* and operetta. A symbol of French national identity revered as a verbal form as much as a musical form, *chanson* carried aural markers of Frenchness while highlighting the textual appeals that prisoners would need in order to defy their position as the vanquished soldiers of a fallen nation.[11] Operetta, a form of light opera that first appeared in the mid-nineteenth century and featured political satire, erotic jokes, and romantic plotlines, offered soldiers a model of musical performance already suited to the project of challenging Nazi power and recovering their lost manhood.[12] Ultimately, by combining melodies of both genres into new, original operettas, the prisoners marked themselves as proud Frenchmen who refused to accept the emasculation of defeat.

The most vital component to the operetta's reclamation of the prisoners' masculinity was the powerful illusion of a feminine presence. Wearing carefully styled wigs and fashionable dresses, the female impersonators— or *travestis*, as they were called in French—were a mainstay of the camp stage. Like the American female impersonators who rose to stardom in the mid-nineteenth and early-twentieth centuries, the men who played these roles were not excessive, overembellished drag queens, but imitators who aimed to reproduce femininity as convincingly as possible.[13] In the process, the men privileged certain representations of womanhood over others, exerting power over the construction of appropriate gender boundaries. Jill Dolan has theorized this phenomenon, arguing that male cross-dressing allows both the performer and spectator to "conspire to construct a male-identified subject," a mythical woman born out of male desire and dominance.[14] Sharon Ullman echoes this observation in her study of American female impersonators, noting that the process of imitating women gave men the opportunity to take power over normative femininity and reinforce male authority.[15] Thus, the "women" who elicited the lustful gazes of French POWs confirmed the prisoners' power, as they were always already reflections of their preferred version of womanhood.

These women, formed in man's own image and for his pleasure, cemented the prisoners' masculinity by facilitating the maintenance of a patriarchal brotherhood. Indeed, as footage from *Sous le Manteau* reveals, prisoners did not experience heterosexual desire as an insular, private yearning, but as a communal affirmation of their gender dominance. When the two beautiful starlets strutted across the stage, for example, the film captured prisoners exchanging glances and elbowing each other's ribs, bonding over their shared desire for, and dominion over, women. Eve Sedgwick has explained the constitutive nature of male heterosexual longing, arguing that it works to "consolidate partnership with authoritative males in and through the bodies of females."[16] Extending René Girard's concept of the erotic triangle—a model of heterosexual desire that identifies a third axis of power in sexual relationships—Sedgwick notes that the relationship between men, even rivals, is "even stronger and more determinant of actions and choices" than their desire for beloved women. This manly bond—elicited by the sexual pursuit of women—is "definitive of masculinity."[7] Thus, as men gathered in makeshift theaters to participate in the communal ogling of representations of sexy leading ladies, they strengthened their understanding of belonging to that special system of domination: patriarchy.

Yet, just as the exhibition of representative female bodies offered men the opportunity to experience and express manly virility, it also undermined their manhood. Prisoner diaries and camp newspapers confirm the destabilizing nature of the female impersonations, documenting that the feelings they elicited occupied a slippery position between sanctioned heterosexual desire and transgressive homoeroticism. Judith Butler has explained this slippage, demonstrating that cross-dressing displaces "the entire enactment of gender significations from the discourse of truth and falsity."[8] In other words, in established normative hierarchies where people are assumed to have a stable, internal identity that is marked on the body, female impersonations confuse the distinction between interior identities and readable exteriors, exposing the notion of essentialized gender as a lie. Thus, the POW theater offered an imperfect means of securing the prisoners' positions as powerful, virile men and required additional discourse in order to police the porous boundary between heterosexual and homosexual desire.

Disarmed and Dismantled: The Emasculation of Capture

Even before France's official defeat in June 1940, the experience of war with Germany was interpreted through gendered terms that heralded a crisis in French masculinity.[19] Outmatched by the size, youth, and technological superiority of the German army, the French military proved unable to defend the nation's borders or shield civilians from combat. Indeed, as the German army penetrated France with alarming speed, the illusion of a safe civilian zone apart from the official war "front" evaporated, forcing the nation's women, children, and elderly out of their homes in search of safe shelter. In what is known as the *Exode*, between eight and ten million French citizens and Belgian refugees fled the fighting, transforming the nation's streets into chaotic labyrinths. Accounts of this period emphasize the feminine nature of this national fleeing, highlighting the tales of mothers leading children through the panic-stricken mob, and desperate women selling their bodies for gasoline.[20] In his memoir, Jean Vidalenc describes the horror in vivid detail, recalling the "craters that blasted out of the roads by bombs, houses that were falling down or in flames . . . and everywhere, alas the dead." Amongst the destruction and carnage, one sight struck him as particularly terrible: Lying against a wall was "a woman who was fatally wounded, holding in her arms a baby of about two, whose skull was completely split open. At her side two children of three and five years old crying."[21] The suffering endured by women and children, perceived to be the nation's most vulnerable demographic, validated the notion that French manhood had been weakened. The resolved and valiant soldiers who so victoriously defended the nation in 1919, it seemed, were nowhere to be found.

While French civilians struggled to escape combat zones, the French army withdrew in confusion and dismay. After just six weeks of fighting, the French army surrendered, having sustained twice as many casualties as Hitler's army. When combat ceased, the Germans took 1.8 million French soldiers as prisoners of war, making them the highest number of men ever captured at one time in the history of warfare.[22] While soldiers who had served in World War I and those who had four or more children were repatriated, 1.6 million Frenchmen were held captive in Germany, nearly 1 million imprisoned for five years. The men held in German prisoner-of-war camps accounted for the nation's youngest and most robust men. As historian Yves Durand reports, 65 to 70 percent were between the ages of twenty-five and thirty-five, the average age being just over thirty years old. Most were married and had young children.[23] The Germans had not only defeated the French, they had beaten and captured the nation's strongest and most virile men.

Although Vichy leader Philippe Pétain sought to deflect criticism from the soldiers by blaming capitulation on the decadent individualism of the Third Republic and the nation's low birth rate, the vanquished soldiers felt the sting of defeat with particular acuteness. The experiences of most captured soldiers did not square with contemporary notions of military valor, especially since most were taken prisoner without ever seeing active combat.[24] According to Yves Durand, "the captives were seized by a feeling of powerlessness," sickened by "having participated in the collapse of the nation."[25] Former POW Raymond Henri recalled reading about the soldiers' disgrace in an editorial while imprisoned. "The prisoners are France's shame," he remembers reading. "They should have gotten themselves killed rather than accepting a life of luxury [*la vie de chateaux*] in Germany." François Mitterrand, an imprisoned soldier who would later become the nation's president, also noted the nation's disdainful attitude toward the prisoners, writing in 1945 that "we were defeated soldiers and therefore contemptible."[26]

The prisoners' own experiences of disarmament and imprisonment lent even greater resonance to their national shame. In their testimonies and memoirs, former POWs often recall the humiliation of being stripped of their weaponry and uniforms. Describing his capture, Captain Arnoult remembered the shame of surrendering his equipment: "Each man passed through the hands of a few [German] soldiers: one tore off my bag, another my identity cards [*porte-cartes*], they made us throw away our helmet and gas mask, and it was in jacket and bare head, possessing nothing more than a satchel, that I took my place in the troop."[27] After spending several weeks in hastily built and unsanitary provisional camps known as *Frontstalags*, the troops were hauled across the Rhine in overcrowded cattle cars where they endured horrible thirst, hunger, and filth on their way to undisclosed locations. Sergent Depoux described the inhuman conditions that he and his men suffered during their three-day journey to Stalag 1 A: "What a voyage! Piled to sixty or seventy in cattle cars with almost no provisions; a stop every 24 hours for the satisfaction of natural needs," he wrote. When it was time to sleep, "Big fights took place every night" as men tried to find room to stretch their legs. In the end, as Depoux remembers, they scrambled for a place at the edges of the cart where they could sit with their legs crossed and lean their heads against the slopes of the train. Immobilized there until the train stopped, "it was a true torture."[28] Upon their arrival in Germany, many prisoners were paraded through city streets, where local residents mocked and ridiculed them. One soldier remembered women and children hurling insults at him while they drew their fingers across their throats in gestures of execution.[29]

Once in German territory, the prisoners were divided among eighty-seven different camps, located across Germany, Poland, and Austria. The officers, who the Geneva Convention of 1929 specified could not be forced to work in enemy territory, were separated from their troops and divided across seventeen *Oflags*. The enlisted men, who made up the vast majority of the prisoners, were dispersed among seventy *Stalags*, where they would await assignment to one of the 82,000 work camps known as *Kommandos*.[30] While most prisoners credit the German soldiers with treating the French with professionalism and even compassion, their testimonies underscore the struggle to maintain a sense of dignity and self-respect inside the camps. One of the most frequently recounted experiences of captivity was the embarrassment of mass cleansings and delousings. In his diary, former officer Georges Mongrédien described the emasculation he and his comrades experienced as they undressed and surrendered all their clothing, bedding, and bags to the Germans for disinfection. The men's heads and genitals were then shaved before they were subjected to a shower, the application of a gray anti-lice ointment, a soda cleaning, and a second shower. Afterwards, the naked men walked in single file to the German doctor's office who examined all their (formerly) "hairy parts." For the next two hours, the men waited for the return of their clothing and personal effects in a cramped and cold room. Mongrédien remembers the humiliation of the experience, noting that "nothing was more ridiculous than these fifty men, crammed together, completely naked, chatting as though in a salon . . . we suffered an inexpressible sense of embarrassment." In a final demeaning gesture, the Germans threw their clean laundry and bedding "pêle-mêle" in the grass of the camp courtyard, leaving the naked men shivering and exposed as they searched for their belongings.[31] Forced nakedness was a common experience throughout captivity, particularly in the first months when soldiers eagerly awaited a second set of clothing from their families or the Red Cross. Former POW François Lalin remembers that "during many months, you had to wash your clothes in Adam's suit [*en costume d'Adam*] and watch over them as they dried . . . because all unguarded laundry was regularly stolen."[32]

The intense humiliation of the first few weeks of captivity yielded only to an acute awareness of the loss of one's personal autonomy. Prisoners' daily lives were regulated by German guards who planned their meals, assigned their work detachments, and organized their daily schedules, including the times at which they would wake, submit to "roll call," and go to bed. The Reich even controlled the men's contact with their own friends and families. Prisoners and their wives could only exchange two letters and two postcards per month, with letters restricted to twenty-seven lines and postcards limited to seven lines. All correspondence was heavily censored to prevent prisoners and their families from discussing political topics.[33] For men in *Oflags*, constant confinement to the camp meant that personal autonomy was especially constrained. For five years, these men never heard the running water of a stream or felt the cool shade of a large tree. And while the enlisted soldiers enjoyed greater freedom of movement when working on labor detachments, they, too, lived in social isolation as they were strictly forbidden from fraternizing with German civilians.

One of the greatest hardships for both groups of prisoners was the lack of female contact. Men in the *Oflags* were confined behind the barbed wire of their camps for the entire war, deprived of even the sight of a woman for the duration of their imprisonment. In their diaries, the imprisoned soldiers repeatedly lamented the absence of women, remarking that they had not seen a woman's face or heard a woman's voice for the entire five years of their captivity. Camp newspapers often featured drawings and sketches that poked fun at the officers' desperation for female contact. In a drawing entitled "Nostalgie" (Nostalgia) created by the prisoners in Oflag III C in July 1941, for example, a group of soldiers gathers to gaze upon a pair of women's undergarments that hang on a clothesline just beyond the barbed wire.[34] Holding their heads in their hands, the men stare at the bloomers with mixed expressions of fascination and yearning (figure 8).

So desperate were the prisoners for female contact that many risked severe reprisals when presented with the rare opportunity for female interaction. Georges Mongrédien recalled such an event in his diary, writing that "This afternoon, a young comrade watched some walkers pass by: six young girls passed; one of them blew him a kiss; at the risk of ten

Figure 8. "Nostalgie," July 1941.

years in prison, he responded with the same gesture!"[35] Even in *Stalags* where prisoners were more likely to interact with the German civilian population on their work detachments, access to women was limited to prevent the formation of romantic relationships. Given the paramount importance of protecting the purity of the nation's bloodline, punishment for "interracial" sexual relationships was severe. On September 10, 1939, Hitler announced that German women who committed "crimes against the race" would have their heads shaved publicly and would be deported to concentration camps for at least one year. Prisoners of war who slept with German women risked imprisonment or death.[36] Thus, not only were prisoners prevented from socializing with women, but they were confined to a homosocial space where heterosexual acts were virtually impossible. While mention of homosexual relationships is rare within the writings of the prisoners, some did note their existence. Former prisoner Robert Christophe, for example, described learning of a German lecture given to Frenchmen on "the danger, the shame, and the immorality of relationships between men."[37] In his pamphlet "To Understand the Prisoners," Joseph Folliet, in a homophobia characteristic of the time, decried the presence of "sex maniacs—fortunately very rare—who looked for arousal in imitation and sometimes, alas, substitute lovers."[38]

Despite their feelings of humiliation and deprivation, prisoners in both the *Oflags* and *Stalags* organized elaborate cultural centers in the heart of their camps. Almost immediately upon their arrival in German territory, the prisoners arranged themselves into orchestras, choirs, and theatrical troupes and began petitioning their families and the Red Cross for sheet music, musical instruments, and scripts. While the artistic groups often performed separately—the orchestra playing an evening of Chopin, for example, or the actors reviving a classic Molière play—they also pooled their talents to put on original operettas. These musicals responded directly to the prisoners' feelings of emasculation and powerlessness, inviting them to see themselves once more as manly agents. Indeed, as one prisoner wrote in *Confins*, the newspaper of Stalag 1 A, the theater proved that they "always succeed in what they truly want," that no amount of adversity and isolation could kill their proud French spirits.[39] Yet, as we shall see, the reassertion of the prisoners' virile pride and masculine power did not rely primarily upon the quality of their sets or the sound of their orchestra, but on the "women" the stage brought before their eyes.

Looking at "Women": Female Impersonation and the Male Gaze

On January 22, 1942, members of the theatrical troupe Théâtre des Aspirants (Theatre of Cadets) debuted their original operetta *Au Temps des*

Crinolines (In the Time of Crinolines) for their comrades in Stalag 1 A.[40] The musical tells the story of two poor artists, Marcel and Rodolphe, struggling in nineteenth-century France to live off of the meager earnings made from the sale of their paintings and poetry. On the day of a peasants' Bohemian ball, two serendipitous events occur that promise to change the pair's bad luck. First, they meet and fall in love with Estelle and Véronique, the young, beautiful nieces of their landlord. Second, the men make the acquaintance of Monsieur Glandaine, an idiotic *nouveau riche* whom they con into buying their work. With the help of their friend Colline and landlord Agathe, Marcel and Rodolphe pose as established artists and bring Glandaine to the Bohemian ball—an event, they tell him, that is really designed to honor the highly esteemed and wealthy Duke of Palikao. All goes according to plan until Estelle and Véronique, whom Agathe had ordered to stay at home, sneak out of the house and come to the ball, disguised as allegorical representations of France's colonies. Marcel and Rodolphe, unaware of the true identity of the indigenous women, praise their beauty and declare them the queens of the ball. Véronique and Estelle, horrified at their new lovers' duplicitous behavior, suffer brief fits of jealousy before exposing their true identities. After a series of dramatic protestations of love, the couples are reunited and live happily ever after, supported by the money they procured from the gullible Monsieur Glandaine.

The characters of Estelle and Véronique are vital to the operetta's ability to cast prisoners as powerful, virile agents because they give men visual access to "female" bodies. In her seminal essay on the power of looking, film scholar Laura Mulvey has demonstrated the ways in which the visual consumption of women's bodies works to reify male dominance by offering men control over the styling and representation of the female body.[41] In the case of *Au Temps des Crinolines* and other POW operettas, however, the male gaze operates less through the mechanics of determinism than through the expression of heterosexual desire. Indeed, beginning with the girls' first onstage appearance, the dialogue and songs encourage audience members to yearn for the girls' innocent "smiles, youth, and frills." First, Marcel, the painter, asks Estelle to pose for him. As he studies her face, he sings of her charming "sweet smile that makes one dream," and her wheat-colored, blonde hair:

Devant mes yeux son doux visage	Before my eyes, her sweet face
Vient me troubler	Begins to disturb me
Et je sens près de son image	And I feel, close to her image,
Ma main trembler . . .	My hand tremble
Mais quand je vois ce doux sourire	But when I see this sweet smile
Que fait rêver	That makes one dream
Dans mon cœur tout bas j'ose dire	Deep in my heart I dare to say
En suis-je aimé	Does she love me?

In this song, Marcel explicitly brings Estelle "before his eyes," so that he can revel in the pleasure of her "sweet face." By demonstrating his heterosexual desire, Marcel marks himself as a virile agent and offers the audience a surrogate through whom they may also experience manly sexual longing.

The relationship between Rodolphe and Véronique is also negotiated through the act of looking. As the two get to know each other, Véronique reveals that she is a hat maker. Immediately, Rodolphe notes the fine quality of her own hat and adds that her dress is just as lovely to look upon. "Will you permit me to admire it?" he asks. "Walk a little, will you?"

Véronique shyly acquiesces, singing of the way his gaze "intimidates her" even as she desires his approval:

Tout ceci est bien modeste	All this is very modest
Et devant vos yeux je reste	And before your eyes, I remain
Intimidée . . .	Intimidated . . .
Cependant, monsieur, pour vous plaire	However, sir, to please you
Je veux bien essayer de faire	I really want to try to do
Ce que vous demandez	That which you ask
Voyez par ci, voyez par là	Look here, look there
Comment trouvez-vous ceci	How do you find this?

In this scene, a timid Véronique submits to Rodolphe's gaze, twirling before him despite the fact that he "intimidates" her. As she elicits his feedback ("look here, look there / how do you find this?"), she reifies his right to visually consume and judge her body, shoring up his sexual dominance. By the end of scene two, Marcel and Rodolphe's status as powerful agents has been made clear, predicated upon their desire for and access to Estelle and Véronique's bodies.

The process of consolidating masculine power continues as the play progresses, achieving its climax through allusions to the racial and sexual politics of colonialism.[42] Once at the ball, given in honor of France's colonial expeditions, Marcel and Rodolphe consume a series of tableaux representing France's imperial might. Together, these colonial scenes work to secure imperial power by constructing the white colonizer as the civilized, knowing agent and the indigenous colonist as the barbaric, ignorant subordinate.[43] *Au Temps des Crinolines* deploys these tropes, seeking to transform the nation's imperial strength into a metonym for the men's own virility. In the first colonial scene, for example, an Algerian official pleads with his friend, a French officer, not to destroy the Casbah or central market, as its disappearance would be "as cruel to our hearts as the disappearance of old Paris would be to yours." The subtext here is clear: from the perspective of the refined Frenchman, the Casbah appears impoverished and dilapidated. Yet, because this crumbling city center is all the Algerians know, they value it just as much as their colonizers treasure the beautiful, cosmopolitan Paris. In a style befitting his status as the benevolent imperialist, the French officer reassures his Algerian friend that France will allow the colonists to "remain as the centuries made you," and that "France will conserve for you all the poetry of your Orient." This exchange establishes France as the knowing, paternalistic protector of an ignorant and weakened Algeria. Indeed, by promising to guard Algerian culture, the Frenchman lays claim to knowledge of the nation, asserting that France can make proper decisions about what to conserve and what to discard. At a time when France's postwar autonomy and independence were in question, this reference to the nation's imperialism attempted to shore up French virility and reassure prisoners that far from becoming the colonized, they would retain their status as manly colonizers.

The next six scenes continue to build the masculine character of the French nation by taking the audience on a tour of France's empire, represented in allegorical form by a variety of beautiful indigenous women from Indochina, Senegal, and the Antilles. Here, the operetta makes explicit use of the sexualized component of imperial rule, deploying women's bodies in order to characterize France's colonies as effeminate countries that a patriarchal France has a natural right to subordinate. Reprising the familiar colonial strategy of securing political domination through sexual domination, the scenes confer power and might on the French nation through the visual consumption and possession of beautiful indigenous women.[44] As the male audience members gaze upon exotic dances and steamy love scenes, the brown bodies of these beautiful colonial subjects confirm the prisoners' status as manly agents, suggesting that the French are so powerful that indigenous men no longer represent a sexual threat. At the conclusion of the colonial tableaux, Rodolphe and Marcel explicitly proclaim their right to domination, both sexual and regional. For example, while dancing with Véronique, whom he believes to be a representation of Martinique, Rodolphe marvels that "only a few moments ago I was a simple poet, now here I am a colonist, landing on Martinique." Meanwhile, a similar conversation occurs between Marcel and Estelle, disguised as the representation of Guadeloupe. As they dance, Marcel remarks that he has "always had a marked preference for her, the most beautiful, the largest" of the Antillean islands. "How many times have I traveled up and down it in my dreams as a youth," he asks. Guadeloupe uncovers the true meaning of his remark, jealously observing that "now you travel up and down it with your gaze." Throughout the colonial tableaux, the operetta works to build white French authority through the old gendered tropes of colonial domination.

In the case of *Au Temps des Crinolines*, and in general, making the male gaze a viable process of building male virility and sexual power required theatrical troupes to make the female impersonations believable. In camp theaters across Germany, directors recruited tailors and hairdressers to fashion beautiful dresses and stylish wigs, and required actors to shave their legs and underarms.[45] Photographs from the POW stage reveal the impressive results of these efforts, showing the ways that male actors transformed themselves into Estelle, Véronique, and other heroines (figures 9–11).[46]

As these photographs document, prisoners took the task of performing female roles seriously, adopting womanly physical characteristics (dress, hair, makeup, etc.) as well as body language and postures. Beveling their hips and raising their pinkie fingers, the actors' mastery of feminine style

Figure 9. Photograph from *Au Temps des Crinolines*, Stalag 1 A.

Figure 10. Prisoner dressed as a woman for a performance of *Le Bal des Voleurs*.

Figure 11. Prisoner dressed as a woman for a performance of *Barbara* by Michel Duran.

not only created the conditions necessary for their comrades' expression of heterosexual desire, but also demonstrated considerable manly control. As historian Alon Rachamimov has demonstrated in his analysis of Russian WWI theater, the "perfection" of a female performance allowed men the power to enact womanhood, in some cases offering "more authentic representations of femininity than women themselves could."[47] Convincing impersonations cast men as ultimate creative masters who could make woman, breathe life into her, just as Adam created Eve. By "perfectly" embodying their preferred representation of femininity, they evidenced ultimate artistic and gender mastery.

These efforts were not lost on audience members. Indeed, reviews of performances published in camp newspapers and written in private diaries attest to the authenticity of the female impersonators. One anonymous critic, for example, wrote that in one performance at Stalag XVII B, "the difficulties that can arise from feminine roles were surmounted to the point that they seemed to no longer exist."[48] Georges Mongrédien, an officer imprisoned in Oflag IV D, also testified to the quality of the female performers in his diary, writing that a friend was so "perfect" in a new female role that he "truly forgot he was a prisoner for four hours."[49] Another prisoner, reviewing a new performance in Oflag XVII A, wrote that the performance had been so convincing that "it took several instants after the show to realize that the doors didn't open onto Boulevard de Clichy," a busy street in Paris's nightclub district.[50] Thus, the theater offered not only symbolic means of enacting the male gaze, but the material means as well. When characters like Marcel and Rodolphe invited the audience to measure their sexual power against the figures of Estelle and Véronique, they did so not only through songs and dialogue, but through the exhibition of "real" female bodies.

Yet, paradoxically, the authenticity of these feminine performances undermined the very notion of manliness that the men sought to embrace. Indeed, in the process of inviting men to ogle men dressed as women, the theater exposed the lie of a stable gender identity, throwing the concepts of essentialized manliness and heterosexual desire into confusion. Indeed, given the believability of the performances, how were soldiers to prevent the destabilization of gender and maintain sex difference? In the process of soliciting heterosexual desire, how were they to prevent their comrades from experiencing homosexual desire? In their attempts to work through the gender trouble that they experienced at the POW theater, prisoners printed reviews and cartoons in the camp press that reminded prisoners that the women were fakes, that their leading ladies were really just unattractive, unkempt men. For example, in one newspaper review of a variety show, jazz musician Jules Ruwet spoke of being afraid to look underneath the performers' bras because he knew he "would find cotton balls."[51] Another critic, writing for the paper of a work camp, reported that during a female dance solo in the jazz variety show *Knock*, a prisoner pointed to the stage and shouted, "She has hair between her boobs!"[52] Comments about the disappointing character of the "women's" breasts both reified the desirability of the female body and upheld the notion of a stable interior and exterior manly identity. While the actors could pretend to have breasts, the article suggested, they could never escape their hairy, flat chests—the biological fact of their gender.

A drawing entitled "Avant, Pendant, Après" ("Before, During, After"), published in *Le Chic Os*, the newspaper of Kommando E. 44, offers a rich example of the tension between authenticity and falseness that constrained the rhetoric of prisoners' theatrical performances (figure 12).[53] The cartoon chronicles the experiences of prisoners before, during, and after the theatrical performance. In the first frame, the men read an advertisement for *J'te Veux* (I Want You), a performance that features their fellow prisoners Toto and Ignace in the leading roles. The next frame depicts the men at the performance, ogling the heroine, a sexy woman dressed in a beautiful, revealing evening gown. In the final frame, the love-struck men wait outside the cast's dressing room, eager to get the heartthrob's autograph. Their hopes are dashed as their comrade, a featureless, slovenly man dressed in women's undergarments, exits. As the illusion vanishes, the men stand with their jaws agape, readjusting to the reality of their captivity.

Here, the artist's humorous interpretation of the theater points to the dual emphasis on believable but transparent female impersonations. Representing the men's enjoyment of the show as predicated upon their desire for the authentic "woman" on stage, he disciplines this desire in the third frame by confronting his subjects with the inescapable fact of the starlet's biology. Paradoxically, the cartoon suggests, the believable,

Figure 12. "Avant, Pendant, Après," March 1943.

authentic female impersonators could only succeed in rehabilitating French masculinity if they were combined with reminders of their false-ness—reminders that would close off opportunity for sexual confusion and reinforce the gender hierarchy. Given the prevalence of similar cartoons and reviews, it is no wonder that their ideology crept into the writings of the prisoners themselves. In the words of Robert Desvernois, an officer imprisoned in Oflag VI A, the impersonations "demanded on the part of the audience a tacit agreement. You had to enter into the game."[54] Paul Juif echoes this description, documenting that "the prisoners knew well that the chests were empty and that, underneath the shimmering dresses, under the wigs and under the make-up, one would find nothing but a hairy, clumsy friend."[55] As these testimonies reveal, the newspaper reviews and cartoons worked alongside the performances, eliciting an authentic *feeling* of heterosexual desire while maintaining the integrity of a fixed, essentialized gender system where inner and outer identities always match.

The complexity of the rhetoric of these female impersonations is perhaps best illustrated in the cartoon "Les Oflagirls," printed in the newspaper of Oflag III C in July 1941.[56] Depicting the actors as they prepare to perform the female leads, the artist captures the theater's delicate balance between enacting believable feminine performances that would elicit heterosexual desire and issuing reminders that the beautiful starlets were really unkempt and unattractive men.

Take, for example, the man seated in front of the mirror, applying his makeup while wearing a woman's bra and man's underwear. The beer

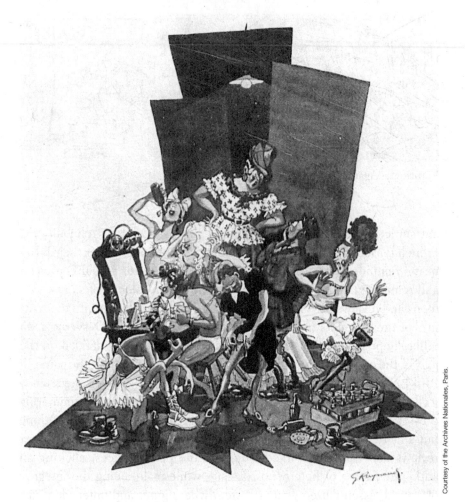

Figure 13. "Les Oflagirls," July 1941.

mug in his hand and the bulge at his pelvis reveal his true identity, even
as he strains to apply his lipstick properly. Seated on a crate in front of
him, another actor wears a bra, tutu, and ballet shoes; "her" true identity
as a man is only made clear by "her" boyish posture and the pipe "she"
smokes. The combination of female and male features operates to discipline the prisoners' desire by reminding them that the performance of
female identity is always an illusion, convincing though it may be. Other
characters in the drawing, however, have fully executed their gender

transformation, becoming women so realistically that they even feel violated by the presence of a man in their dressing room. Indeed, the woman in the background hovers over the male intruder, her hands perched on her hips in a sassy gesture of feminine disapproval. The man clasps his mouth, presumably cowed by the woman's forceful language and intimidating bearing. This interaction underscores the convincing nature of the female impersonations and the skill with which male actors performed an authentic femininity. When the men completed their transformations, the cartoon suggests, they so masterfully mimicked female behavior that they even adopted womanly subject positions. In all, "Les Oflagirls" makes a forceful argument for the actors' mastery of an illusion of femininity. Adjusting their wigs, applying makeup, and pulling up their stockings, the men become women before our very eyes, even adopting a female sense of decorum and privacy. Yet, as the bulging underwear, pipes, and discarded boots reveal, these women are really men, masterfully bringing to life the bodies of women.

Virginal Vixens: Idealized Women and Male Desirability

The operettas reclaim prisoners' sense of agency and power not only through the enactment of the male gaze, but also by grounding manly worth in their male desirability. By creating female characters with healthy libidos and sexual appetites, the prisoners consolidated their sexual value and self-esteem. Nowhere is this more evident than in *D'Amour et d'Eau Fraiche*, an operetta written and performed by the actors of Cabaret La Haut (The High Cabaret) in Oflag VI A.[57] The musical tells the story of two young girls living a confined existence in a boarding school, tightly surveilled by their teacher and caretaker, a middle-aged spinster named Mademoiselle Puce. The girls, Arlette and Beatrice, yearn to experience romantic love, much to the consternation and chagrin of Mlle Puce. As the play progresses, we learn that Puce harbors her own romantic desires and also longs for a man despite her advanced age. As night falls, all three women ask Santa to bring them a Prince Charming. When Christmas morning arrives, young Beatrice awakes to find her wish granted. Santa has brought her Francinet Moyen, the "hope of New France." Due to France's dire need of children, the two decide to skip the engagement and marry immediately. Mlle Puce wishes them well, but confesses her doubts that the couple will be happy, living within the restrictions of wartime France. As Francinet and Puce reminisce about the good old days, Santa overhears their complaining and chastises them for missing the point of his gift. Love, Santa tells them, is the only thing anyone needs. Love, he sings, is abundant in France and can never be forbidden or rationed.

At first glance, *D'Amour et d'Eau Fraiche* seems an odd operetta for a group of soldiers to create and perform, as the story unfolds from the perspective of two young women rather than Francinet, the handsome and desirable Prince Charming. While *Au Temps des Crinolines* features the male protagonists Marcel and Rodolphe, this story advances from the point of view of female agents who issue their request to Santa and bring about Francinet's arrival. Yet, the focus on three "women," all of whom desire romantic and sexual relationships with men, performed a critical task in the reclamation of the prisoners' virility. Indeed, the choice to develop the story from the women's perspective allowed the men to perform a sexualized version of femininity that flattered the prisoners' own egos. In the characters of Beatrice and Arlette, the authors and actors built upon the old stock character of the innocent and naive ingénue, blending the familiar, fetishized damsel in distress with the modern woman to create their ultimate fantasy—an ignorant sexpot with an obsession with marriage. In turn, these virginal vixens flattered the prisoners' notions of their own sexual prowess and value.

The characterization of Arlette and Beatrice as naive, traditional women begins early in the operetta. In scene one, the two women reveal themselves to be uneducated in politics and warfare, but considerably dedicated to their training as mothers and wives. Reading a letter from her aunt, Arlette tells Beatrice of her aunt's desires that the girls take advantage of their education. In her correspondence, the aunt expresses regret over her own squandered opportunities, alluding to her ignorance about the geographical location of Tobruk, the site of one of the first and most important Allied victories in North Africa. Beatrice interrupts her roommate in defense of the kind aunt: "There is nothing to be embarrassed about," she interjects. "Until now, I thought that Sidi Omar was an

Arab leader." Here, the women establish themselves as domestic women with no interest in public life. As evidenced by their ignorance about the city of Sidi Omar, the location of another battle in the North African campaign, Arlette and Beatrice care little for the business of the war, but are very interested in men, an interest the aunt warns against. As young women of sixteen and eighteen, the aunt writes, the girls must "beware of men, especially soldiers" as these are "the dirtiest" (*les plus dégoûtants*) of all. Here, the aunt's advice casts the prisoners as hypersexual predators whom the two eager girls should avoid. In all, the first scene firmly establishes the main characters as silly, ignorant women while representing the soldiers as the proud associates of Allied victory and possessors of sexual skill and knowledge.

While the girls have little interest in current events, they do wish to know all they can about sex and men. Bemoaning the sheltered and restricted education offered at their boarding school, they complain to their governess, Mlle Puce, about the futility of studying "the care to give to children without having more details on the way in which we bring them into the world." Singing to the tune of Ray Ventura's "Je Voudrais en Savoir Davantage" (I Would Like to Know More about It), the girls give voice to the prisoners' fantasies about women's sexual innocence and eagerness:

On voudrait en savoir davantage	We would like to know more about it
On voudrait qu'on nous renseigne un brin	We would like someone to teach us a bit
Sur les secrets du mariage	About the secrets of marriage
Dont il est triste, qu'à notre âge	Which, it's sad, at our age
Nous ne connaissons rien.	We know nothing of.
Quand on pense qu'en parlant des abeilles	When we think that when speaking of the bees
On nous vante les joies du vol nuptial,	People boast about the joys of the nuptial flight,
Mais qu'on nous tire les oreilles	But that one draws our ears
Quand on remarque, quelle merveille!	When someone remarks, what a marvel!
Qu'y a un gros dard chez le mâle	There is a big stinger in the male

Here, the girls reveal themselves to be inexperienced but eager lovers. They want Mlle Puce to teach them about men's "stingers," presumably so that they can be ready to fulfill their roles as housewives and mothers. Deploying this representation of the virginal vixen, the operetta fulfills prisoners' fantasies of the ideal woman—the innocent, lustful siren—and invites them to feel desirable, thus restoring their self-worth.

As the operetta continues, even Mademoiselle Puce, the middle-aged governess, intervenes to stroke the audience's ego. In her biggest solo, Puce reveals that she "isn't what one thinks," she "isn't what one says." While she may appear "stiff and straight," she has a heart that "burns like a volcano":

Je rêve souvent d'un beau garçon	I often dream of a handsome guy
Qui me donnerait le grand frisson,	Who would give me the big shiver,
J'en frémis toute.	I quiver all over.
Il me prendrait sur ses genoux	He would take me on his lap
En dirait en me frôlant le cou:	Saying as he brushed against my neck:
Ma grande choucoute	My big pet

In this verse, Puce bemoans the absence of a male lover and fantasizes about the physical pleasure that men provide. She is so desperate to "calm her aspirations" that she has resorted to "a practical solution." Each night, "instead of correcting your tests," she admits, "I compose pornographic writings," a vague reference to what one can only assume is the act of masturbation. For men who feared that their wives and girlfriends were cheating on them in France as they remained in Germany, the invitation to believe in their own sexual worth was seductive. In this song and others, Mlle Puce links male desirability to male dominance, offering sexual prowess as a rationale for patriarchy. Indeed, Puce's song suggested that women submitted to male authority because to resist meant to go unloved. Men were, after all, the only purveyors of physical love.

Appeals to male desirability resonated well with the prisoners, as they were rooted in the sexual component of French national identity. The historian Fabrice Virgili, in his study of the sexual lives of the prisoners, writes that "the French were generally convinced of the reality of their reputation as seducers and skillful lovers," a conviction that "consti-tuted one of the rare elements of national pride" upon France's defeat.[58] Evidence from prisoners' diaries confirms Virgili's assessment, suggesting that the belief in a heightened French sexuality was one of the standards by which the men measured their national superiority. Writing from a *Frontstalag* in France in August 1940, Robert Christophe described the German authorities' efforts to contain allegedly excessive public displays of affection between French prisoners and their beautiful wives. Recount-ing an incident in which a French doctor was lying in the grass next to his "very pretty, very primped up, and well-dressed" wife, he boasted that the couple gave the voyeuristic Germans "an eyeful." The next day, Chris-tophe wrote that the Germans had to institute a new policy to facilitate quick goodbyes, because "the French are the most romantic people in the world!"[59] Thus, given the existing connection between French manliness and romantic prowess, the operetta's appeals to male desirability tapped into a unique source of national pride for the prisoners. By deploying rep-resentations of hot and bothered French femininity, the operetta invited the prisoners to reclaim their status as virile Frenchmen.

Yet, Mlle Puce's solo did not stop at her confession about her sexual desire. In the last chorus, she converts her message about having a stron-ger libido than people expect to a rallying cry for resistance within the camp. "Don't always be what people think, don't always be what people say," she sings. Urging her audience members to "keep [their] independ-ence" because "liberty doesn't have a price," she advises them to care-fully pursue clandestine activities, whatever the consequences may be:

N'soyez pas toujours ce que l'on pense	Don't always be what people think
N'soyez pas toujours ce que l'on dit	Don't always be what people say
Sachez n'montrer dans l'existence	Know to show in life
Votre vrai visage qu'à vos amis	Your true face only to your friends
Conservez votre indépendance	Keep your independence
La liberté, ça n'a pas de prix	Liberty doesn't have a price
Et foutez-vous de ce que l'on pense	And fuck what people think
Et foutez-vous de ce que l'on dit	And fuck what people say

Here, the song moves from a sexual confession to a thinly veiled call for resistance. Having restored the prisoners to the position of virile agents through the figures of Arlette, Beatrice, and Mlle Puce, the operetta channels this power toward support for more openly defiant political activities. Thus, the female impersonations did not simply attempt to alleviate depression and sadness among emasculated POWs, but attempted to direct their newfound power toward resistant ends.

No Love Lost: France Reunited with "Her" POWs

Thus far, I have demonstrated the ways in which POW theater helped to consolidate male power by eliciting the expression of heterosexual desire and testifying to male sexual worth. Yet, these representations of sexy men and women also served a vital role in the rehabilitation of the prisoners' relationship to their wives and their nation. By depicting France's estrangement from the POWs in terms of heteronormative romantic love, the theater deployed the masculine power derived from men's sexual difference toward a project of familial and civic belonging. At a time when the prisoners felt increasingly abandoned by the nation and forgotten by their own wives and families, the theater represented romantic love as an allegory for the POWs' relationship to France.

In May 1942, the same comrades who brought Oflag VI A the story of sexually repressed Mlle Puce and eager Arlette and Beatrice debuted their newest operetta, *Blanche-Neige* (Snow White).[60] The tale takes place during wartime, some years after the marriage of Snow White and Prince Charming. Immediately, the operetta makes explicit its allegorical nature, revealing the wicked witch to be none other than a personification of the war itself. The witch has again cursed Snow White, the allegorical representation of both the prisoners' wives and the nation. The new spell plunges Snow White into a deep sleep every day, but allows her to wake briefly each evening at midnight. The evil witch has also imprisoned Prince Charming in a faraway haunted forest, preventing him from returning to his suffering and beloved Snow White. The seven dwarfs accompany the lovers. Bashful, Grumpy, Happy, and Sneezy tend to Snow White as she sleeps and help her gather flowers to send to the

Prince each evening when she wakes. Doc, Dopey, and Sleepy endure captivity with the Prince, each one representing a strategy for surviving in the terrible forest, far from Snow White. In the end, the witch dies and the lovers reunite to live happily ever after.

Early in the operetta, the dwarfs make Snow White's status as a symbol for France explicit, describing the princess as a formerly abundant and fertile land that has now been driven to decay. In scene one, Sneezy laments "seeing her sunk into such weakness . . . she who was so beautiful and so strong before!" He goes on to contrast Snow White's weakened condition to her former days of glory: "She reigned over the earth, the sunniest, the richest, the most fertile, she was like the garden of the world. All the nations envied her, and now, it's been two years since she's been condemned to live no longer . . . it is as if she is dead!" In this passage, Sneezy makes a clear comparison between the slumbering princess and Occupied France. Using Snow White's forced sleep as a metaphor, he suggests that the Nazi Occupation has driven France to a temporary decline. Like Snow White, who can only be saved by Prince Charming, France must wait for her own savior, the prisoners of war. Upon their return, the prisoners' allegory suggests, the nation will embrace the prisoners as its heroes and recapture its former splendor.

The notion that the prisoners were responsible for rescuing France did not originate with the POWs, but was part of Vichy's earliest efforts to explain the purpose of their imprisonment. As historian Sarah Fishman notes, Vichy attempted to give meaning to their capture by positioning the prisoners as those whose suffering would atone for France's former sins. In a tricky discursive pairing, Vichy insisted that even though the prisoners were not to blame for the nation's defeat, they were "defeat's ransom," whose captivity would pay for the irresponsible decadence of the Third Republic.[61] Yet, while Vichy paid lip service to the importance of French prisoners and their status as national redeemers, the government betrayed a deep ambivalence about their welfare. Indeed, while the Geneva Convention specified that a neutral country should oversee the prisoners of belligerent nations, Vichy declined to designate the United States as the protector of its men and agreed to Germany's suggestion that France maintain responsibility for its own prisoners. As Fishman argues, this decision was not motivated by concern for the POWs, as it was unlikely that defeated France, who held no German prisoners to use as leverage, would be able to forcefully represent the men's interests or intervene on their behalf.[62] The prisoners, from Vichy's perspective, presented another opportunity to demonstrate a good-faith effort at collaboration.

Vichy's attempts to demonstrate their willingness to work alongside the Reich not only deprived the prisoners of a powerful, independent watchdog, but also contributed to a crisis of identity for French soldiers. As historian Yves Durand writes, the POWs struggled to maintain a sense of their national, soldierly pride in the face of France's new relationship to Germany.[63] The armistice meant that France and Germany were no longer belligerent nations, yet the Reich refused to release the defeated nation's men. This inconsistency was unsettling, shrouding the POWs' political and national allegiances in ambiguity. Traditional codes of honor dictated that good soldiers should resist their captivity and attempt escape, yet modern politics asked the prisoners to accept seemingly unnecessary captivity. As these opposing forces vied for the prisoners' loyalty, Vichy alienated them even further through the publication of erroneous reports on their welfare. Representing life in the *Oflags* and *Stalags* as either a monastic retreat or extended summer camp, Vichy sought to appease the families of captured men and gain public approval for its politics.[64] However, reading these accounts in their camps, French prisoners were horrified by the rosy depiction of their lives. A group of officers from Oflag IV D insisted:

> We are neither heroes nor saints . . . The POWs of this Oflag . . . have
> had enough of this perfectly suffocating life. In short, we dread the rose-
> colored clichés, the image of conventional prisoners matured by camp
> life which have led many people to view our captivity as a monastic
> retreat, a term at the University of Redemption, or a meditation cure.[65]

In all, Vichy's lack of concern for the nation's prisoners, the ambiguous relationship between France and Germany, and the false reports of happy camp life complicated the prisoners' sense of national loyalty and soldierly pride.

The promise of *Blanche-Neige* was its ability to ease complex worries over the prisoners' national standing through the allegory of romantic love. By recasting the nation as a female lover, the operetta invited the prisoners to see themselves as indispensable to the nation's health, just as *D'Amour et d'Eau Fraiche* argued that they were indispensable to the satisfaction of feminine desire. In one song, for example, Sneezy sings of the relationship between Snow White and the Prince before the war, painting a portrait of domestic bliss. Apparently, "if they argued at night, Grumpy was always the cause." Each night, "when the delicious instant would come / where, in their little bed, they would go to stretch out / they would chase Sleepy and call Happy." Here, Sneezy alludes to the act of sex in order to deploy prisoners' sexualized self-worth to the project of redeeming their national significance. Just as Snow White's well-being requires the love of the Prince, France's rebirth requires the return of its prisoners. In another song, Snow White herself sings of her desire to tell the prince all the "secrets that one cannot write . . . the ineffable words / that one only whispers cuddled up in bed." Here, again, the operetta uses heterosexual love as a metaphor for the prisoners' importance to France. As the "lover" of France, the prisoners lay claim to a civic position of possessive dominance. It is only men who can satisfy the nation's needs.

Anecdotes recorded in prisoners' diaries reveal that, consciously or otherwise, prisoners drew upon this metaphor of heterosexual love to understand their unique claim and continued significance to France. In his diary, for example, Paul Juif described an incident in which a German officer visited the theater's female wardrobe room and unfolded "the silk dresses and frilly undergarments with a sort of crook's pleasure." As he indulged in touching the women's garments, the German guard whispered, "Just like Paris." For the German, the theater's believable female impersonators worked all too well, eliciting fantasies not only about French women, but about the nation itself. Indeed, commenting on the nature of Paris while caressing women's costumes, the guard conflates French women with the French nation, a confusion made more resonant by centuries of allegorical depictions of France as beautiful Marianne. Juif noted the German's lust in his diary, ending his description of the encounter in a possessive huff: "When they speak of Paris, one doesn't know whether it's the capital of romance or the capital of world thought—they are full of a respect that bothers me a bit, because I have the impression that *their* Paris doesn't have much to do with *my* Paris."[66] Here, Juif responds to the German's desire for France by denying his ability to know it. Differentiating *his* Paris from the guard's Paris, Juif refutes Germany's domination of France. Relegating the officer to the status of an ignorant foreigner, an outsider who will never understand the true nature of French women or culture, Juif lays claim to knowledge of, and access to, France rooted in his native status. He and his fellow Frenchmen alone know which women's fashions are "just like Paris" and have a natural, consensual relationship with their women and their nation.

Conclusion

Facilitating expressions of heterosexual desire, the operettas written and performed by French prisoners of war from 1940 to 1945 helped to combat the emasculating nature of their defeat and captivity. By giving POWs visual access to convincing "female" bodies, the operettas encouraged men to participate in the consumption and objectification of women, a process that helped them to measure their sexual power. Reacting to the ways in which the female impersonations destabilized the boundary between homosexual and heterosexual desire, prisoners published reviews and cartoons in camp newspapers that worked to police homoerotic behavior and maintain the integrity of the gender hierarchy. By simultaneously applauding the believability of the starlets and underscoring their falseness, these discourses attempted to rehabilitate the notion of an essential gender identity that grounded French virility. The operettas also appealed to the men's own sexual appeal, inviting them to ground their self-worth in male sexual prowess. By deploying representations of what I have called the virginal vixen, operettas encouraged men to see themselves as the sole purveyors of female sexual satisfaction. As the war continued, these efforts to construct prisoners as virile Frenchmen became useful ways to reassure the men of their national worth. Alienated by Vichy's politics of collaboration and increasingly worried about their wives' fidelity, the prisoners looked to the theater to ease their anxieties about returning to the nation. Operettas like *Blanche-Neige* asked men to measure their civic worth in terms of their sexual value and to experience themselves as possessive and dominant national patriarchs.

While suitable to the exigencies French soldiers faced in German POW camps, this model of male citizenship would complicate the situation facing French men as they returned from captivity. Back on French soil, these men witnessed the female "infidelity" they had feared all along, only instead of Nazi soldiers, it was American GIs that were usurping their allegedly natural role as the rightful sexual partners of French women. Well-provisioned, well-dressed, and emboldened by burgeoning American power, the GIs made no secret of their feelings of desire for and entitlement to French women. Hosting lavish private parties in French cafés and American military camps, the GIs ensured intimate access to these women, spinning them across the dance floor to the tunes of new American jazz. Yet, jazz not only facilitated the display of American virility and strength, but provided key inventional resources with which the French could vie for power in the postwar world.

CHAPTER 5

GI Jazz

Music and Power in Liberation France

———•◆•———

M ichel Adam was just fifteen years old when he witnessed the Allied liberation of his home in Normandy during the summer of 1944. It was an extraordinary time for the French, marked by both profound suffering and joy. But Adam's account dwells neither on the devastation wrought by the Allied invasion, nor on the euphoria of expelling the German occupiers. Instead, his recollection features the sonic landscape shaped by the American GIs stationed in his city. "It was a fabulous shock that I didn't recover from," he remembered of his first encounter with new American jazz.[1] While Adam was familiar with Django Reinhardt and other prominent French jazz musicians, recent hits from Americans like Benny Goodman struck him as something altogether different and unexpected, "a drug" he could not quit.[2] Yet, Adam's admiration of this music was not shared by all. Writing a few months later for the critical periodical *Jazz Hot*, an unnamed columnist represented American jazz as a perverse corruption of the genre. Exclaiming that "now, more

than ever 'our music' is under attack," the author warned of the "exploita-
tion" and "vulgarization" that jazz was suffering at the hands of American
musicians and audiences. Calling upon those who considered themselves
"dedicated to defending our patrimony," he urged his French compatriots
to "attack" those who "defame our music."[3]

The coexistence of these two different perspectives during the period of France's liberation belies a fundamental disagreement over which
country owned the genre of jazz. For Adam, jazz was the cultural product
of the United States, a nation responsible for its creation and subsequent
stylistic evolution. It was, after all, the music of Benny Goodman that
inspired Adam, not the work of the French artists he had heard during the
Occupation. Yet, the column in *Jazz Hot* represented jazz as "our music,"
as a French art form bound up in the nation's cultural heritage. As good
custodians of the genre, the author suggested, French people must protect jazz from American corruption. While jazz's national belonging had
been disputed in French jazz criticism as early as the 1920s, the context
in which the debate now circulated was radically different from that of
the interwar period.[4] Indeed, as Adam and the anonymous author of *Jazz
Hot* were formulating their divergent opinions, the end of the war was
reordering the international hierarchy. Poised on the brink of victory, the
United States prepared to assume its new role as global superpower while
France, reeling from German defeat and four years of Occupation, now
confronted its international decline and uncertain political future. Thus,
in 1944, the question of jazz's national belonging did not circulate within
a politically stable France, confident of its world standing and capabil-
ity to resume political sovereignty. Rather, the issue reemerged within a
broader struggle over international influence and political power. What,
we are left to wonder, was the relationship between jazz and this changing
moment? What symbols were likely to accrue to the American music
heard by local French people like Michel Adam? How did the notion that
jazz was actually French work alongside these symbols to either reify or
challenge American dominance? What, in sum, was the rhetorical conse-
quence of American jazz for the emerging postwar relationship between
France and the United States from 1944 to 1945?

To answer these questions, I interrogate in this chapter the performance and criticism of jazz in France from 1944 to 1945, arguing that the

genre emerged as an important axis of struggle between the French and their American liberators. On one hand, jazz parties confronted locals with American hegemony by enacting the GIs' considerable power. In the context of widespread gender damage brought on by the German Occupation and Allied invasion, the *soirées dansantes* deepened the assault on French manhood by facilitating the displacement of French men from heterosexual social spaces and providing the GIs with unrestricted access to French women. The preponderance of material goods available at the parties worked to augment the performance of American power. From the physical structures that housed the events, to the chocolate and candy bestowed upon female guests, to the orchestrated big band tunes that were often performed, the parties flaunted the GIs' incredible wealth, a display that contributed to a conflation between the music and consumer culture itself. And while the understanding of jazz as a material product like Coca-Cola and cigarettes did supply some French men with a convenient way to explain the appeal of these parties, it also reified the threat of the Americanization of French culture. Indeed, the popularity of American jazz only exacerbated fears over France's diminished international standing, suggesting that France's political losses might be accompanied by cultural decline.

Yet, jazz also worked as a tool through which the French could challenge American hegemony. Critics writing for the popular periodical *Jazz Hot* worked to contain American domination by divorcing jazz from the United States and realigning it with France. Emphasizing the essential blackness of all "good" jazz, these critics used American racism to disqualify the United States as the rightful guardian of jazz. Representing France as not only colorblind but endowed with unusual musical talent, these critics transferred cultural ownership of jazz to their own nation. This rhetorical move offered a symbolic means to protect against the Americanization of French culture, as it recast jazz as a cultural form more properly belonging to France. Moreover, this discourse allowed France to reclaim some of its lost international standing, as it framed its people as the world's ethical and cultural leaders. The United States might have emerged from the war with unmatched wealth and military power, this framing suggested, but it was France that led the world when it came to the humanist pursuits of art and ethics. Ultimately, jazz, at

once a sign of American opulence and strength and of French high taste
and open-mindedness, offered an ideal prism through which the French
could refract the struggle over political power in the wake of their nation's
liberation.

Examining music as a rhetorical site where political power was exercised and contested between 1944 and 1945 helps to complicate our
understanding of jazz in France in the era of the Second World War.
Overwhelmingly, this scholarship emphasizes jazz's function as a symbol
of resistance and freedom among a public struggling against Nazi Occupation. Matthew Jordan, for example, argues that the Germans' opposition to jazz established the genre as a symbol of both "Resistance
to Vichy and true Frenchness" by war's end.[5] Colin Nettlebeck offers a
similar appraisal, stating that, for the French, jazz was a "music whose
essence was freedom, of personal expression."[6] While recent scholarship
has challenged jazz's ability to symbolize resistance to the Nazis, there
are good reasons for such interpretations.[7] First, as the case of the zazous
makes clear, official Nazi cultural policy did not embrace jazz. While Hitler did not ban jazz in France or prevent German officers from enjoying
the live concerts performed in Parisian concert halls and cabarets, his official position remained that the allegedly "racially degenerate" music was
unfit for European audiences. It was this "condemnation by the Nazis,"
as Tyler Stovall writes, that made jazz into a ready-made "cultural symbol of antifascism."[8] Second, jazz's association with African Americans
positioned the music as a sonic symbol of liberty even to those outside
America's borders. Indeed, the French were familiar with the reality of
American racism, having heard tales of the Jim Crow South from the
African American musicians who animated the nightclubs in Cannes,
Nice, and Paris.[9] Rashida Braggs argues that it was this connection to the
oppression suffered by African Americans that drew French audiences to
jazz during their own *années noires*. "The desire for freedom one day soon,
despite Nazi occupation," she writes, "helped French jazz fans relate to
jazz and to bond. Not only did jazz become even more Frenchified; it
became a universal representation of freedom."[10]

While jazz certainly did operate as a symbol of resistance and freedom for some French people in certain contexts, criticism published in
the popular quarterly *Jazz Hot* in the year after the nation's liberation

reveals that "resistance" was not the only meaning embedded in the genre. Rather, a rich history of French jazz criticism had imbued it with symbols of Frenchness that would be useful in the political struggle now facing the nation. First appearing in 1935, *Jazz Hot* was the first periodical to be dedicated solely to the genre of jazz. Begun by Charles Delaunay and Hugues Panassié, it was the official voice of Le Hot Club de France, a private fan club where both neophytes and connoisseurs could gather to listen to new records, discuss musicians, and hear lectures devoted to style and technique. Boasting a list of collaborating critics from England, the United States, France, Romania, and Holland, the periodical aimed to legitimize jazz before a worldwide audience, publishing articles in French and English that would "make known under its true nature a music still so unappreciated, so misunderstood."[11] While *Jazz Hot* stopped publication during the Occupation, it resumed in October 1945, printing French articles only. Over the next two years, its readership grew substantially as local chapters spread throughout provincial cities and towns. According to Ludovic Tournès, twenty-nine Hot Clubs existed in mid-1944, a figure that expanded to thirty-seven by January of 1945 and to seventy by December 1946. By the height of the Hot Club movement in 1947, membership fluctuated from between 2,200 and 5,000 people.[12]

Analyzing *Jazz Hot* in the era of France's liberation helps to trouble the association between jazz and freedom by drawing our attention to the ways that musical culture emerged to help resituate France as it struggled to identify its place in the geopolitical climate that took shape after Occupation and Liberation. As historians have shown, culture has long been linked to French national identity. Representing the consumption of food, art, music, and literature as evidence of French people's alleged cultural superiority, political and economic leaders have worked to establish French people as the setters of international taste for centuries. Leora Auslander, for example, writes that "as early as the seventeenth century the French understood themselves as possessing, as a nation, more refined taste than other European nations," a notion that would help drive demand for French goods amidst increasing global competition in the nineteenth century.[13] Whitney Walton echoes this appraisal, writing in her account of bourgeois consumption that cultural critics often attributed "the tastefulness of French goods to the discriminating standards of French

consumers." The perception that "French industry produced beautiful
things because French consumers settled for nothing less" helped support a widespread belief that the French "were inherently more tasteful,
more sensitive to beauty, than other nationalities."[4] In 1944, as France
took stock of its weakened international position, crippled economy, and
shattered infrastructure, this cultural capital became a crucial means by
which to reclaim some of its lost prestige. As Herman Lebovics has suggested, it was culture that could give France "a comparative advantage in
the new international competition."[5] Jazz, a musical form created by the
United States but promoted and legitimized by France, offered a unique
opportunity to leverage that cultural superiority to challenge American
dominance in the aftermath of war.

In order to see the ways that a battle over international political
standing unfolded on the pages of *Jazz Hot*, we must first take stock of
deteriorating Franco-American relations during the Liberation. While the
French and Americans enjoyed an amicable beginning, the relationship
soured as the French learned of Washington's disrespect for French autonomy, endured the humiliation of incredible wealth disparity, and suffered pervasive sexual assault. The situation was particularly bad near the
port cities of Le Havre, located in the region of Normandy, and Marseille,
located in Provence, where the largest concentration of American GIs
were stationed. The principal point of entry for the European Theater,
Le Havre saw approximately four million soldiers as they embarked or
disembarked from the war zone during 1944–1945.[16] Marseille also hosted
a large population of GIs, as it was there that the U.S. military headquartered the Delta Base Section (a large supply base) and a large staging
area for GIs preparing to travel to the Pacific Theater. At any given time,
the staging area alone housed 100,000 men.[17] Anecdotes and testimonials
from French people who lived in these cities implicate jazz in the deteriorating relations with the soldiers, revealing jazz performances themselves to have been instrumental in the performance of American wealth
and strength. It is in relationship to these testimonials, I maintain, that
the rhetorical and political significance of *Jazz Hot* emerges. By reading
these articles in tandem with French accounts of the GIs' jazz parties, I
aim to tease out the ways that jazz signified both American hegemony
and French cultural supremacy. Jazz, I maintain, was a medium through

which French people confronted their fears about American hegemony and negotiated a discursive space wherein France could retain its claim to social and cultural prestige in a postwar world.

France at the Liberation: The Threat of Americanization

For the French, the joy of liberation in the summer of 1944 was tempered by deep despair. Allied bombings, intended to immobilize the German army and prepare France for invasion, destroyed the nation's infrastructure and killed tens of thousands of civilians. Beginning in the fall of 1943, the Allies demolished the roads, bridges, and railways that would transport troops and supplies for Hitler's army, obliterating French homes, farms, schools, and workplaces in the process. In the year 1944 alone, the Allies dropped 503,000 tons of bombs on France, killing 35,317 civilians.[18] Eyewitness accounts help to reconstruct the ravaged nature of the visual landscape. According to American Frank Freese, for example, the destruction in the village of Saint-Lô made the city appear "as though it had been pulled up by its roots, put through a giant mixmaster then dumped back out again."[19] "Familiar places appeared unrecognizable," recalled Frenchman Charles Lemeland. "It seemed there was now something horrible and monstrous hiding there. The endless road, bordered by houses and farms, was absolutely deserted except for dead animals—a German shepherd and a pig side by side—and a few dead men."[20] American Andy Rooney sympathized with the emotional toll such destruction took on local populations, noting that "it was true that they were being freed but at the cost of the total destruction of everything they had."[21] Indeed, the Allies were not the only ones to make sacrifices in the battle for Normandy. For those who lived in its villages and worked its farms, the invasion was truly a stunning combination of the "beautiful" and the "cruel."[22]

The collateral damage sustained by the French was just the beginning of a series of events that would ultimately contribute to an abiding distrust of their American liberators. Not only did the bombings strike civilians unaware and unprepared, but because their utility and strategic purpose often went unexplained, they seemed to indicate the Allies' disregard for French safety. German authorities quickly filled the void in the public's knowledge, launching a propaganda campaign that depicted the United States as a power-hungry nation that hoped to conquer and colonize France.[23] Of course, suspicion about American imperial ambitions was not unfounded. Roosevelt's hesitance to recognize Charles de Gaulle as France's political authority and plans to interfere in France's political system lent credence to this fear. As historian Julian Hurstfield explains, Roosevelt privately regarded France with a great deal of contempt, believing that the nation had "proven incompetent at social and economic reform, unable to defend itself against its neighbor even while claiming a preemptive right to rule underprivileged peoples."[24] In lieu of restoring French sovereignty, then, Roosevelt intended to place the nation under the control of the Allied Military Government for Occupied Territories (AMGOT), a military government controlled by the United States, Great Britain, and the Soviet Union.[25] Although these plans had been abandoned by May 1944, AMGOT remained "a powerful myth" among Gaullists who feared American intervention into French politics.[26] The French would not rest easy until FDR finally recognized De Gaulle's provisional government in October 1944, nearly five months after D-Day.[27]

While the White House charted a plan for postwar France, hundreds of thousands of American GIs began pouring into the nation, primarily passing through the port cities of Le Havre and Marseille. The French welcomed the Americans with warmth and gratitude, offering precious bottles of wine and Calvados in celebration.[28] But as the euphoria of liberation faded, relations between the local residents and the GIs began to deteriorate. One of the most significant problems was the extreme disparity in wealth. Donning well-tailored uniforms, feasting on plentiful K-rations, and speeding along in muscular Jeeps, the GIs humiliated the locals who had recently witnessed the destruction of their infrastructure and who still suffered extreme shortages of food and clothing. While children begged in the streets and adults queued up for meager meat and bread rations, the GIs became the richest men in town, using their chocolate and cigarettes as currency in the pervasive black market. Nothing was beyond their purchasing power, not even the one item unavailable at the local PX—prostitutes.[29] As Mary Louise Roberts has demonstrated, the frequency with which American soldiers bought sex from French women worked as a particularly potent symbol of American dominance in the postwar world, nurturing an "arrogant, even imperialist attitude among the Americans" and symbolizing France's status as a conquered, shamed nation among the civilians who witnessed their mothers, sisters, and lovers soliciting on the streets.[30] For the citizens of Reims, this gendered display of power and privilege was transforming the Liberation into "a second Occupation . . . as unbearable as the last one."[31] "We expected friends who would not make us ashamed of our defeat," another Norman remembered. "Instead there came incomprehension, arrogance, incredibly bad manners, and the swagger of conquerors."[32]

French anxiety about Washington's growing power and influence, potent though it was, coexisted nonetheless with curiosity about American people and enthusiasm for American popular culture, especially jazz. Having first heard it from the African American soldiers deployed across the Atlantic during the First World War, the French had quickly developed a taste for New Orleans–style jazz. Once home, African American musicians set out to return to France, eager to pursue professional musical careers and escape the racism endemic to the United States. During the twenties, African American musicians established a veritable Harlem Renaissance in Paris, setting up nightclubs and dance halls for the well-heeled in Montmartre and, later, the bohemians in Montparnasse.[33] Before long, their "hot," improvisational style began to reach French musicians. Inspired by the records of Duke Ellington and Louis Armstrong, Django Reinhardt, the Belgian-born Gypsy, was perhaps the most influential in developing a French style of jazz. Performing with the Quintette du Hot Club de France, he departed from the typical American brass orchestration in favor of an all-string band made up of three guitars, bass, and violin. Despite the collaboration between the Quintette and American expat musicians, coverage of the jazz scene in the pages of *Jazz Hot* emphasized jazz as an art form that, despite French interest, was essentially an American cultural form. Central to this representation was Panassié's insistence on jazz as an essentially *nègre* music, a style that came most naturally to black musicians. "While the negro masses among themselves have an instinctive feeling for this music," he wrote, "white people approach it with resistance and assimilate it slowly."[34]

When African American musicians left France upon the outbreak of war in 1939, many wondered how French jazz would continue, cut off as it now was from the epicenter of creation and innovation.

Despite the proliferation of French jazz that occurred during the Occupation, the return of American GIs in 1944 was thus greatly anticipated by French jazz fans. As they discovered American cigarettes, chocolate, Coca-Cola, and chewing gum—products that collectively became known as the 4 C's—the French also looked to the GIs for news of the latest hits from their favorite American artists. Recall, for example, Michel Adam's account of the "hole" left by the years of deprivation and the "fabulous shock" he experienced as a teenager when he first heard Benny Goodman's music at a party hosted by the GIs.[35] Michel Gaudry, also a teenager during the summer of 1944, remembered how desperate he was to listen to American jazz upon France's liberation. "I was ready to do whatever it took to get a jazz record, he recalls. "In the end, I was able to get one in exchange for a piece of pork that I had stolen."[36] Summarizing the state of jazz music across the nation, Hugues Panassié, cofounder of the French Hot Club, recalled the excitement as "an explosion."[37] Jazz was in high demand as French citizens, previously cut off from American music, finally saw the reappearance of recent recordings by popular artists like Duke Ellington, Louis Armstrong, Count Basie, and Coleman Hawkins.[38]

For those living among the highest concentration of GIs, opportunities to listen to American jazz abounded. Musical activity was vigorously encouraged by the U.S. military, which believed that singing was crucial to the maintenance of troop morale.[39] Not only did the Special Services arrange for military bands to be permanently installed in some camps, it also supplied soldiers with sheet music and instruments so that they might form informal bands and small ensembles.[40] To keep soldiers connected to the musical scene at home, the Special Services sent the troops millions of V-discs, small plastic records that contained tunes from across several genres, but especially featured jazz and swing.[41] Thus armed with musical equipment and inspiration, the GIs formed jazz bands and swing combos to entertain their comrades as they relaxed on base or participated in the "dance classes" held in local French bars and cafés.[42] Often, these performances brought the GIs into contact with French locals. Nitoune Conrad, for example, recalls frequenting the Pélissier, a café near her apartment in Marseille that regularly hosted African American jazz orchestras. Together with her best friend, Conrad learned new swing dances from the GIs who gathered there.[43] In Le Havre, a group of African American soldiers played jazz for a regular "dance class" before locals began complaining that the classes were really "clandestine balls" that allowed GIs and French women to violate the nation's ban on dancing.[44] The GIs also participated in jam sessions with aspiring French musicians who were eager to learn new styles and techniques. In Marseille, these Franco-American musical exchanges were so popular that Paul Mansi, president of the local Hot Club, established a weekly jam session every Sunday morning.[45] As Panassié joked, "this was without a doubt the first time in the history of jazz that concerts took place from 10:00 a.m. to noon!"[46]

While the GIs' jazz concerts and parties were a source of great fun among those who attended, their popularity nonetheless exacerbated existing concerns over France's ability to withstand pressure from Washington. Those who had experienced the nation's many wartime losses now wondered if France was to also suffer an erosion of its own culture. That this degradation should come at the hands of the Americans was particularly alarming. For the French, America was a nation of soulless industry and unbridled mass consumerism, skilled at producing wealth but devoid of the kind of intellectual acuity and cultural sophistication characteristic of Europe in general and France in particular. The trope that American culture was yet another commodity, hastily made and easily discarded, was well known in the interwar period, appearing frequently in criticisms of both high and popular art, music, and film. Journalist Joseph Kessel, for example, described Hollywood as "a factory town" that "makes moving images like Ford makes automobiles." "All is organized, hierarchized, standardized. From thought to inspiration."[47] Even America's most respected creative talents could not effectively challenge the stereotype. "No matter how many Hawthornes, Melvilles, Twains, Faulkners, or Hemingways the nation produced," as historian Richard Pells writes, the notion that "American culture was shallow, derivative, second rate, lacking in social texture and intellectual complexity . . . would not subside."[48] So entrenched was this opinion that even the Axis powers appealed to it in their propaganda, representing American music as composed and

performed by "money grubbers and jazz addicts, drinkers" who produced
second-rate ersatz instead of "real" art. "All good music," the Germans
preached, was "either German or Italian."[49] Whatever the source, the
message that American culture suffered from an obsession with profit circulated widely, casting a suspicious pall on the GIs' jazz. The Liberation,
it seemed, threatened to decimate not only French farms and homes, but
the nation's culture as well.

The threat of American jazz seemed even more potent in light of
the United States' efforts to promote American culture. Fearful that
widespread stereotypes about commercialized culture would constrain
Washington's ability to win international support and contain the spread
of Communism, the U.S. War Department invested heavily in its own
propaganda campaign, using American concert music to build trust and
cooperation among foreign nations. In 1942, it created the Office of War
Information (OWI) to serve as the primary branch of America's cultural
offensive. Best known for its extensive domestic and international radio
programming and pro-American Hollywood films, the OWI believed
that music could be especially useful in building pro-American sentiment.[50] For the OWI, music offered the chance to engage in "friendly
propaganda" that could transcend language barriers and make "friends
out of strangers" by evoking "the natives' feelings."[51] In addition to these
pragmatic virtues, it offered an ideal medium through which to combat
fears related to Americanization. Music, the OWI believed, could help
frame the emerging superpower as a benevolent nation committed to
diversity, inclusiveness, and democracy. By broadcasting radio programs
that featured American musicians playing the works of British, French,
Italian, and even German composers, the OWI aimed to demonstrate
America's respect for foreign culture.[52] Likewise, broadcasts of American
orchestras playing the symphonic works of homegrown composers like
Aaron Copeland, Roy Harris, Robert Russell Bennett, and William Grant
Still were intended to establish America's cultural legitimacy and unique
musical heritage.[53] Ironically, though, these efforts to portray the United
States as a sophisticated, tolerant contributor to Western music excluded
jazz. Despite the genre's status as one of the most salient musical expressions of American culture and diversity and its position as the most
popular American art form among the French, the OWI did not consider

it the kind of "good music" that could promote the nation among foreign audiences.[54]

Despite the fact that jazz was not featured in the OWI's propaganda campaign, French enthusiasm for the genre worked to establish it, nonetheless, as one of the most effective weapons in the American cultural arsenal. Indeed, testimonials indicate that the French understood jazz as part of the United States' broader strategy to build support and acceptance of American policy, regardless of the OWI's intent. Take, for example, Michel Adam's recollection that "the Americans had understood that [jazz] was also a means . . . to make us love their culture."[55] Another woman remembered jazz as integral to the formation of friendships with American GIs, most of whom did not speak French very well: "Ties of friendship were formed between black Americans and the young Havrais. It was mostly a question of music!"[56] Jazz was a particularly powerful arm of the American offensive because it gave expression to fun and excitement in an era of deprivation, despair, and boredom. Indeed, even as the Germans left French territory, wartime bans on dancing persisted, making American jazz parties even more desirable in the eyes of French youth.[57] "Everywhere," as Adam recalled, "there were balls, parties, various meet-up points designated for young people."[58] Elizabeth Coquart's description of the scene further underscores the exhilaration that the French felt: "Badaboum! The syncopated rhythms set behavior [*les moeurs*] free." All across France, "wherever a garrison of GIs was stationed," one could find "a pianist, a sax, a drummer, or a trumpet player to make the couples twirl."[59] Jazz, with all its energy and dynamism, both expressed and accompanied the reclamation of normal life for teens and young adults. In so doing, it worked alongside the symphonies and folk songs that the OWI hoped would build a love of American culture, supplementing the campaign of "friendly propaganda."

Thus, as this history shows, American jazz did not come to France in 1944 as apolitical entertainment, but was bound up in a culture war over international influence on the eve of the United States' rise to the position of global superpower. As the French faced the reality of their nation's diminished position, Allied bombings, Roosevelt's disdain, and the arrogant attitudes of many American GIs left them suspicious of America's intentions and concerned about their nation's bid for political sovereignty. These concerns were magnified by the popularity of American jazz among French youth, a music that, though increasingly mainstream, was nonetheless associated with America's allegedly "commercial" and inferior culture. The United States' efforts to combat the fear of Americanization took the form of a cultural offensive in which music played a crucial role in assuring civilians that their way of life would not be diluted or dismantled upon war's end. Pumping American concert music into France over the airwaves of the OWI's networks, propagandists converted the skill and talent of American musicians into an argument for French cooperation. And while jazz was not a major pillar of the OWI's campaign, it nonetheless accompanied the organization's efforts, flooding into France with the GIs who played it on V-discs or performed it live for enthusiastic French youth. Yet, for the French, jazz was not always heard as the "friendly propaganda" that the OWI intended, but a powerful performance of American dominance in the postwar world.

Jazz: A Confrontation with American Hegemony

In the first issue of *Jazz Hot* to appear since the Occupation, an anonymous author complained about the decision to extend France's ban on dancing until the conclusion of all fighting and repatriation of French POWs. This kind of wartime propriety was foolish, he held, not only because it would result in fewer paid gigs for French musicians, but because it would provide the GIs, most of whom were "immoral," with even more access to French women. "The Allies," he wrote, "have always danced at home. They are going to, then, in light of the French ban, open private clubs with French *danseuses* and their own orchestras." From a moral and social point of view, he asked, "is this the desired outcome?"[60] The answer, of course, was no. The GIs, whose predilection for prostitution and sexual assault was well known, should be kept away from French women, not driven into their arms by a French ban on dancing. Such a ban, the author, argued, would allow American soldiers to invite French women to their own parties completely unencumbered by competition from French men. Given the substantial gender damage France had already suffered throughout the German Occupation and Allied Liberation, such a monopoly on female interaction could not be tolerated, as it would compromise France's ability to display the kind of strength necessary to demonstrate its capacity for sovereignty.[61] As we shall see, testimonials from citizens living in Marseille and Le Havre corroborate the fear expressed in this column, revealing that jazz parties hosted by American soldiers facilitated a gendered display of American power rooted in the GIs' access to French women and possession of material wealth. In response, French men attempted to mitigate this damage by reviving old assumptions about America's obsession with consumerism and subsequent cultural inferiority. French women wanted to go to GI dance parties, the rationale went, not because they were attracted to American men or American jazz, but because they wanted to feast on American whiskey and chocolate.

In a marked parallel to the concerns listed in the 1945 article quoted above, the most striking feature of the testimonials recorded by French men about their experiences with jazz and the GIs is the repeated charge that the Americans were able to skirt the nation's ban on dancing and monopolize local nightlife, hosting regular dance parties for the local women at the exclusion of local men. Famous jazz critic Hugues Panassié recalled, for example, that in Marseille, "white men or men other than soldiers were not admitted" to dance parties hosted by African American GIs. He himself was only granted access when a friend told the doorman that "he [was] one of the fellows."[62] Max Bengtsson, a teenager living in Normandy, also had trouble getting through the doors. He remembered having to pass "incognito," disguised in an American military uniform lent to him by friendly GIs.[63] On the rare occasion that French men were granted access, their entry was conditional upon their ability to bring a female companion. In a letter to the chief of civil affairs, for example, the prefect of Bouches-du-Rhône complained about the *réunions dansantes* (dance meet-ups) hosted four times a week by the "colored workers associated with the American army" in the town of La Ciotat. The prefect was vexed that entry was being denied to "French soldiers and sailors" but granted to any man who was accompanied by a woman.[64] Captain Ralph Horton Jr.'s response clarified U.S. policy in La Ciotat, explaining that due to a "lack of adequate accommodations for all French civilians and military personnel, only males who are accompanied by female guests are permitted to the dances."[65] Thus, while no universal rule seems to have applied, these accounts reveal that access to American jazz parties was enthusiastically given to French women and actively denied to French men.

The problem of GIs having such exclusive access to French women extended even to the parties hosted in bars and clubs owned by French people. Noting the demand for jazz, enterprising residents with black market connections scraped together the resources to build nightclubs and *bars américains*, or bars that sold beverages only. To skirt the national ban on dancing, owners presented their establishments as dance schools or cabaret theaters, charging admission for the "classes" or "performances." Before long, though, residents began complaining that the bars were operating as mere façades for Franco-American dancing. One letter to the *sous-préfet* of Le Havre complained, for example, that "two or three houses called 'Dance Schools'" were really "veritable public balls." On one evening, the author noted, "40 couples, civilian and military, French and American," could be found, "abandoning themselves to dance" while a jazz orchestra from the American army played.[66] In a similar tone of disapproval, another resident complained that the "dance classes" were disreputable places where "a notable quantity of alcohol is consumed and the clientele is composed, for the most part, of soldiers of the Allied Armies."[67] What a "sad spectacle," wrote former *maquisard* Lt. Montagnac, to put before the eyes of so many people haunted by the present hour."[68] Not only were these bars providing GIs with even more access to French women, but they were becoming hotbeds of violence and prostitution. One letter to the mayor of Le Havre, for example, complained about the "black and white Americans" who frequently invaded a local café and "set off numerous fights."[69] A report filed in Marseille indicated that "three or four women of loose morals 'worked' with black Americans" in the furnished flat belonging to a bar called the Julot.[70] So grave was the situation that city officials petitioned the *commissaire* régional de la République to prohibit the opening of all "new establishments of this genre."[71]

Unsurprisingly, the fact that the jazz parties allowed American soldiers—men whose ample provisions and wealth permitted them to host and attend the events—such intimate access to French women was deeply upsetting to French men. Recalling the evening he spent at an American camp, disguised as a GI and sipping whiskey, Bengtsson writes that he "was very ill at ease in this environment, in a space where French boys didn't have their place."[72] Despite his ability to "pass for an American," something he had often fantasized about, the young teenager felt uncomfortable at the sight of "the girls there, who weren't behaving themselves very well." "It bothered me," he explained, "because it was, in fact, false. All of it was false."[73] On one level, Bengtsson's emphasis on the "falseness" of the evening operates as an indictment of French women by resurrecting familiar notions of femininity that position women as inherently dishonest, changeable, and fraudulent. We might interpret Bengtsson's remarks, therefore, as a denunciation of what he perceived to be female manipulation of American GIs. To be sure, young women spent a great deal of time primping for these parties, hoping to compete for manly attention. Emilienne Ciesielski-Prevots remembered, for example, that the women of Le Havre attempted to outdo one another by wearing the "new-look"—a sartorial ensemble consisting of a dress "cinched at the waist, gathered atop layers of starched tulle petticoats, perched atop high-heeled shoes."[74] The effect was topped off with a ponytail, which could be whipped around while dancing.[75] For jealous French men who resented the female attention paid to American soldiers, these attempts at seducing the GIs could be denigrated as a manifestation of feminine nature. By representing women as deceitful and dishonest, Bengtsson charged women with attempting to make the body over, to mask its truth and present only the kind of idealized image of femininity that could ensnare the powerful GI.

Yet, Bengtsson's comment speaks to a more consequential falsehood, as it suggests that the jazz parties were disturbing the nation's social order and deepening widespread anxiety over France's manly strength and fitness for sovereignty. The sight of French girls dancing with American GIs was false not just because it relied on the female body's alleged trickery, but because it violated French men's presumably natural position of dominance and control. As the *chef de famille* (head of the family), the position given to French men in the Napoleonic Code of 1804, men bore the responsibility to act on behalf of women and children. However, because of their inability to protect their families from the destruction wrought by Hitler's army, the horrendous conditions of Occupation, or the Allied bombs dropped during the Liberation, French men worried that they had ceded their positions as heads of the family and, by extension, their sexual privileges with French women.[76] The proliferation of jazz parties at the Liberation, whether in military camps or French bars, lent credence to this fear, as these events literally displaced French men from heterosexual social space. "Having no place," as Bengtsson put it, French men confronted the possibility that the GIs were displacing them from their position as *chefs de famille*.

The spectacle of GI dance parties deepened the assault on French manhood by putting American wealth on display. First, the construction of night clubs and bars was expensive, as it required raw materials that were incredibly scarce. French residents who suffered the lack of proper housing, schools, and government buildings were understandably aghast to see precious concrete, glass, and metal go to construct entertainment venues that would cater to the GIs. In a letter to a friend, one *Marseillais* captured the frustration and dismay of the city's residents, reporting that "from the immense hole that engulfed twenty houses at the corner of Rue de Rome and Rue de la Darse, a small and colorful American night club is beginning to emerge. It is impossible to change a roof or to patch up a house, but we can build these vile clubs. It's sickening."[77] Not only did building these venues divert resources from rebuilding French infrastructure, but the parties themselves put American bounty on display. To entice young women to attend the events, American soldiers provided transportation in their exotic Jeeps and tantalizing refreshments. For women who were still subsisting on fake coffee and bread made with wood chips, a night at the American buffet line offered temporary relief from incredible scarcity, especially if one managed to take home a bit extra. As Claude-Michel Langanay remembers, "the *mômes* [young girls] returned home" from the GI camps "with their gleanings of cigarettes, different flavors of chewing gum, magazines, or less often, chocolate taken from a K-ration."[78] Hugues Panassié writes that even the mothers who accompanied their daughters as chaperones "hurled themselves on the free buffet and filled up their stomachs, their pockets, or their purses."[79] That French women were looking to American men for basic provisions offered humiliating evidence of the nation's decline. France, once a powerful empire, now could not supply its people with adequate food and shelter.

Yet, while the jazz *soirées* drew attention to the incredible wealth disparity between the two nations, these material goods also provided local men with a comforting way to explain the popularity of the GIs. Jean Lerussé, for example, remembers that it was "pastries" that attracted women to hear the GIs play, despite his admission that this particular group of black soldiers did, in fact, boast a "superb orchestra."[80] Panassié's own account of the parties sums up this line of thinking well: "If the women followed the black soldiers around, it was because they had rare commodities or some *galettes*, the usual thing."[81] Ironically, then, even though the jazz parties humiliated French men, the material goods that they made available offered a convenient defense of their manhood and preserved stereotypes about American cultural inferiority. By underscoring American wealth, French men claimed that local women did not really prefer American men—especially black men—or American music, but were using the GIs for their own financial gain. Appealing to the same market logic that drives prostitution, these men portrayed French women as selling themselves in exchange for commodities to either be enjoyed or used as currency on the black market. It was, in their eyes, only the pastries and *galettes* that drew women to the parties.

The notion that French women were primarily attracted to jazz parties because of the availability of foodstuffs and cigarettes worked in tandem with a widespread association between GI jazz and consumerism. Take, for example, the many testimonials that represent jazz as another American consumer good such as cigarettes or chocolate. One drummer described jazz as the "hymn" of the moment that brought "the Jeep, bourbon, and the *série noire*" to France.[82] Max Bengtsson's account of the GIs listed jazz alongside the "artifices"—"blankets, sandwiches, cigarettes, chewing gum, dollars"—that the men used to "seduce" French women. Panassié's account of the Liberation also bears evidence of this conflation between jazz and consumerism. Describing the GIs' purchasing power, he writes that they took full advantage of the black market, "having such rare commodities as coffee, sugar, chocolate, cigarettes, soap, toothpaste, shaving cream, etc." As evidence, he describes a trombonist who "always walked around with two cases: one contained his trombone, the other a pile of products he sold left and right." Taken together, these testimonials reveal a persistent tendency among local French men to imagine jazz as another American material good that, like cigarettes, chocolate, and Coca-Cola, threatened to weaken France's world-class culture and subvert the natural social order. Jazz, the argument went, was but another cheap commodity to be bartered in the interests of the United States.

Even the musical preferences of the American GIs worked to bolster the representation of American jazz as a mass-produced consumer good that failed to live up to French cultural standards. While French jazz enthusiasts longed to hear new works from Duke Ellington and Count Basie, the GIs often requested symphonic arrangements by white composers like Glenn Miller and Artie Shaw. Recalling Miller's biggest wartime hit, for example, Michel Adam described "In the Mood" as the "grand moment of the liberation." Jazz critic Frank Ténot echoes this account, noting that "the vast majority of GIs who came to chase out the Germans were ignorant of jazz except for 'In the Mood' and 'Moonlight Serenade' by Glenn Miller."[83] For French jazz fans, many of whom had been reading sustained denouncements of arranged, "straight" jazz in the pages of *Jazz Hot* since the 1930s, the proliferation of big-band swing offered evidence to support long-standing stereotypes about the commercial nature of American culture. In the words of Claude Leon, a French musician who performed for GIs, "we quickly realized that America wasn't at all the country of encyclopedic knowledge of jazz. In the facts of jazz, the Americans were often totally uncultured." Leon and his band grew so tired of playing "straight" jazz that they adopted a "philosophy . . . of refusing to execute the pieces that [they] didn't like." "Our sacred GIs always called out for 'Besame Mucho' and other big hits of the era," Leon remembered. We responded "*non*, we will not play 'Besame Mucho,' we will play Duke Ellington." In the end, Leon, recalled, "it worked out well . . . the soldiers danced and we, we played 'our music.'" For French fans who had read consistent denigrations of symphonic, arranged jazz as "commercial" and "false" in the pages of *Jazz Hot* since before the Occupation, these encounters with American GIs corroborated rather than refuted long-standing stereotypes that situated France as America's cultural superior.

Thus, while American jazz was very popular in France, its performance confronted French people with the reality of American hegemony. By facilitating the displacement of French men from important sites of heterosexual social life and by putting American bounty on display, the jazz parties operated as reminders that the GIs were in charge. The discourse of anti-Americanism helped to contain this challenge to French standing, as it supplied the convenient trope of consumerism to explain French women's interactions with GIs and to denigrate the quality of the music that the GIs often requested. But even these arguments weren't perfect, as they reified rather than diffused fears of Americanization of French culture. After all, the notion that French women were being seduced by material goods and a commercialized, second-rate music did little to ease widespread fear about the loss of France's culture, even as it perhaps assuaged feelings of jealousy among individual men. It is within this context that we turn to the pages of *Jazz Hot*, reading closely for a performance of resistance that could acknowledge France's love of American jazz while preserving its cultural heritage and national pride.

Critical Interventions: Writing Resistance in Jazz Hot

Writing in 1945, Charles Delaunay begins his first post-Occupation column of *Jazz Hot* with a tone of great anticipation. Having been "separated from America for five years," he describes the "impatience," "enthusiasm," and "infinite curiosity" with which the French greeted the arrival of new American records and critical reviews. Yet, Delaunay quickly dashes his readers' high hopes, reviving stereotypes about American cultural inferiority to denigrate the jazz heard in Liberation-era France. He reports that the "first indications" demonstrate that "American jazz has followed the tendencies in which it has been engaged before the war . . . commercialism and exhibitionism." The problem, for Delaunay, is that big bands, musical ensembles that play arranged jazz instead of improvisational jazz, are attracting large audiences and stealing the spotlight from the true masters. Citing the popular orchestras led by white band leaders like Harry James, Glenn Miller, and Tommy Dorsey, Delaunay argues that symphonic jazz bands, talented and skilled though they may be, are degrading the quality of jazz by playing virtuosic, "neo-symphonic" arrangements that are "more and more *spectaculaire*." Such trumped-up arrangements, he writes, only "use and contaminate swing"; they lack the "essential vitality that animates the true jazz orchestras." In order to reverse this troubling trend, Delaunay calls upon jazz players to emulate Duke Ellington and recognize that "improvisation must remain the primordial element in all executions of jazz." Only then, in his view, can the legacy of the true masters—"Louis Armstrong, Béchet, Johnny Hodges, . . . Duke Ellington"—be protected from imposters like "Roy Eldridge, Benny Goodman, or Harry James."[84]

At first glance, Delaunay's article operates merely as an indictment of recent American jazz. However, in the process of differentiating between good and bad music, Delaunay subtly revives an old feature of French jazz criticism, the racialization of jazz. Indeed, while he never makes explicit mention of race in this article, his emphasis on the superiority of black musicians and his allusions to a sort of unteachable *esprit de jazz* evoke long-standing racial assumptions to reinforce the music's relationship to the black body. Indeed, in all cases except one, Delaunay's examples of jazz heroes and villains fall along a racial divide. Only black musicians like Sidney Bechet, Duke Ellington, and Louis Armstrong are offered as examples of those who possess the "genius" and "essential vitality" that lend jazz its "primordial element." Likewise, Delaunay faults white musicians like Roy Eldridge, Benny Goodman, and Glenn Miller as those responsible for turning jazz into a profit-driven, highly stylized circus show.[85] Even his description of the problem with contemporary jazz works to strengthen this racialized understanding of good and bad jazz, as it relies upon essentialized notions of primitivism to make jazz into a musical form that can only be properly performed by the black body. Indeed, while Delaunay describes white musicians as "masters of written research and the finish of execution" (*maîtres dans les recherches d'écriture et le fini de l'execution*), all their expertise and skill cannot restore to jazz "its purity of inspiration and vitality." Presumably, only the black body, endowed with innate soulfulness, can produce "true" jazz.

While Delaunay's racialization of jazz was not new to French jazz criticism, the trope takes on special rhetorical significance here, as it lays the discursive groundwork necessary to position jazz as at odds with American society. By characterizing jazz as the product of the black body, a body excluded from American political and social life, Delaunay sets the genre within the context of American racism. Subsequent articles seize this framing, working to divorce jazz from the United States and recast it as more properly belonging to France. Consider, for example, another column penned for the same edition. Here, an anonymous author opens with an explicit attack on America's possession of jazz, arguing for France as the rightful custodian of the genre. "Although jazz was born in the United States," the author writes, "it was in Europe that it was given its titles of nobility." Using the history of the Hot Club as evidence, the editorial represents the Hot Club as an organization of anti-racists, tirelessly working to bring knowledge to all "five corners of the world" about a music "still poorly understood, but already heavily resisted."[86] Deploying the same essentialized notion of black jazz embraced by Delaunay, the author lists African American musicians Louis Armstrong, Bessie Smith, Coleman Hawkins, "Fats" Waller, and Duke Ellington as examples of "real" jazz, reminding readers that these masters were not recognized in their home country. In fact, as the article stresses, it was the Hot Club that first "defended this 'music of savages.'" Putting the word "savages" in quotation marks, the author makes a pointed reference to American racism, suggesting that it is this ideology, rather than any artistic deficiency, that precludes jazz from being celebrated in the United States. France, a nation of open-minded, tolerant citizens, the article implies, has long been capable of hearing the real merit in jazz.

Not only did linking jazz to the black body allow columnists to recruit American racism for the purpose of severing the nation's ties to the genre, it also helped French columnists to differentiate the music from the rest of the nation's allegedly overly commercialized popular culture. "Real," black jazz, the argument went, was unlike the rest of America's half-rate culture that could be so easily produced and sold. Indeed, the articles repeatedly represent African American musicians as the embodiment of originality and "vitality"—the opposite of American mass culture and commodification. Take, for example, Delaunay's later column on French musician André Ekyan. Here, Delaunay acknowledges that some may find it strange to see him doling out praise for a white player like Ekyan, since readers "imagine for better or for worse my bias for all that is black," adding that such a reverence comes from "a very French tendency to admire that which comes from abroad, at the expense of our own resources."[87] Instead of denying this negrophilia, Delaunay embraces it, explaining that he does, in fact, "generally consider black musicians to be far superior to their white brothers." Not only did "blacks create jazz," but, as Delaunay explains, "their musical instinct and their creative power have always remained unequaled." It is this innate jazz sensibility, for Delaunay, that has insulated them from the "commercial influences that have so corrupted jazz music."[88] Here again, Delaunay's column uses blackness as a foil for white commercialism. By portraying black people as endowed with a natural creative genius, he suggests that jazz could never properly belong in a nation known for the mass production of cheap, tasteless art.

From a rhetorical perspective, two important consequences emerge from this representation of real jazz as black, and therefore more properly belonging to France. First, the cultural seizure of jazz helped to mitigate the threat of Americanization. In the context of widespread fear of American influence over French politics and culture, the popularity of the GIs' jazz threatened to signify an acceptance of American dominance and France's international decline. The utility of positioning black jazz as a cultural form belonging to France was that it provided a way to understand the music heard at GI jazz parties as less American and more French. It was, after all, in France that the great pioneers of jazz had been nurtured and encouraged. Rooted in French culture and tradition, then, jazz was not an arm of American consumer culture, aimed at diluting French patrimony, but a homegrown art form that would promote French cultural prestige. Second, the argument that (black) jazz belonged in France restored some of France's lost dignity by positioning the nation as inherently egalitarian. Repeated references to American racism and French tolerance offered locals a source of pride, even as they faced incredible economic hardship and a lack of political autonomy. Stripped of military, political, and economic power, France, the articles suggested, was still the ethical superior of the United States.

Having positioned jazz as black and therefore at odds with American society, *Jazz Hot* can then proclaim the critical prerogative for France and deny American knowledge and mastery of jazz. Perhaps the best example of this cultural seizure appears in the article "American and British Jazz Reviews," published in 1945 in the third edition of *Jazz Hot*. Here, an anonymous author writes, "We were surprised that American fans, with the information that they can draw from the source, haven't been able to do more careful work, as not only is the information far from complete, but its authenticity is often doubtful."[89] Another edition intensified this attack, charging jazz reviews printed in the United States, Great Britain, Belgium, Holland, Denmark, Australia, and Switzerland with being motivated by "commercial necessities" rather than by a "rigorous musical aesthetic." These reviews, the author claims, neglect "the study of true jazz music" by privileging "corporate gossip, journalistic surveys, and musicians and orchestras that are in vogue."[90] By Christmas, French critics were intensifying the attack, writing that American jazz criticism, "whose level was already not very high," had become "in the majority of cases, scandalously idiotic."[91] The journal's allusions to American racism supplied a rationale for this failure. Blinded by their racism, the implication went, American critics surely could not offer objective criticism of a black musical form.

In light of the alleged deficiency of other leading jazz periodicals, the authors of *Jazz Hot* proclaim the right to judge jazz for themselves. Referring to the Hot Club's historical record of defending jazz, the authors give the critical prerogative to France. In an article entitled "What French Jazz Musicians Think about the Hot Club of France," Roger Chaput, a founding member of the Hot Club's famous Quintette, remembered the ways that the organization taught him to "know and love jazz music" and instilled in him the ability to "distinguish from the crowd the real, the good jazz."[92] Claude Laurence summed up the legacy of the Hot Club this way: "If I was a dabbler in metaphors, I would say that the Hot Club is the Temple of Jazz, or even the Academy of Swing where one learns the pure traditions of this very particular musical genre."[93] Jerry Mengo echoed this representation of the Hot Club as the only legitimate organization for the promotion of jazz, calling the club the "place where we can hear real jazz, where we can play real jazz, where we can talk about real jazz."[94] For Mengo, the HCF's importance is tied directly to its promotion of improvisational jazz over the allegedly inferior symphonic arrangements. "It managed to stay outside the commercial arrangements of 'swing traffickers,' who think only about exploiting the increasing popularity of *our* music" (emphasis mine). Together, these musicians' memories work to elevate the significance of the French Hot Club, portraying it as a disinterested, noble protector of an art that is under threat from those who lack knowledge and integrity. It is up to the French, they suggest, to intervene in the international art scene to defend "their" music, even from the Americans on whose soil it originated.

To bolster claims to French ownership of jazz, the Liberation-era articles repeatedly argue for the quality of white French musicians, players whose skill and finesse is *only* rivaled by African American jazz masters. In the first issue published in 1945, Panassié reported on the "Five Great Figures of French Jazz." Predictably, the article focuses the majority of its reporting on the infamous Django Reinhardt, a player who was not the "equal" of other guitarists, but their "master." Writing that he "mak[es] his guitar speak just like Louis Armstrong makes his trumpet speak," Reinhardt offers incontestable proof that "the French can play jazz music just as well as the Americans." Even the other, lesser-known jazzmen support this claim. In Stéphane Grappelli, France claimed the kind of "violinist we have searched for in vain among the Anglo-Saxons." Philippe Brun possessed "an extremely developed sense of jazz" that allowed him to "improvise choruses with admirable beauty." "Who is the Anglo-Saxon trumpet player who has ever played better?" Panassié asks. The implied answer, of course, was no one. Only black musicians whose innate skill and passion ignited the genre, this column argued, could compete with the French.

As proof of these players' skill, the journal repeatedly emphasizes American desire for French music, featuring accounts of GIs searching for the great Django across Parisian nightclubs, or of the American Forces Network recruiting the Quintette to record special broadcasts alongside American musicians. French readers learned, for example, that American soldiers on leave in Paris were frustrated with the "difficulty that they meet listening to our best artists in favorable circumstances." "The number of these people surpasses that which we can imagine," the writer continues, making it difficult "to accommodate the fans in uniform who come, either to ask where they might hear Django Reinhardt, to obtain a copy of *Hot Discographie*, or to procure French records."[95] Under the headline "French Jazz Honored Abroad," the periodical pronounced that "French jazz is followed with interest by connoisseurs across the world" and chastised readers for being surprised that "our musicians are so sought after by American and English stations."[96] Reporting an upcoming

Franco-American radio broadcast, another columnist boasted that French players were so good that "the American officials immediately realized [their] interest and quality."[97] Appearing so frequently, such declarations of American regard for French jazz help establish France as the proper parent of the genre. So gifted are French musicians, the journal tells us, that Americans must now travel across the Atlantic to keep abreast of new trends in jazz performance.

Conclusion

Taken together and viewed within the context of the GI jazz parties that proliferated throughout France after the Liberation, the articles published in *Jazz Hot* in 1945 emerged as a rhetorical response to the performance of American power. By deploying an essentialized understanding of good jazz as black jazz and alluding to American racism, the authors argued that the United States could never claim jazz. Instead it was France, a nation whose racial tolerance and special musical skill was apparent, who was its rightful guardian. In the context of the United States' meteoric rise to global dominance, this rhetorical move worked to restore some of France's lost stature, as it represented the nation as an ethical and cultural world leader, regardless of the substantial losses sustained over the previous five years. As Ludovic Tournès has argued, this strategy would prove useful even as France faced the consolidation of American power during the Cold War era.[98] By 1947, for example, *Jazz Hot*, complaining about the American radio program *Voice of America*, wrote sarcastically about America's "liberalness concerning blacks." This kind of "narrow-mindedness" was polluting the airwaves with fake jazz. The antidote, the journal wrote, was a visit to France, a nation that could provide Americans with "a freedom of thought and a sincerity that is not practiced in their home."[99] The scars of war, though deep, had not undone France's international relevance. A nation of special cultural sophistication and moral uprightness, it still had something to teach the United States.

To be clear, this interpretation of *Jazz Hot*'s discourse is not meant to deny the reality that American racism was indeed a barrier to the careers of important jazz musicians or to the genre's acceptance as a legitimate art

form. Nor is it my intent to deny the fact that many African American artists *did* enjoy greater personal and artistic freedom in France during this
era than in their home country. However, as Andy Fry notes, these facts
have gone untroubled in much of the historiography, helping to crystallize
a myth of French egalitarianism that obscures the ways in which "ideals
for the fraternity of races coexisted with an everyday reality of racism."[100]
As Carole Sweeney eloquently puts it, "The widespread popularity of
l'art nègre and *le jazz hot* in the clubs and salons of bourgeois Paris did
not make fashionable Parisians aware of the 1919 Pan African Congress
in Versailles led by WEB DuBois or the formation of the Union Inter-
Coloniale in 1921."[101] Similarly, French enthusiasm for the works of Duke
Ellington and Louis Armstrong in 1945 did not prevent the nation from
entertaining racist fantasies about African American soldiers' designs on
French women or from pursuing imperial ambitions in Syria, Vietnam,
and Algeria. In short, the nation's love of jazz should not be mistaken for
evidence of a national politics of racial inclusion.

What I have hoped to show, rather, is that jazz operated in France as
a key signifier of political dominance and a conduit through which France
resituated itself in the modern geopolitical order. Jazz's connection to
the myth of French egalitarianism allowed cultural critics writing in the
aftermath of war to give a disempowered people the rhetorical means to
assert their national worth and confront an uncertain political future. As
citizens took stock of France's deficiencies in military might, economic
power, and political influence, the notion that the nation surpassed the
United States at least in social and cultural sophistication provided a
much-needed source of national confidence and a powerful antidote to
the anxiety over Americanization. Perhaps it is for these reasons that jazz
has continued to accompany French remembrances of the war's end. In
1995, for example, the city of Marseille hosted a party in honor of both the
fiftieth anniversary of the Liberation *and* the fiftieth anniversary of bebop,
the experimental jazz pioneered by Charlie Parker in New York.[102] That
the city should have celebrated these two anniversaries together belies
the significance of jazz to the nation's interpretation of the war. Groov-
ing to the esoteric, complex harmonies of bebop jazz, these *Marseillais*,
like the generation before, tempered the pain of remembering national
defeat and disempowerment with a performance of their own cultural

discernment. The virtuosic style of Charlie Parker and Dizzy Gillespie may have been out of the musical mainstream, but for these French, this highbrow, artistic jazz may have been just the kind necessary to call forth a performance of French cultural superiority that would ease the remembrance of the past.

Conclusion

———•◆•———

Shortly before soldiers of the Resistance and French army liberated
Paris in the summer of 1944, humorist Pierre Dac aired his parody
of famous singer Maurice Chevalier's wartime hit "Et tout ça, ça fait
d'excellents français" (And all that, that makes for excellent Frenchmen)
on Radio Londres, the BBC's French station. Recorded during the escala-
tion of the threat of German attack in 1937, Chevalier's original song told
the tale of Frenchmen from a variety of different professions and political
parties, banding together to fight in defense of the Republic. However, in
the new parody, "Et tout ça, ça fait de mauvais français" (And all that, that
makes for bad Frenchmen), Dac reversed the tale of moral and upright
men, telling instead the story of the opportunistic singers and musicians
who collaborated with Vichy and the Reich. Making direct reference to
Chevalier, Dac sang that "The creator of this little song / used to pass
for a true *chevalier* [knight]." However, instead of behaving with patriotism, Chevalier and his musician friends "smiled at the Germans" while

padding their wallets and "safeguarding their interests." The song closes by praising the Resistance, who "without reproach and fear, fought so that France will always be in the vanguard of honor."

While Dac's song appears to have only played over the airwaves for a brief time, it set off a long and, for Chevalier, painful investigation of his politics during the Occupation. In his memoirs, the singer described how extensively the rumors traveled, writing that "the horrible accusation spread everywhere, through all the cities and villages."[1] Soon, radio stations across Germany, London, Algeria, and Paris were even announcing that the *maquis* had assassinated him. In Périgueux, city officials added his name to their list of *fusillés*, or traitors who had been executed by a firing squad. Publically denounced as a collaborationist, Chevalier went into hiding with friends in the Dordogne, but was eventually found and arrested. During his interrogation, he argued that he was innocent of collaboration, swearing that he had only performed once in Germany, for a group of POWs imprisoned in the same camp that he had been held in during the First World War. "After the recital, instead of money," he testified, "I asked for the freedom of ten prisoners, which was promised to me." The German propaganda machine, he added, was responsible for spinning his visit into a "German tour." Chevalier swore that he had always behaved as a loyal Frenchman, citing evidence that since his concert in Germany, he had "abstained from singing at galas, soirées, and performances that had any political tendencies" and had even refused to appear in films.[2] Despite his testimony, and his previous military service, suspicion of Chevalier's collaborationist activities continued. After his interrogation, the singer fled to Toulouse, where he waited for public opinion to turn. It was not until 1949 that his name was officially cleared.

Chevalier's story accounts for a small portion of the backlash against those suspected of aiding the occupiers. During a brief period of time known as the *épuration sauvage* (savage purification), Resistance members and sympathizers—whose numbers increased dramatically after the Liberation—rounded up scores of French citizens who had purportedly committed crimes against the nation, and doled out an array of extrajudicial punishments ranging from the shearing of hair to public execution.[3] By December 1944, de Gaulle's provisional government had taken control of the purging, setting up a series of courts to investigate hundreds of thousands of accusations of collaboration. The High Court of Justice tried a small number of senior Vichy politicians like Philippe Pétain and Pierre Laval, both of whom were sentenced to death, though the former was spared on account of his old age. The Courts of Justice handled the bulk of the most grievous cases of collaboration, sentencing 6,760 people to death. Of these, only 767 executions were actually carried out. No one involved in organizing the deportation of French Jews stood trial.[4] Finally, the lower Civic Courts heard cases against French citizens accused of the new crime of *indignité nationale*, or national unworthiness. Those convicted were sentenced to prison or to *dégradation nationale*, a suspension of the right to vote, hold governmental office, and work in a series of professions.[5]

Of special interest to those directing the *épuration* was the activity of the nation's most famous citizens, its writers, artists, and musicians.[6] To root out the treasonous, the courts authorized the cultural disciplines to form their own *comités d'épuration*—committees who could investigate crimes of collaboration, dole out professional sanctions, and recommend cases for trial by the courts. While these committees often overlapped and caused a great deal of confusion, the best organized and most active was the Comité National des Écrivains (CNE). The CNE went after the editors and journalists of pro-German newspapers like *Au Pilori* and *Aujourd'hui*, sending 165 writers to trial where many were sentenced to death.[7] Writers were easy targets in the early days of the *épuration*, when passions ran high but evidence proved difficult to gather. While other committees were force to delay their decisions until interrogations could be completed and witnesses interviewed, the CNE had only to look to the latest fascist newspapers for the evidence they needed.[8] Not only did the printed word facilitate the conviction of journalists, but collaborationist writing struck some contemporaries as particularly treasonous. In a 1945 edition of the newspaper *Carrefour*, the novelist Vercors explained his view that journalists had gone too far, taking advantage of a medium that was not open to rebuttal under the German occupation. "When writing that is protected by arms cannot be refuted, nor fought against," he contended, "the consequences become entirely attributable to the author."[9] From this perspective, collaborationist writers were guilty not only because of what they wrote, but because other French people could not write back.

While musicians were not treated as severely as the editors and journalists of collaborationist newspapers, they nonetheless endured intense
scrutiny and harsh sentences. In the realm of classical music, three cases
demonstrate the severity of the crime of musical collaboration. Alfred
Cortot, a renowned concert pianist, had spent the Occupation as the
musical advisor to Vichy and had frequently performed in Germany. After
his arrest on September 1, 1944, Cortot was dismissed from his position
as professor at the Conservatoire de Paris and banned from public performance for one year. When he returned at the end of 1945, he was booed
off stage.[10] Soprano Germaine Lubin and conductor André Cluytens were
not as lucky. Known for her performance of Wagner's operas and her frat-
ernization with German officers, Lubin was arrested shortly after the Liberation and interrogated in the town hall of Paris's eighth *arrondissement.*
After a brief release, she was arrested again and held for two months
in the internment camp Drancy and the Fresnes prison. After another
series of new arrests and interrogations, Lubin was finally brought to trial
in December 1946 where a Court of Justice convicted her of *indignité
nationale* and sentenced her to a lifetime of *dégradation nationale*, the
confiscation of her property, and a twenty-year banishment from Paris.[11]
Cluytens shared a similar fate. Accused of assisting German intelligence,
befriending members of the Gestapo, and adopting Hitler's salute, he
was also sentenced to permanent *dégradation nationale*, stripped of his
property, and prohibited from traveling in certain regions of France.[12]

Singers of popular music escaped *dégradation nationale*, but still paid
for their alleged collaboration. While few cases lasted as long as that of
Maurice Chevalier, many others were arrested for crimes ranging from
performing on the collaborationist Radio-Paris, singing for German audiences, or befriending Gestapo officers. Tino Rossi, for example, was arrested in October 1944 and held for three weeks in Fresnes prison before
serving a temporary ban from public performance.[13] Charles Trenet was
also interrogated and banned from performing. To escape conviction and
preserve his career, he fled to the United States, only returning to France
two years later.[14] Léo Marjane, arrested in December 1944, was accused
of singing for German troops, raising money for collaborationist organizations, and having "relations with numerous German officers."[15] Although
she was acquitted of the charges, the public had so turned against her

that she was unable to resume her career.[16] The notable exception to this list is Edith Piaf. Though questioned, Piaf was never tried for collaboration. Her reputation as a resister, cemented by numerous testimonies that she had used her performances in POW camps to smuggle French soldiers out of enemy territory, was so firmly entrenched in the public psyche that her loyalty was never really questioned.

As this brief outline makes clear, the *épuration* was a difficult affair, particularly for the nation's artists and cultural leaders. While those most responsible for the violence and suffering endured by the French—the Vichy police officers who organized the deportation of twenty-three thousand French Jews to German concentration camps, the senior-level Vichy administrators who worked directly with the Germans, the manufacturers who supplied the German army with equipment, and the publishers and broadcasters who provided the outlets for collaborationist propaganda—escaped death and often trial, individual writers, artists, actors, and singers became the nation's scapegoats. From the perspective of the modern researcher, this imbalance is striking. How was it, one wonders, that Léo Marjane paid for her crimes with her career, Germaine Lubin with her civic rights and property, but the head of the Gestapo in France, Karl Oberg, avoided execution and eventually received a pardon from de Gaulle himself?[17] Given the presence of so many collaborationist politicians and administrators, why did the behavior of French cultural figures matter to those who lived through the Occupation? What, in short, was so disgraceful about artistic collaboration?

A number of explanations run through the scholarly literature, scant though it is. First, and most common, historians note that the épuration was subject to the same contingencies as all trials. Differences across a number of circumstances—the date and location of the trial (later was better), the willingness of witnesses to testify for or against, the skill of the attorneys, etc.—contributed to the variety in sentencing and the incommensurability between the severity of the act and that of the punishment. For example, since evidence against journalists was so easy to produce, these men were the first to be tried and, as a result, the targets of French anger at its peak. Building cases against other artists and politicians took longer, so when these trials occurred, if they ever did, the desire for vengeance had cooled and lighter sentences became more prevalent. Second, important government officials like Vichy police officers avoided trial because of their insider status. As Frederic Spotts writes, "government officials were understandably not keen to prosecute other government officials."[8] While Spotts does not elaborate, we can imagine that opening such an investigation threatened to weaken public trust in government at a time when the nation's institutions were struggling to regain control. Questions about officials' activities might, in short, have revealed more than *épuration* officials wanted to expose. A third explanation for the vengeance against musicians and entertainers during the *épuration* surfaces perennially in the popular press.[9] Those who do comment on the nation's impulse to denounce artists and performers explain the phenomenon in economic terms. While a whole nation went hungry and without warm clothes, this line of reasoning goes, Tino Rossi and Maurice Chevalier were buying steak and champagne with the money they earned from performances in Germany or on behalf of Vichy.

My study of music in France during the Second World War suggests yet another explanation for the nation's need to identify and punish those musicians who collaborated—that citizens recognized culture, and music especially, as a powerful resource for resistance. As I have argued, by 1940 the act of singing had been imbued with republican meaning, established by soldiers of the Revolutionary and Great Wars as a democratic mode of communication available to all people. Decades of cultural debate over musical genres made the act of singing even more nationalistic, as it identified *chanson* as the true musical expression of the French nation while relegating jazz to the periphery of a traditional, inward-looking France. Armed with this unique cultural history, French citizens living through the Occupation seized upon the relationship between nationalism and music, appropriating *chanson* and jazz alike into new rhetorics of nationhood that contested the politics of German collaboration. While Resistance fighters and POWs borrowed from *chanson* to envision a virile, republican France, Parisian teenagers drew from "degenerate" jazz in order to imagine a cosmopolitan, modern nation, blurring the lines of racial belonging and transgressing normative gender. Across all three cases, music helped the French to resist Nazi Germany and Vichy's rearticulation of their national identity and insist upon different versions of a free, republican France. In light of these creative musical repurposings, it makes sense that musicians who did not actively participate in resistance activities would come under fire. Indeed, perhaps the vitriol against Chevalier was not just about profiting while most people suffered, but about the singer's missed opportunities to defy Nazi and Vichy control. Given the rich and abundant resources that music provided for the subversion of collaboration, Chevalier's behavior may have struck citizens as an intentional squandering of such opportunity.

We also gain insight into the nation's need to identify and expunge musicians who had collaborated by viewing the *épuration* alongside France's reemergence as an independent nation at war's end. As we have seen, the period immediately after the Liberation was marked by considerable anxiety about France's uncertain political future and the burgeoning power of the United States. New jazz came across the Atlantic as a form of unintentional propaganda, reaching enthusiastic audiences as a part of America's bid for international dominance. Drawing French women to well-stocked American dance parties, the genre facilitated the display of American dominance and challenged French manhood. However, as I have argued, jazz also provided discursive resources through which the French could resist America's influence. Looking to their nation's historical championing of jazz, cultural critics converted the genre from a symbol of American hegemony to one of French cultural superiority. By deploying old tropes of jazz's essential blackness, journalists writing in the popular periodical *Jazz Hot* suggested that it belonged more properly to France, a nation whose reputation for special cultural discernment and racial tolerance had been evidenced, they argued, by decades of defense of *le jazz nègre*. In this way, columnists made music into a signifier of French political power and a warrant that undergirded the nation's bid for a position as a major world power. In light of this discursive resituation of the nation, the project of punishing musical collaboration was paramount. If France's claim to renewed international standing was to be supported by its historic position as a cultural and ethical leader, then the arts had to be purified to avoid the appearance of inconsistency or hypocrisy. "Traitors" like Maurice Chevalier simply could not be ignored.

Finally, this study suggests an explanation for the relative leniency with which musicians were treated in comparison to their journalist counterparts. Unlike written discourse, music is an open medium of communication that resists censorship and control. After all, while French writers could not write back to the collaborationist journalists who printed pro-German propaganda, they could sing back. An ephemeral mode of communication particularly well-suited to the material constraints of war, the performance of music offered soldiers and civilians alike the opportunity to constitute their national community and determine who belonged within it. Freed from the centralized hierarchy of spoken and written discourse, and capable of transforming emotions into symbolic form, songs stood as participatory, performative events through which dissident citizens contributed to the construction of national identity while deriving unique interpretations of it. In short, music was a symbol system that accommodated multiple perspectives on what it meant to be French during the war. As such, no German politician, Vichy administrator, or American liberator could monopolize music for their own ideological purposes.

In these ways, the case of popular music and resistance in WWII France draws the critic's attention to music's ability to mediate the means by which people understand, constitute, and represent their nations. But, as the lyricist Maurice Druon astutely observed, the Second World War did not mark "the first time in history that a song served as a moral weapon. Since the dawn of time, all armies—both national and revolutionary—have sung."[20] If one of our collective efforts is to illuminate the ways people use discourse not only to interpret the world around them, but to select their very realities, I hope that this book draws humanists of all kinds to examine music's considerable power to construct nationalism, assert political power, and express resistance in the face of repression and control.

Notes

————— •◆• —————

PREFACE

1. Jean Laurent, "Tout finit par des chansons," *Les Nouveaux Temps*, December 14, 1940.
2. See, for example, Myriam Chimènes, ed., *La vie musicale sous Vichy* (Brussels: Complexe, 2001); Nathalie Dompnier, *Vichy à travers chants* (Paris: Editions Nathan, 1996).
3. In the context of France, republicanism emerged as a political form that would promote and protect individual liberty through the equal treatment of all citizens. As a result, French republicanism has emphasized universality over difference. As Joan Scott has eloquently written, "equality is achieved, in French political theory, by making one's social, religious, ethnic, and other origins irrelevant in the public sphere; it is as an abstract individual that one becomes a French citizen." See Joan Scott, *The Politics of the Veil* (Princeton, NJ: Princeton University Press, 2007), 11–12. Another, more recent study also centers universality as the key tenet of French republicanism. The Republic seeks, the authors write, to produce a society "in which each individual enjoyed full equality in the eyes of a democratic

state uninterested in its citizens' particularistic distinctions—their religion, ethnicity, gender, and social class theory." Edward Berenson, Vincent Duclert, and Christophe Prochasson, *The French Republic: History, Values, Debate* (Ithaca, NY: Cornell University Press, 2011), 1–3.

4. Liberal individualism was the guiding political philosophy of the Third Republic, France's government from 1870 until 1940 when it fell to Germany. This political orientation tried to strike the ideal balance between protecting individual liberty, especially from what nineteenth-century theorists considered undue religious influence, and promoting a sense of solidarity that could mitigate societal injustice. To achieve these ends, political leaders emphasized the importance of civic education as a means of freeing one's thinking, and the role of social reform in combating inequality. For a more thorough treatment of liberal individualism, see Laurent Dobuzinskis, "Defenders of Liberal Individualism, Republican Virtues and Solidarity: The Forgotten Intellectual Founding Fathers of the French Third Republic," *European Journal of Political Theory* 7 (2008): 287–307.

5. James R. Irvine and Walter G. Kirkpatrick, "The Musical Form in Rhetorical Exchange: Theoretical Considerations," *Quarterly Journal of Speech* 58 (1972): 273. See also Stephen Kosokoff and Carl W. Carmichael, "The Rhetoric of Protest: Song, Speech, and Attitude Change," *Southern Speech Journal* 35 (1970): 295–302.

6. For a sampling of work on the persuasive nature of song lyrics, see G. P. Mohrmann and Scott Eugene, "Popular Music and World War II: The Rhetoric of Continuation," *Quarterly Journal of Speech* 62 (1976): 145–56; David A. Carter, "The Industrial Workers of the World and the Rhetoric of Song," *Quarterly Journal of Speech* 66 (1980): 365–74; William D. Harpine, "'We Want Yer, McKinley': Epideictic Rhetoric in Songs from the 1896 Presidential Campaign," *Rhetoric Society Quarterly* 34 (2004): 73–88. For work that seeks to analyze the musical tropes within musical texts, see Robert Francesconi, "Free Jazz and Black Nationalism: A Rhetoric of Musical Style," *Critical Studies in Mass Communication* 3 (1986): 36–49; Deanna Sellnow and Timothy Sellnow, "John Corigliano's 'Symphony No. 1' as a Communicative Medium for the AIDS Crisis," *Communication Studies* 44 (1993): 87–101.

7. Lawrence Grossberg, "Another Boring Day in Paradise: Rock and Roll and the Empowerment of Everyday Life," *Popular Music* 4 (1984): 225.

8. Della Pollock, ed. *Exceptional Spaces: Essays in Performance and History* (Durham: University of North Carolina Press, 1998), 1–45, quoted in Greg Dimitriadis, "Hip Hop to Rap: Some Implications of an Historically Situated Approach to

Performance," *Text and Performance Quarterly* 19 (1999): 357.

9. Dimitriadis, "Hip Hop to Rap," 357, 358.

10. I borrow this word from Dwight Conquergood, "Performance Studies: Interventions and Radical Research," *Drama Review* 46 (2002): 151–52.

11. Joshua Gunn, "Mourning Speech: Haunting and the Spectral Voices of Nine-Eleven," *Text and Performance Quarterly* 24 (2004): 92.

12. Greg Goodale, *Sonic Persuasion: Reading Sound in the Recorded Age* (Urbana: University of Illinois Press, 2011), 3.

13. See, for example, Fernando Delgado, "Chicano Ideology Revisited: Rap Music and the (Re)Articulation of Chicanismo," *Western Journal of Communication* 62 (1998): 95–113; Fernando Delgado, "All along the Border: Kid Frost and the Performance of Brown Masculinity," *Text and Performance Quarterly* 20 (2000): 388–401; Lisa Foster, "The Rhetoric of Heavy Metal Resistance: Musical Modalities in Iraqi Public Life," *Middle East Journal of Culture and Communication* 4 (2011): 320–38; Bryan McCann, "Contesting the Mark of Criminality: Race, Place, and the Prerogative of Violence in N.W.A.'s Straight Outta Compton," *Critical Studies in Media Communication* 29 (2012): 367–86.

14. Of special note here is Lisa Foster's work to account for the musical and cultural contexts that condition the meaning of musical performances. See Lisa Foster, "Populist Argumentation in Bruce Springsteen's *The Rising*," *Argumentation and Advocacy* 48 (2011): 61–80.

15. Christopher Small, *Musicking: The Meanings of Performing and Listening* (Hanover, NH: University Press of New England, 1998), 2. Small's emphasis on music as an activity reflects a broader, historical shift in the field of musicology to move beyond methods of analysis that locate meaning primarily within the musical score. Under the banner of New Musicology or Critical Musicology, these scholars have pushed to problematize the social, performative, and cultural processes through which meaning accrues to music. For a helpful overview, see Dai Griffiths, "What Was, or Is, Critical Musicology?," *Radical Musicology* 5 (2010–2011), http://www.radical-musicology.org.uk.

16. See, for example, Richard Raskin, "'Le Chant des Partisans': Functions of a Wartime Song," *Folklore* 102 (1991): 62–76; Charles Rearick, *The French in Love and War: Popular Culture in the Era of the World Wars* (New Haven, CT: Yale University Press, 1997); Christopher Lloyd, "Divided Loyalties: Singing in the Occupation," in *Popular Music in France from Chanson to Techno: Culture, Identity, and Society*, ed. Hugh Dauncey and Steve Cannon (Aldershot, UK:

Ashgate, 2003), 153–70; Keith Reader, "Flaubert's Sparrow, or the Bovary of Belleville: Edith Piaf as Cultural Icon," in *Popular Music in France from Chanson to Techno*, 205–24; Chimènes, *La vie musicale sous Vichy*.

17. André Halimi, *Chantons sous l'Occupation* (Paris: Marabout, 1976), 9.

18. Rearick, *The French in Love and War*; Reader, "Flaubert's Sparrow, or the Bovary of Belleville," 205–23.

19. Chimènes, *La vie musicale sous Vichy*; Dompnier, *Vichy à travers chants*; Ursula Mathis, "Politique "via ether": La chanson francaise de la BBC pendant la 2ᵉ Guerre mondiale," in *1789–1989: Musique, histoire, démocratie*, ed. Antoine Hennion (Paris: Fondation de la Maison des Sciences de l'Homme, 1992), 481–98.

20. Stephen Olbrys Gencarella and Phaedra C. Pezzullo, eds., *Readings on Rhetoric and Performance* (State College, PA: Strata Publishing, 2010), 2.

21. Dwight Conquergood, "Ethnography, Rhetoric, and Performance," *Quarterly Journal of Speech* 78 (1992): 80–123.

22. Conquergood, "Performance Studies, 148.

23. James C. Scott, *Domination and the Arts of Resistance: Hidden Transcripts* (New Haven, CT: Yale University Press, 1990), 19.

24. Cheryl R. Jorgensen-Earp, *Discourse and Defiance under Nazi Occupation: Guernsey, Channel Islands, 1940–1945* (East Lansing: Michigan State University Press, 2013), 4.

25. Throughout this book, I use the term "nationalism" to refer to the feeling of belonging to one's nation. As Benedict Anderson has argued in his seminar study, these emotional ties are "imagined" through discourse; interlocking symbol systems work to establish the dominant characteristics of the nation and to delineate boundaries of belonging. Benedict Anderson, *Imagined Communities: Reflections on the Origins and Spread of Nationalism* (London: Verso, 1983).

26. John MacAloon, quoted in Marvin Carlson, *Performance: A Critical Introduction* (New York: Routledge, 2004), 20.

27. Elin Diamond, ed., *Performance and Cultural Politics* (London: Routledge, 1996), 1. Understanding performance as located within a preexisting discursive terrain is well established in the fields of rhetoric and performance studies. For examples, James Jasinski has theorized the ways in which past speech acts offer inventional resources for current rhetorical action. See James Jasinski, "Instrumentalism, Contextualism, and Interpretation in Rhetorical Criticism," in *Rhetorical Hermeneutics: Invention and Interpretation in the Age of Science*, ed. Alan G. Gross and William M. Keith (Albany: State University of New York Press, 1997),

195–223. Anthropologist Richard Bauman has argued that the form and meaning of performance is "rooted in culturally defined scenes or events" that "constitute meaningful contexts for action, interpretation, and evaluation." See Richard Bauman, *Story, Performance, and Event* (Cambridge: Cambridge University Press, 1986), 3–4.

28. Jasinski, "Instrumentalism, Contextualism, and Interpretation in Rhetorical Criticism," 195–223.

29. Bauman, *Story, Performance, and Event*, 3.

30. Ibid., 4.

31. Karlyn Kohrs Campbell, "Agency: Promiscuous and Protean," *Communication and Critical/Cultural Studies* 2 (2005): 5.

32. Kendall R. Phillips, "Rhetorical Maneuvers: Subjectivity, Power, and Resistance," *Philosophy and Rhetoric* 39 (2006): 326.

33. I refer here to Campbell's argument that "texts have agency." See Campbell, "Agency: Promiscuous and Protean," 7.

34. Conquergood, "Performance Studies," 151.

35. After France's defeat in 1940, more than 1.8 million French soldiers were made prisoners. While some men were immediately repatriated, approximately 1.6 million were held captive in Germany. Nearly 1 million of these men remained interned in German camps for the entire duration of the war. Yves Durand, *Prisonniers de guerre dans les Stalags, les Oflags et les Kommandos, 1939–1945* (Paris: Hachette, 1994), 11.

36. Small, *Musicking*, 2.

CHAPTER 1. REPERTOIRES OF RESISTANCE: MUSICAL RESOURCES FOR REIMAGINING THE NATION

1. Paul Meurisse, *Les éperons de la liberté* (Paris: Editions Robert Laffont, 1979), 153–54.

2. In several popular press biographies, Piaf is credited with all sorts of resistant acts, including arranging for her photograph to be taken with prisoners of war so that the men could make a forged identity card and escape their captivity. See, for example, David Bret, *Piaf: A Passionate Life* (London: Robson Books, 1998), 44–45. Whether or not this is true, Piaf was remembered as a resister at the end of the Occupation and, unlike many of her colleagues in the music business, was not accused of having collaborated.

3. Philippe Pétain, quoted in Philippe Burrin, *France under the Germans:*

Collaboration and Compromise, trans. Janet Lloyd (New York: New Press, 1993), 6–7; and H. R. Kedward, *Occupied France: Collaboration and Resistance, 1940–1944* (Oxford: Blackwell, 1985), 1–3.

4. H. R. Kedward, "Patriots and Patriotism in Vichy France," *Transactions of the Royal Historical Society* 32 (1982): 176.

5. Kedward, *Occupied France*, 2.

6. Sarah Fishman, *The Battle for Children: World War II, Youth Crime, and Juvenile Justice in 20th Century France* (Cambridge, MA: Harvard University Press, 2002), 51.

7. Yves Durand, *Prisonniers de guerre dans les Stalags, les Oflags et les Kommandos, 1939–1945* (Paris: Hachette, 1987), 11.

8. Fishman, *The Battle for Children*, 51. For details about the terms of the armistice, see also Burrin, *France under the Germans*, 11–14.

9. Roger Austin, "Propaganda and Public Opinion in Vichy France: The Department of Hérault, 1940–44," *European Studies Review* 13 (1983): 470.

10. Paul Simon, *One Enemy Only—the Invader* (Hodder and Stoughton, 1942), 27, quoted in Kedward, *Occupied France*, 10.

11. Laura Mason, *Singing the French Revolution: Popular Culture and Politics, 1787–1799* (Ithaca, NY: Cornell University Press, 1996), 2.

12. See Mason, *Singing the French Revolution*, 2–3, for more on the ease with which songs were disseminated and learned within both cultures.

13. Mason, *Singing the French Revolution*, 11.

14. Ibid., 7.

15. Ibid., 71.

16. Ibid.

17. Quoted in Elizabeth C. Bartlet, "The New Repertory at the Opéra during the Reign of Terror," in *Music and the French Revolution*, ed. Malcolm Boyd (Cambridge: Cambridge University Press, 1992), 109.

18. Mona Ozouf, *Festivals and the French Revolution*, trans. Alan Sheridan (Cambridge, MA: Harvard University Press, 1991), 98; and Cynthia M. Gessele, "The Conservatoire de Musique and National Music Education in France, 1795–1801," in *Music and the French Revolution*, ed. Malcolm Boyd (Cambridge: Cambridge University Press, 1992), 201–2.

19. Gessele, "The Conservatoire de Musique and National Music Education in France, 1795–1801," 200.

20. Mason, *Singing the French Revolution*, 70.

21. Ibid., 71.

22. Ibid., 72.

23. Herbert Schneider, "The Sung Constitutions of 1792: An Essay on Propaganda in the Revolutionary Song," in Boyd, *Music and the French Revolution*, 236–75.

24. Mason, *Singing the French Revolution*, 2–3.

25. Ibid., 109–10.

26. Eugene Weber, *Peasants into Frenchmen: The Modernization of Rural France, 1870–1914* (Stanford, CA: Stanford University Press, 1976), 435.

27. Weber, *Peasants into Frenchmen*, 441.

28. Ibid., 442.

29. Gerald Bordman, *American Operetta: From H.M.S. Pinafore to Sweeney Todd* (Oxford: Oxford University Press, 1981), 10.

30. Richard Traubner, *Operetta: A Theatrical History* (New York: Doubleday and Co., 1983), 22–23.

31. Quoted in Sterling Mackinlay, *Origin and Development of Light Opera* (Philadelphia: David McKay Co., 1927), 126.

32. Charles Rearick, *The French in Love and War: Popular Culture in the Era of the World Wars* (New Haven, CT: Yale University Press, 1997), 2.

33. Ibid., 9.

34. Regina M. Sweeney, *Singing Our Way to Victory: French Cultural Politics and Music during the Great War* (Middletown, CT: Wesleyan University Press, 2001), 10.

35. Rearick, *The French in Love and War*, 20, 26.

36. Sweeney, *Singing Our Way to Victory*, 12–13.

37. Ibid.

38. Rearick, *The French in Love and War*, 29, 25–28.

39. Nearly all histories of WWII France emphasize the shock of French defeat. See Kedward, *Occupied France*, 1; and Burrin, *France under the Germans*, 5.

40. The German military killed 92,000 Frenchmen—twice as many casualties than it sustained—and injured over 200,000 Frenchmen. Even German generals, who had followed Hitler with apprehensive flashbacks to the disastrous Battle of the Marne, did not dream of such a swift and decisive victory. Ultimately, French high command—a disorganized group with antiquated military strategies—was to blame for the defeat. Despite the substantial size of the French ranks, their military's concentration on upholding the strong fortifications along the Maginot Line left the country open to attacks from the northern Ardennes region, near the Belgian border.

41. Kedward, *Occupied France*, 8–9.

42. Both of these quotations were taken from Burrin, *France under the Germans*, 188.

43. Fishman, *The Battle for Children*, 53.

44. Ibid., 54–55.

45. Lynne Taylor, "The Black Market in Occupied Northern France, 1940–4," *Contemporary European History* 6 (1997): 154.

46. Fishman, *The Battle for Children*, 58–59.

47. John F. Sweets, *The Politics of Resistance in France, 1940–1944* (Dekalb: Northern Illinois University Press, 1976), 4.

48. Sarah Fishman, *We Will Wait: Wives of French Prisoners of War, 1940–1945* (New Haven, CT: Yale University Press, 1991), 40. For more on the competing political ideas vying for power at Vichy, see Fishman's summary of the competing goals of Vichy traditionalists, technocrats, and fascists, 39–42.

49. Philippe Pétain, *Discours aux Francais: 17 juin 1940–20 août 1944*, ed. Jean-Claude Barbas (Paris: Albin Michel, 1989), 361.

50. Ibid., 361–62.

51. Julian Jackson, *France: The Dark Years, 1940–1944* (Oxford: Oxford University Press, 2001), 149.

52. Kedward, *Occupied France*, 22–23.

53. Alan Riding, *And the Show Went On: Cultural Life in Nazi-Occupied Paris* (New York: Alfred A. Knopf, 2010), 51–52.

54. Ibid. The quotation from Fritz Werner is also available in the original French in Manuela Schwartz, "La musique et la propagande culturelle des Nazis," in *La vie musicale sous Vichy*, ed. Myriam Chimènes (Brussels: Complexe, 2001), 90.

55. "La nouvelle Allemagne revendique aussi la domination culturelle en Europe et qu'elle est en mesure de prouver par ses présentations le bien fondé de cette revendication." Quoted in Schwartz, "La musique et la propagande culturelle des Nazis," 94.

56. Quoted in Leslie Sprout, *The Musical Legacy of Wartime France* (Berkeley: University of California Press, 2013), 5.

57. Ibid., 6.

58. Ibid., 15.

59. Ibid.

60. Jules Michelet, *The People*, trans. John P. McKay (Urbana: University of Illinois Press, 1973), 47, quoted in Matthew F. Jordan, *Le Jazz: Jazz and French Cultural Identity* (Urbana: University of Illinois Press, 2010), 27–28.

61. Ned Rorem, quoted in Simon Frith, *Performing Rites: On the Value of Popular Music* (Cambridge, MA: Harvard University Press, 1996), 170.

62. Seth Schulman, "The Celebrity Culture of Modern Nightlife: Music-Hall, Dance, and Jazz in Interwar Paris, 1918–1930" (PhD diss., Brown University, 2000), 42.

63. Kelley Conway, *Chanteuse in the City: The Realist Singer in French Film* (Berkeley: University of California Press, 2004), 32–33.

64. Rearick, *The French in Love and War*, 118.

65. Ibid., 130.

66. Sweets, *The Politics of Resistance in France, 1940–1944*, 6–7.

67. Burrin, *France under the Germans*, 185.

68. Jordan, *Le Jazz*, 96.

69. Rearick, *The French in Love and War*, 219.

70. Ibid., 220.

71. Ibid., 197.

72. Jordan, *Le Jazz*, 185–86; and Ludovic Tournès, *New Orleans sur Seine: Histoire du jazz en France* (Paris: Fayard, 1999), 59–61. Richard Regnier argues that even American jazz was not completely banned from the radio, writing that "it played without interruption on Radio-Paris, most often under camouflaged titles, but not always." Quoted in Andy Fry, *African American Music and French Popular Culture, 1920–1960* (Chicago: University of Chicago Press, 2014), 181.

73. Jean Cocteau, *Le coq et l'arlequin: Notes autour de la musique, 1918* (Paris: Stock, 1978), 43, quoted in Jordan, *Le Jazz*, 41.

74. Emile Vuillermoz, *Musique d'aujourdhui* (Paris: Editions Georges Crés, 1923), 196, quoted in Jordan, *Le Jazz*, 77.

75. Jordan, *Le Jazz*, 40–42.

76. Quoted in Jeffrey H. Jackson, *Making Jazz French: Music and Modern Life in Interwar Paris* (Durham, NC: Duke University Press, 2003), 25.

77. Jordan, *Le Jazz*, 28.

78. Jackson, *Making Jazz French*, 89.

79. Schulman, "The Celebrity Culture of Modern Nightlife," 54.

80. Albert Flament, "L'Olympia," *La Revue de Paris*, February 1, 1927, quoted in Schulman, "The Celebrity Culture of Modern Nightlife," 55–56.

81. Gustave Fréjaville, *Au Music Hall*, 5th ed. (Paris: Aux Editions du Monde Nouveau, 1923), 36, quoted in Schulman, "The Celebrity Culture of Modern Nightlife," 56.

82. Pierre Fontaine, "Est-ce l'agonie de la chanson française?," *Comoedia*, November

15, 1926, quoted in Rearick, *The French in Love and War*, 89.

83. Fréjaville quoted in Conway, *Chanteuse in the City*, 62.

84. Yvonne Moustiers, "Deux époques," *L'ami du peuple du soir*, May 18, 1929, quoted in Rearick, *The French in Love and War*, 89.

85. While women still experienced rampant discrimination under the Third Republic, several new laws granted them some measure of independence from their husbands. For example, in 1920 a woman could join a union without her husband's permission. In 1927, she could keep her French nationality if she married a foreign man. By 1938, she could get a passport, open a bank account, and attend university without her husband's authorization. See Conway, *Chanteuse in the City*, 74.

86. Mary Louise Roberts, *Civilization without Sexes: Reconstructing Gender in Postwar France, 1917–1927* (Chicago: University of Chicago Press, 1994).

87. Jackson, *France: The Dark Years*, 156.

88. Fishman, *The Battle for Children*, 62.

89. Jackson, *France: The Dark Years*, 149.

90. Miranda Pollard, *Reign of Virtue: Mobilizing Gender in Vichy France* (Chicago: University of Chicago Press, 1998), 57.

91. Ibid., 2.

92. Matt. 7:24–27 NIV.

93. I borrow from Miranda Pollard's excellent analysis of this poster. See Pollard, *Reign of Virtue*, 3–4.

CHAPTER 2. *LA FRANCE EN CHANTANT*: THE RHETORICAL CONSTRUCTION OF FRENCH IDENTITY IN SONGS OF THE RESISTANCE MOVEMENT

1. According to historian Raymond Josse, between 3,000 and 10,000 students were involved in the protest. The exact number of participants is unknown, as many ran away to avoid arrest and left no record of their activities. Also, it is difficult to separate the protesters from the onlookers who came to watch the protest or happened to be on the Champs Elysées that day. See Raymond Josse, "La naissance de la Résistance étudiante à Paris et la manifestation du 11 novembre 1940," *Revue d'histoire de la Deuxième Guerre mondiale* 47 (1962): 22.

2. Josse, "La naissance de la Résistance étudiante à Paris," 17. Josse notes that the protest was patriotic in nature, rather than political.

3. For more on the politics of "La Marseillaise," see Nathalie Dompnier, "Entre La Marseillaise et Maréchal, nous Voilà! Quel hymne pour le régime de Vichy?" in *La*

vie musicale sous Vichy, ed. Myriam Chimènes (Brussels: Complexe, 2001), 69–89. While "La Marseillaise" was banned in the Occupied zone, it was allowed in the Unoccupied zone, controlled until 1942 by the Vichy government.

4. All information about the November 11, 1940, protest was taken from Josse, "La naissance de la Résistance étudiante à Paris," 1–31.

5. Archives de la Préfecture de Police, box BA 2361, Paris, France.

6. Occasional access to printing presses meant that some songs could be distributed on paper. In Ardèche, WWI veteran Achille Coevet gave copies of his song to Resistance trucks that carried it to another Resistance group in Les Vans (see Sylvain Chimello, *La Résistance en chantant* [Paris: Editions Autrement, 2004], 211). So great was the fear of arrest, however, that most people did not keep written copies of the songs. Jean Melamed, for example, was arrested in Paris on August 25, 1941, when authorities found subversive songs in his apartment.

7. Jean Maurin, *Chansons et poésies de la Résistance*, a collection of songs and poems from the French Resistance, Institut d'Histoire du Temps Présent, ARC 074–72, Paris, France. Maurin's manuscript provides the lyrics and melodies of nearly thirty songs. Half were written by members of the *maquis* and half were created and broadcast by the BBC. In addition, my archival research also uncovered two Resistance songs, "Chanson du Maquis Vasio," and "La Ballade des Pendus." These song sheets were mixed in with other WWII pamphlets and indicate the presence of other songs still undiscovered in France's archives.

8. Chimello, *La Résistance en chantant*; T. Barthoulot et al., eds., *Paroles et musique: Les chansons et la Deuxième Guerre mondiale* (Besançon: Musée de la Résistance et de la Déportation, 2003). These anthologies contain the words and sometimes music of Resistance songs, but offer no analysis of their rhetorical function.

9. For example, Jeanne Lerouge, a nurse in the Dordogne region, remembers hearing a song she wrote for a local group sung by soldiers from several neighboring regions. She was "surprised to hear it whistled or hummed . . . in other places and by men that [she] didn't know," a testament to the fact that "the song was a bit widespread" despite the fact that it had not been printed. Lerouge's quotation comes from Chimello, *La Résistance en chantant*, 246.

10. While musicologists have written extensively on the role of art music (such as symphonies and operas) in wartime France, they have ignored the abundance of vernacular and popular songs that circulated widely throughout the country. One important exception, however, is Richard Raskin, "Le Chant des Partisans: Functions of a Wartime Song," *Folklore* 102 (1991): 62–76. For a sampling of the

scholarship on WWII art music in France, see Lilise Boswell-Kurc, "Olivier Messiaen's Religious War-Time Works and Their Controversial Reception in France (1941–1946)" (PhD diss., New York University, 2001); Chimènes, *La vie musicale sous Vichy*; Jane Fulcher, "French Identity in Flux: Vichy's Collaboration and Antigone's Operatic Triumph," *Proceedings of the American Philosophical Society* 150 (2006): 261–95; Fulcher, "Musical Style, Meaning, and Politics in France on the Eve of the Second World War," *Journal of Musicology* 13 (1995): 425–53; Fulcher, "The Preparation for Vichy: Anti-Semitism in French Musical Culture between the Two World Wars," *Musical Quarterly* 79 (1995): 458–75; Daniel Matore, "Le modernisme musical français a la veille de la Seconde Guerre mondiale," *Revue Internationale de Musique Française* 18 (1985): 69–78; Caroline Potter, "French Music and the Second World War," in *French Music since Berlioz*, ed. Richard Langham Smith and Caroline Potter (Aldershot, UK: Ashgate, 2006); Nigel Simeone, "Messiaen and the Concerts de la Pléiade: 'A Kind of Clandestine Revenge against the Occupation,'" *Music and Letters* 81 (2000): 551–84; Yannick Simon, "Les périodiques musicaux français pendant la Seconde Guerre mondiale," *Fontes Artis Musicae* 49 (2002): 67–78; Leslie A. Sprout, "Music for a 'New Era': Composers and National Identity in France, 1936–1946" (PhD diss., University of California Berkeley, 2000).

11. John F. Sweets, *The Politics of Resistance in France, 1940–1944* (Dekalb: Northern Illinois University Press, 1976), 6–7.

12. Philippe Burrin, *France under the Germans: Collaboration and Compromise*, trans. Janet Lloyd (New York: New Press, 1993), 185.

13. Ibid., 188.

14. Julian Jackson, *France: The Dark Years, 1940–1944* (Oxford: Oxford University Press, 2001), 408–9.

15. H. R. Kedward, *Resistance in Vichy France: A Study of Ideas and Motivation in the Southern Zone, 1940–1944* (Oxford: Oxford University Press, 1978), 233.

16. Claude Bourdet, *L'aventure incertaine* (Paris: Stock, 1975), 26–27, quoted in Jackson, *France: The Dark Years*, 403.

17. Jackson, *France: The Dark Years*, 404–5; Patrick Valérin, *Chansons et chanteurs des années noires: Une approche de l'histoire au travers de la chanson et de ses serviteurs* (Malemort: Proanima, 1996), 191.

18. R. Austin, "The Cult of the Outlaw," in *Vichy France and the Resistance: Culture and Ideology*, ed. Roger Austin and H. R. Kedward (London: Croom Helm, 1985), 240–45.

19. Ibid., 242.

20. Chimello, *La Resistance en chantant*, 119.

21. Christopher Small, *Musicking: The Meanings of Performing and Listening* (Hanover, NH: University Press of New England, 1998), 2.

22. Benedict Anderson, *Imagined Communities: Reflections on the Origins and Spread of Nationalism* (London: Verso Editions, 1983), 36.

23. Alban Vistel, *Héritage spirituel de la Résistance* (Lyon: Éditions Lug, 1955), 63, 81, quoted in Sweets, *The Politics of Resistance in France*, 11.

24. Copy of Saliège's letter, reproduced in *Ville de Toulouse Bulletin Municipal* (Numéro spécial consacré à la liberation de Toulouse, October 1944 [Marseille: Imprimerie Gaussel & Cie]), 28, quoted in Sweets, *The Politics of Resistance in France*, 11.

25. *Ville de Toulouse Bulletin Municipal*, 12, quoted in Sweets, *The Politics of Resistance in France*, 12.

26. Archives de la Préfecture de Police, box BA 2105, Paris, France.

27. Ibid.

28. Roger Tabar, quoted in Chimello, *La Résistance en chantant*, 158.

29. Raskin, "Le Chant des Partisans," 68.

30. Ibid., 76.

31. Composer Anna Marly quoted in Raskin, "Le Chant des Partisans," 69.

32. Anna Marly, *Mémoires* (Paris: Little Big Man, 2000), 85. Marly and her family fled Russia during the Russian Civil War in 1919, eventually settling in France and taking French citizenship. When the fighting broke out in 1940, she and her husband escaped France and traveled to London in 1941. It was there where she wrote the famous "Le Chant des Partisans."

33. Michael C. McGee, "In Search of 'The People': A Rhetorical Alternative," *Quarterly Journal of Speech* 61 (1975): 249; Maurice Charland, "Constitutive Rhetoric: The Case of the Peuple Québécois," *Quarterly Journal of Speech* 73 (1987): 140–41; Karlyn Kohrs Campbell and Kathleen Hall Jamieson, *Deeds Done in Words: Presidential Rhetoric and the Genres of Governance* (Chicago: University of Chicago Press, 1990), 55.

34. James R. Irvine and Walter G. Kirkpatrick, "The Musical Form in Rhetorical Exchange: Theoretical Considerations," *Quarterly Journal of Speech* 58 (1972): 279.

35. Alberto Gonzalez and John J. Makay, "Rhetorical Ascription and the Gospel According to Dylan," *Quarterly Journal of Speech* 69 (1983): 4.

36. Deanna Sellnow and Timothy Sellnow, "'The Illusion of Life' Rhetorical

Perspective: An Integrated Approach to the Study of Music as Communication," *Critical Studies in Media Communication* 18 (2001): 397.

37. "Le Chant des Partisans," in Chimello, *La Résistance en chantant*, 113.

38. "Pas de Kollaboration," in ibid., 96.

39. "Liberté," in ibid., 191.

40. "Pas de Kollaboration," in ibid., 96.

41. "Francs-Tireurs Partisans de France," in ibid., 131.

42. "Les Fifis," in ibid., 128. "Francs-Tireurs Partisans de France," in ibid., 131.

43. "Chant des Maquisards Chauvinois," in ibid., 259. "La Marche du Maquis," in ibid., 197.

44. "Le Chant des Maquis Ardéchois," in ibid., 208. "Le Chant Héroïque de la Résistance," in ibid., 200.

45. "Le Chant des Partisans," in ibid., 113.

46. "La Marseillaise du Maquis," in ibid., 238.

47. Chimello, *La Résistance en chantant*, 250.

48. Regina M. Sweeney, *Singing Our Way to Victory: French Cultural Politics and Music during the Great War* (Middletown, CT: Wesleyan University Press, 2001), 43–55.

49. For more information about the history and uses of these songs, see the indexes of Sweeney, *Singing Our Way to Victory*, and Mason, *Singing the French Revolution*.

50. This anecdote was taken from François Musard's testimony in Valérin, *Chansons et chanteurs des années noires*, 192–93.

51. Julien Helfgott, quoted in Valérin, *Chansons et chanteurs des années noires*, 193.

52. "Haut les Coeurs," in Chimello, *La Résistance en chantant*, 168.

53. Ibid.

54. "Les Libérateurs," in Chimello, *La Résistance en chantant*, 179.

55. "Maquisards," in Chimello, *La Résistance en chantant*, 119.

56. Anecdote taken from Valérin, *Chansons et chanteurs des années noires*, 196.

57. Linda Hutcheon, *A Theory of Parody: The Teachings of Twentieth-Century Art Forms* (New York: Methuen, 1986), 6–7.

58. Hutcheon, *A Theory of Parody*, 32. Like Hutcheon, Robert Hariman theorizes parody as a neutral act of "placing speech beside itself" that often "turns whatever was being used for effect into a joke." See Robert Hariman, "Political Parody and Public Culture," *Quarterly Journal of Speech* 94 (2008): 249.

59. Mikhail M. Bakhtin, *The Dialogic Imagination*, ed. Michael Holquist, trans. Caryl Emerson and Michael Holquist (Austin: University of Texas Press, 1981),

55, quoted in Jonathan Gray, *Watching with the Simpsons: Television, Parody, and Intertextuality* (New York: Routledge, 2006), 4.

60. "Maréchal, Nous Voilà!" in Barthoulot et al., *Paroles et musique*, 62–63.

61. "Maréchal et Laval," in Maurin, *Chansons et poésies de la Résistance*.

62. "L'Espoir des Gars du Maquis," in Chimello, *La Résistance en chantant*, 282.

63. "Les Voilà, Nos Soldats," in Barthoulot et al., *Paroles et musique*, 81.

CHAPTER 3. ZAZOUS IN ZOOT SUITS:
RACE PLAY IN OCCUPIED PARIS

1. While jazz and swing are technically two different genres of music, the zazous did not distinguish between them in the creation of the yellow stars. Indeed, the popular songs of the era also used the terms interchangeably, collapsing the two styles into the same genre.

2. Archives de la Préfecture de Police, Paris, box B/A 2436.

3. Ibid.

4. Sophie Roberts, "A Case for Dissidence in Occupied Paris: The Zazous, Youth Dissidence, and the Yellow Star Campaign in Occupied Paris (1942)," *French History* 24 (2010): 89.

5. Patrice Bollon, *Morale du masque* (Paris: Editions du Seuil, 1990), 135–36.

6. Jon Savage, *Teenage: The Creation of Youth Culture* (London: Chatto & Windus, 2007), 390.

7. Roberts, "A Case for Dissidence," 82–103.

8. Emmanuelle Rioux, "Les zazous: Enfants terribles de Vichy," *L'Histoire* 165 (1993): 37. See also Emmanuelle Rioux, "Les zazous: Un phénomène socio-culturel pendant l'Occupation" (mémoire de maîtrise, Université de Paris X-Nanterre, 1987).

9. Matthew Jordan, *Le Jazz: Jazz and French Cultural Identity* (Urbana: University of Illinois Press, 2010), 194.

10. Ibid.

11. I refer here to Edwin Black's seminal essay "The Second Persona," *Quarterly Journal of Speech* 56 (1970): 109–19.

12. John Storey, "Rockin' Hegemony: West Coast Rock and Amerika's War in Vietnam," in *Cultural Theory and Popular Culture: A Reader*, 4th ed., ed. John Storey (London: Pearson Education Ltd., 2009), 90.

13. Noel Burch and Geneviève Sellier refer to the movie as a "cult film" for young zazous in *La drôle de guerre des sexes du cinéma français, 1930–1956* (Paris: Editions Nathan, 1996), 135.

14. D. Poulin, "Zazous and Swing Jazz: Cultural Resistance under the Vichy Regime, 1940–1943" (master's thesis, Université de Quebec à Montreal, 1995), 55.

15. See, e.g., W. D. Halls, *The Youth of Vichy France* (Oxford: Clarendon Press, 1981); and Sarah Fishman, *The Battle for Children: World War II, Youth Crime, and Juvenile Justice in Twentieth-Century France* (Cambridge, MA: Harvard University Press, 2002).

16. Fishman, *The Battle for Children*, 60.

17. J. Peyrade, quoted in Halls, *The Youth of Vichy France*, 166.

18. Halls, *The Youth of Vichy France*, 132.

19. Henri Joubrel, "Formation de la jeunesse," *L'Illustration*, March 21, 1942, 201.

20. Fishman, *The Battle for Children*, 61.

21. Abel Bonnard, quoted in Halls, *The Youth of Vichy France*, 36–37.

22. Commissariat Générale à la Famille, *Aux éducatrices*, quoted in Miranda Pollard, *Reign of Virtue: Mobilizing Gender in Vichy France* (Chicago: University of Chicago Press, 1998), 80.

23. Young men received more rigorous training in areas that were gendered masculine, such as physics and chemistry, than did their female counterparts. They were also encouraged to play sports, an activity that Vichy held would prepare them for the mental and physical work of reforming the nation. For more on boys' education, see Pollard, *Reign of Virtue*, 86–89.

24. Maurice-Yvan Sincard, quoted in Halls, *The Youth of Vichy France*, 164.

25. Halls, *The Youth of Vichy France*, 183.

26. Ibid., 330.

27. Ibid., 183.

28. Daniel Vauquelin, "Discours de fondation des Jeunesses Populaires Francaises," *Les Documents de la jeunesse, No. 1*, quoted in Halls, *The Youth of Vichy France*, 183.

29. Halls, *The Youth of Vichy France*, 330.

30. Daniel Vauquelin, "Discours de fondation des Jeunesses Populaires Francaises, salle de la Mutualité à Paris," May 25, 1942.

31. Fishman, *The Battle for Children*, 68.

32. Philippe du Peuty, quoted in Gerard Regnier, "Jazz et société en France sous l'Occupation (1940–1944)" (PhD diss., Université Paris 1 Panthéon–Sorbonne, January 2006), 381.

33. Charles Delaunay, quoted in Regnier, *Jazz et société en France*, 377, 381.

34. Fishman, *The Battle for Children*, 67.

35. José Germain, "Danseront-elles," quoted in Jordan, *Le Jazz*, 111.

36. Pierre de Regnier, commenting on *La Revue Nègre*, quoted in Jordan, *Le Jazz*, 109.

37. Gustave Fréjaville, "Les attractions de la quinzaine," *Comoedia* (May 21, 1930), quoted in Jordan, *Le Jazz*, 145.

38. Fernand Mazzi, "Le rhythme et la musique," *Le Monde Musical*, no. 12 (December 31, 1930): 409, quoted in Jordan, *Le Jazz*, 146–47.

39. Maurice Delage, paraphrased in Jordan, *Le Jazz*, 115.

40. Phil Chidester, "May the Circle Stay Unbroken: *Friends*, the Presence of Absence, and the Rhetorical Reinforcement of Whiteness," *Critical Studies in Media Communication* 25 (2008): 157–74; Thomas K. Nakayama and Robert L. Krizek, "Whiteness: A Strategic Rhetoric," *Quarterly Journal of Speech* 81 (1995): 291–309; Richard Dyer, "White," *Screen* 29 (1988): 44–64.

41. Dyer, "White," 45.

42. When perceived as a universal lack of race, whiteness is always oppressive, as "race" is understood as impurity, as distance from whiteness. According to Deleuze and Guattari, "there is no dominant race; a race is defined not by its purity but rather by the impurity conferred upon it by a system of domination." See Gilles Deleuze and Félix Guattari, *A Thousand Plateaus: Capitalism and Schizophrenia*, trans. Brian Massumi (Minneapolis: University of Minnesota Press, 1976), 379, quoted in Nakayama and Krizek, "Whiteness," 299.

43. Literary scholar Mike Hill has shown the importance of preventing variations within whiteness, arguing that "in order to maintain its categorical salience racial identity must stave off intraracial permutation. This is so because permutation is what identity cannot have if it is to remain categorically defensible." See Mike Hill, *After Whiteness: Unmaking an American Majority* (New York: New York University Press, 2004), in *The Post-Colonial Studies Reader*, 2nd ed., ed. Bill Ashcroft, Gareth Griffiths, and Helen Tiffin (London: Routledge, 2006), 205.

44. Production for *Mademoiselle Swing* began on November 17, 1941, and the film premiered on June 12, 1942. See appendix A of Evelyn Ehrlich, *Cinema of Paradox: French Filmmaking under the German Occupation* (New York: Columbia University Press, 1985), 198. Originally intended for release in April 1942, the film's debut was delayed until June because of the line "il faut braver le destin" (You have to defy destiny), a line that the Nazis thought evoked a sentiment of defiance. See Burch and Sellier, *La drôle de guerre des sexes du cinéma français*, 136, for more information about the release of the film.

45. Matthew Jordan notes that Delaunay's book became "important underground

literature for *les Swings*." See Jordan, *Le Jazz*, 188.

46. Charles Delaunay, *De la vie et du jazz* (Paris: Editions Hot Jazz, 1941), 74–76.

47. Ibid., 76, 89–90.

48. In her memoir *The Prime of Life*, Simone de Beauvoir describes the fashion worn by young zazou men, noting that "they wore their hair long, Oxford fashion, and carefully curled, and carried umbrellas, and dressed in zoot suits." Simone de Beauvoir, *The Prime of Life* (Cleveland, OH: World Publishing Co., 1962), 407, quoted in Roberts, "A Case for Dissidence," 92.

49. Ralph Ellison, *Invisible Man* (New York: Random House, 1947), 380, quoted in Stuart Cosgrove, "The Zoot-Suit and Style Warfare," *History Workshop* 18 (Autumn 1984): 77.

50. Ibid.

51. *L'Illustration*, quoted in Savage, *Teenage*, 386–87.

52. For more information about the zazous and the Yellow Star campaign, see Roberts, "A Case for Dissidence," 82–103.

53. *Pour Elle*, quoted in Regnier, *Jazz et société en France*, 367.

54. *L'Illustration*, paraphrased in Savage, *Teenage*, 386–87.

55. Jeffrey H. Jackson, *Making Jazz French: Music and Modern Life in Interwar Paris* (Durham, NC: Duke University Press, 2003), 27–28.

56. Simone de Beauvoir, quoted in Roberts, "A Case for Dissidence," 92.

57. See, for example, Ferdinand, "Qu'est-ce qu'un Zazou-Zazou?," *Au Pilori*, June 11, 1942; and "Les 'zazous' en vacances," *Au Pilori*, August 6, 1942.

58. Dominique Veillon, *La mode sous l'Occupation: Débrouillardise et coquetterie dans la France en guerre, 1939–1945* (Paris: Editions Payot, 1990), 76.

59. For more about the shortage of shoes, see Veillon, *La mode sous l'Occupation*, 79–97.

60. For a description of the new leg dye, see Veillon, *La mode sous l'Occupation*, 51. For information about clothing restrictions, see ibid., 102–4.

61. Fishman, *The Battle for Children*, 58–59.

62. Dick Hebdige, *Subculture: The Meaning of Style* (London: Routledge, 1979), 102.

63. Ibid., 106.

64. Pierre Ducrocq, "Swing qui peut," *La Gerbe*, June 4, 1942.

65. Ibid., June 18, 1942.

66. Ibid., June 4, 1942.

67. "Zazoutisme . . ." *Au Pilori*, June 22, 1944.

68. "Le dernier cri des jeunes zazous," *Au Pilori*, September 16, 1943.

69. Ferdinand, "Qu'est-ce qu'un Zazou-Zazou?"

70. Ducrocq, "Swing qui peut.".

71. Ferdinand, "Qu'est-ce qu'un Zazou-Zazou?"

72. "Les 'zazous' en vacances."

73. Michael H. Kater, *Different Drummers* (Oxford: Oxford University Press, 1992), 20. While Kater does not validate Nazi claims that the commercial music business was controlled by Jews, he does claim that it was a "truism" that Jewish musicians were highly accomplished jazz players.

74. Ibid., 33.

75. Ibid., 32.

76. Roberts, "A Case for Dissidence," 93.

77. Ferdinand, "Qu'est-ce qu'un Zazou-Zazou?"

78. "La chasse est ouverte," *Au Pilori*, June 18, 1942.

79. Fabrice Virgili, *Shorn Women: Gender and Punishment in Liberation France* (Oxford: Berg, 2002), 182.

80. Jacques Doriot, quoted in Savage, *Teenage*, 389.

Chapter 4. From Prisoners to Men:
Operettas on the POW Camp Stage

1. For histories of POW theater, see Alon Rachamimov, "The Disruptive Comforts of Drag: (Trans)Gender Performances among Prisoners of War in Russia, 1914–1920," *American Historical Review* 111 (2006): 362–82; David A. Boxwell, "The Follies of War: Cross Dressing and Popular Theatre on the British Front Lines, 1914–1918," *Modernism/modernity* 9 (2002): 1–20.

2. According to Gascar, the prisoners, many of whom had been professional architects and tailors before the war, took great satisfaction in designing sets, costumes, and wigs out of scraps of fabric and frayed bits of string. Transforming these discarded materials into convincing and beautiful sets and props, he writes, gave "proof to a cleverness that stupefied the Germans" and helped to distract the men from their imprisonment. The caliber of the performances was so high that prisoners temporarily forgot their status as POWs. In his diary, for example, POW René Lahaye attested to the impressive quality of the performances, remembering that "Honestly, we would've believed ourselves to be in a real theatre in a big city . . . the play was magnificently performed." See Pierre Gascar, *Histoire de la captivité des Français en Allemagne: 1939–1945* (Paris: Gallimard, 1967), 161; and Yves Durand, *Prisonniers de guerre dans les Stalags, les Oflags, et les Kommandos,*

1939–1945 (Paris: Hachette, 1987), 186.

3. For example, in Oflag XVII A, the same camp that produced the film *Sous le Manteau*, prisoners used a set of fake shrubs to disguise a tunnel they were digging behind the theater's walls. See Andreas Kusternig, "Entre université et résistance: Les officiers français prisonniers au camp XVII A à Edelbach," in *La captivité des prisonniers de guerre (1939–1945): Histoire, art et mémoire: Pour une approche europeenne*, ed. Jean-Claude Catherine (Rennes: Presses Universitaires de Rennes, 2008), 66.

4. Here, I draw from Turner's observation that "In this hall of mirrors the reflections are multiple, some magnifying, some diminishing, some distorting the faces peering into them, but in such a way as to provoke not merely thought, but also powerful feelings and the will to modify everyday matters in the minds of the gazers. See Victor Turner, *From Ritual to Theatre: The Human Seriousness of Play* (New York: Performing Arts Journal Publications, 1982), 104–5.

5. Ibid.

6. In the bimonthly newspaper of Oflag II D, *Écrite sur le Sable*, an anonymous theater critic argued for the importance of original productions: "J'avoue ma préférence pour les spectacles dont le texte a été écrit par nous. S'ils sont bons, ils sont mieux adaptés à notre désir" (I confess my preference for the plays whose text is written by us. If they are good, they are better adapted to our desires). See "Monsieur Le Trouhadec saisi par la débauche," *Écrite sur le Sable*, March 25, 1941, Archives Nationales, Paris, box F/9/2901.

7. These quotations are drawn from the following passage: "Le théâtre se trouve être ainsi un puissant agent de diffusion de l'hellénisme et, par conséquent, de toutes les idées et de tous les sentiments qui s'y attachent. Dans un mouvement, en apparence contraire, le théâtre grec a aidé à l'affranchissement de l'homme. C'est en ce sens un théâtre moraliste, mais moraliste au sens noble, non point un théâtre qui moralise mais un théâtre qui construit l'homme et, en l'espèce, l'homme moderne." Paul Juif, *Théâtre et musique des temps de misère* (La Pensée Universitaire, 1958), 50.

8. Joseph Folliet, "Pour comprendre les prisonniers," 1943, 22–25, Archives Nationales, Paris, box 72AJ/2633.

9. *Crossing the Stage: Controversies on Cross-Dressing*, ed. Lesley Ferris (London: Routledge, 1993), 9.

10. Simon Frith, *Performing Rites: On the Value of Popular Music* (Cambridge, MA: Harvard University Press, 1996), 158.

11. Here, I paraphrase Ned Rorem, quoted in Frith, *Performing Rites*, 170.

12. Early composers of operetta, the most famous of whom are Hervé and Offenbach, wrote humorous but scathing critiques of the Second Republic and often featured saucy, vulgar jokes delivered by all-female choruses in very revealing costumes. In the late nineteenth century, after the Franco-Prussian war began, librettists began to soften their political critiques and devote their energies toward writing great love stories. For more information about operetta, see Sterling Mackinlay, *Origin and Development of Light Opera* (Philadelphia: David McKay Co., 1927); Richard Traubner, *Operetta: A Theatrical History* (New York: Doubleday and Co., 1983); and Gerald Bordman, *American Operetta: From H.M.S. Pinafore to Sweeney Todd* (Oxford: Oxford University Press, 1981).

13. In their studies of American female impersonators, both Sharon Ullman and Marybeth Hamilton maintain that these actors did not aim to mock femininity, but to craft believable performances that paid tribute to womanhood. See Sharon R. Ullman, *Sex Seen: The Emergence of Modern Sexuality in America* (Berkeley: University of California Press, 1997); Marybeth Hamilton, "'I'm the Queen of the Bitches': Female Impersonation and Mae West's *Pleasure Man*," in *Crossing the Stage: Controversies on Cross-Dressing*, ed. Lesley Ferris (London: Routledge, 1993), 107–19.

14. Jill Dolan, quoted in Ferris, *Crossing the Stage: Controversies on Cross-Dressing*, 10.

15. Ullman, *Sex Seen*, 53.

16. Eve Sedgwick, *Between Men: English Literature and Male Homosocial Desire* (New York: Columbia University Press, 1985), 38.

17. Sedgwick, *Between Men*, 50.

18. Judith Butler, *Gender Trouble: Feminism and the Subversion of Identity* (London: Routledge, 1999), 174–75.

19. The gendered nature of France's defeat has been well documented in histories of the era. See, for example, Miranda Pollard, *Reign of Virtue: Mobilizing Gender in Vichy France* (Chicago: University of Chicago Press, 1998); and Luc Capdevila, "The Quest for Masculinity in a Defeated France, 1940–1945," *Contemporary European History* 10 (2001): 423–45.

20. Pollard, *Reign of Virtue*, 30.

21. Jean Vidalenc, quoted in Pollard, *Reign of Virtue*, 29.

22. Yves Durand, *Prisonniers de guerre*, 11. Durand notes that only one-third as many French soldiers were captured during World War I as in World War II.

23. Ibid.

24. Ibid., 26.

25. Ibid., 40.

26. Raymond Henri and François Mitterrand, quoted in Sarah Fishman, "Grand Delusions: The Unintended Consequences of Vichy France's Prisoner of War Propaganda," *Journal of Contemporary History* 26 (1991): 243.

27. Captain Arnoult, quoted in Durand, *Prisonniers de guerre*, 28.

28. Sergent Depoux, quoted in Durand, *Prisonniers de guerre*, 45.

29. Durand, *Prisonniers de guerre*, 47.

30. Fabrice Virgili, *Naître ennemi: Les enfants de couples franco-allemands nés pendant la Seconde Guerre mondiale* (Paris: Payot, 2009), 31.

31. This anecdote comes from Mongrédien's account, entitled "Le Saint-Barthélemy des Poux," Institut d'Histoire du Temps Présent, Paris, Fonds Georges Mongrédien, box Causeries Familiers.

32. Memoir of François Eugène Jean Pierre Lalin, recorded in 1956, Institut d'Histoire du Temps Présent, Paris, box 72AJ.290.Captivité.

33. Sarah Fishman, *We Will Wait: Wives of French Prisoners of War, 1940–1945* (New Haven, CT: Yale University Press, 1991), 66.

34. "Nostalgie," drawing from Oflag III C, Archives Nationales, Paris, box F/9/2309.

35. Diary of Georges Mongrédien, February 16, 1941, Institut d'Histoire du Temps Présent, Paris, Fonds Georges Mongrédien.

36. Virgili, *Naître ennemi*, 43.

37. This excerpt comes from a portion of Christophe's wartime journal, published in Marcelle and Robert Christophe, *Une famille dans la guerre: 1940–1945* (Paris: L'Harmattan, 1995), 93.

38. Folliet, "Pour comprendre les prisonniers," 1943, 20.

39. "Theatre," *Confins*, January-February 1944, Archives Nationales, Paris, box F/9/2893.

40. *Au Temps des Crinolines*, Archives Nationales, Paris, box 72 AJ/2633.

41. Laura Mulvey, "Visual Pleasure and Narrative Cinema," *Screen* 16 (1975): 11.

42. While *Au Temps des Crinolines* is the only script that I discovered which makes reference to France's imperial past, prisoners' writings reveal that other plays and operettas contained similar colonial references. Paul Juif, for example, describes a scene from the play *Casanova* in which a female allegorical representation of France stands surrounded by "representatives of the Empire, dressed in exotic costumes." See Juif, *Théâtre et musique*, 67.

43. For more on the consolidation of colonial power, see Edward Said, *Orientalism* (New York: Pantheon Books, 1978).

44. While Said's study of Orientalism references the representation of colonial women in western art, his analysis does not attend fully to the ways in which gender and sexuality operate in the West's subordination of the East. For more on the exoticism and subordination of the indigenous female body, see Lisa Lowe, *Critical Terrains: French and British Orientalisms* (Ithaca, NY: Cornell University Press, 1991).

45. Paul Juif describes one particularly demanding director who fined actors who did not shave their legs before a performance. Juif, *Théâtre et musique*, 65.

46. Archives Nationales, Paris, box 72 AJ/2636.

47. Ullman, *Sex Seen*, 51–55, quoted in Rachamimov, "The Disruptive Comforts of Drag," 377.

48. *Le Gai Mat*, April 15, 1942, Bibliothèque Nationale, Paris, RES 4-LC6-493.

49. Diary of Georges Mongrédien, May 4, 1941, Institut d'Histoire du Temps Présent, Paris, Fonds Georges Mongrédien.

50. *Le Canard en KG*, January 31, 1942, Archives Nationales, Paris, box F/9/2901.

51. *Confins*, March–April, 1944, Archives Nationales, Paris, box F/9/2893.

52. *Le Bébé du BB*, October 1942, Archives Nationales, Paris, box F/9/2901.

53. *Le Chic Os*, March 1943, Archives Nationales, Paris, box F/9/2893.

54. Robert Desvernois, "Théâtre Libre," Archives Nationales, Paris, box 72 AJ 1798.

55. Juif, *Théâtre et musique*, 22–23.

56. "Les Oflagirls," drawing from Oflag III C, Archives Nationales, Paris, box F/9/2309.

57. *D'Amour et d'Eau Fraiche*, Archives Nationales, Paris, 72 AJ 1798.

58. Virgili, *Naître ennemi*, 33.

59. Robert Christophe, *Les années perdues: Journal de guerre, 1939–1945* (Editions Anovi, 2008), 135–37.

60. *Blanche-Neige*, Archives Nationales, Paris, box 72 AJ/2633.

61. Fishman, "Grand Delusions," 234.

62. Fishman, *We Will Wait*, 31–32.

63. Durand, *Prisonniers de guerre*, 14.

64. Fishman, "Grand Delusions," 236.

65. *L'âme des camps: Exposition de la vie intellectuelle, spirituelle et sociale dans les camps de prisonniers* (Paris, 1944), quoted in Fishman, "Grand Delusions," 242.

66. Juif, *Théâtre et musique*, 48.

Chapter 5. GI Jazz: Music and Power
in Liberation France

1. Michel Adam, interviewed by Ludivine Hamel, "Les Américains au Havre et dans sa région, 1944–1946: Réalisations et impacts," (mémoire de maîtrise d'histoire, Université du Havre, 2001), n.p.

2. Ibid.

3. Editorial, *Jazz Hot*, no. 2 (1945).

4. Attempting to overcome racist prejudices against the music, pro-jazz French critics began rewriting the origin story of jazz as early as the 1920s, claiming that the genre was developed by Creole slaves. See Matthew Jordan, *Le Jazz: Jazz and French Cultural Identity* (Urbana-Champaign: University of Illinois Press, 2010), 112–13. However dubious the idea of jazz as a music with French beginnings, the notion resurfaced during the Occupation, when the Nazi ban on American culture threatened to curtail access to the genre. See Andy Fry, *Paris Blues: African American Music and French Popular Culture, 1920–1960* (Chicago: University of Chicago Press, 2014), 186, 202–9.

5. Jordan, *Le Jazz*, 231. This position is also embraced by Denis-Constant Martin and Olivier Roueff in *La France du jazz: Musique, modernité, et identité dans la première moitié du XXᵉ siècle* (Marseille: Editions Parenthèses, 2002), 74–76.

6. Colin Nettelbeck, *Dancing with de Beauvoir: Jazz and the French* (Carlton, Victoria, Australia: Melbourne University Press, 2004), 54.

7. The most strident critique of this interpretation comes from Andy Fry, who argues that Germany's lenient attitude toward jazz in France precluded it from becoming a symbol of resistance. I reject this argument, as social movements from Abolition to Civil Rights to Black Lives Matter teach us that cultural products need not be repressed in order to serve as meaningful symbols of resistance for those who oppose the status quo. See Fry's argument in chapter 4 of his book *African American Music and French Popular Culture*.

8. Tyler Stovall, *Paris Noir: African Americans in the City of Light* (Boston: Mariner Books, 1996), 126.

9. For more about the experiences of African American musicians working in France during the decade before the Second World War, see chapter 4 of William A. Shack, *Harlem in Montmartre: A Paris Jazz Story between the Great Wars* (Berkeley: University of California Press, 2001).

10. Rashida K. Braggs, *Jazz Diasporas: Race, Music, and Migration in Post–World War II Paris* (Oakland: University of California Press, 2016), 69.

11. *Jazz Hot*, no. 1 (March 1935).

12. Ludovic Tournès, *New Orleans sur Seine: Histoire du jazz en France* (Paris: Fayard, 1999), 94.

13. Leora Auslander, *Taste and Power: Furnishing Modern France* (Berkeley: University of California Press, 1996), 25.

14. Whitney Walton, *France at the Crystal Palace: Bourgeois Taste and Artisan Manufacture in the Nineteenth Century* (Berkeley: University of California Press, 1992), 222–23.

15. Herman Lebovics, *Mona Lisa's Escort: André Malraux and the Reinvention of French Culture* (Ithaca, NY: Cornell University Press, 1999), 5.

16. Mary Louise Roberts, *What Soldiers Do: Sex and the American GI in World War II France* (Chicago: University of Chicago Press, 2013), 179.

17. *Marseille et les Américains* (Marseille: Musée d'Histoire de Marseille, 1996), 58.

18. Roberts, *What Soldiers Do*, 21. For information about the bombing of Marseille alone, see *Marseille et les Américains*, 25–32.

19. Quoted in Roberts, *What Soldiers Do*, 25.

20. Quoted in ibid., 26.

21. Quoted in ibid., 27.

22. Roberts, *What Soldiers Do*, 27.

23. *Marseille et les Américains*, 31.

24. Hurstfield, quoted in Holly Cowan Shulman, *The Voice of America: Propaganda and Democracy, 1941–1945* (Madison: University of Wisconsin Press, 1990), 155.

25. For more on AMGOT, see chapter 2 of Régine Torrent, *La France américaine: Controverses de la Libération* (Brussels: Editions Racine, 2004); and Roberts, *What Soldiers Do*, 4–5.

26. Andrew A. Thomson, "'Over There' 1944/45—Americans in the Liberation of France: Their Perceptions of and Relations with France and the French," PhD diss., University of Kent at Canterbury, 1996), 8.

27. Roberts, *What Soldiers Do*, 5.

28. Thomson, "Over There," 57. Roberts documents that the French often risked reprisals by the Germans in order to bury American GIs who died in combat; *What Soldiers Do*, 41.

29. For an extended discussion of the ways that wealth disparities deteriorated Franco-American relations, see Roberts, *What Soldiers Do*, 120–25.

30. Ibid., 115.

31. Quoted in ibid., 76.

32. Quoted in ibid., 75.

33. See William Shack's chapter "Le Jazz-Hot: The Roaring Twenties" for a detailed account of African American musicians working in Paris immediately following WWI; Shack, *Harlem in Montmartre*, 26–62.

34. Quoted in Braggs, *Jazz Diasporas*, 66.

35. Michel Adam, interviewed by Hamel, "Les Américains au Havre et dans sa région, 1944–1946," n.p.

36. Michel Gaudry, quoted in Elizabeth Coquart, *La France des GIs: Histoire d'un amour déçu* (Paris: Albin Michel 2003), 167.

37. Hugues Panassié, *Monsieur Jazz* (Paris: Stock, 1975), 185.

38. Due to the Nazi ban on American music during the Occupation and a strike led by American musicians against recording labels, new American music had not traveled across the Atlantic since the United States joined in the war in 1941.

39. Joe Jordan, an entertainer who served as a music advisor at Fort Huachuca, AZ, believed that "A singing army is a winning army." Similarly Raymond Kendall, music coordinator for the USO, held that "within the armed services . . . singing is primarily a weapon, a medium through which men march straighter, give better commands, fight harder, work longer, and move co-ordinately." Quoted in Annegret Fauser, *Sounds of War: Music in the United States during World War II* (Oxford: Oxford University Press, 2013), 106.

40. Fauser, *Sounds of War*, 107.

41. Ibid., 117. See also Richard S. Sears, *V-Discs: A History and Discography* (Westport, CT: Greenwood Press, 1980).

42. Michel Samson, Gilles Suzanne, and Elisabeth Cestor, *A fond de cale: 1917–2011, un siècle de jazz à Marseille* (Marseille: Wildproject, 2012), 68.

43. Nitoune Conrad, interviewed by Elisabeth Cestor, October 2009.

44. Archives du Havre, Series I', letter dated 4 November 1944.

45. Samson, Suzanne, and Cestor, *A fond de cale*, 63.

46. Panassié, cited in ibid.

47. Quoted in Philippe Roger, *L'ennemi américain: Généalogie de l'antiaméricanisme français* (Paris: Editions du Seuil, 2002), 551.

48. Richard Pells, *Not Like Us: How Europeans Have Loved, Hated, and Transformed American Culture since World War II* (New York: Basic Books, 1997), 6.

49. Charles Seeger, quoted in Fauser, *Sounds of War*, 77.

50. Emily Rosenberg, *Spreading the American Dream: American Economic and Cultural Expansion, 1890–1945* (New York: Hill and Wang, 1982), 209.

51. Fauser, *Sounds of War*, 85.

52. Ibid.

53. Still's *Afro-American Symphony* was especially useful, as it helped propagandists represent the United States as a nation that valued racial diversity. See Fauser, *Sounds of War*, 81.

54. Fauser writes that the term "good music" was used to designate "the symphonic concert repertoire, opera, and—as a form of apparently authentic expression of the people—folk music." Ibid., 118.

55. Interview featured in Hamel, "Les Américains au Havre et dans sa région," n.p.

56. "Ils n'avaient que faire de nous," *Havre Libre*, 12 August 2003, 5.

57. The *commissaire régional* de la République française issued an *ordonnance* on 2 November 1944 stating that it would be "premature to allow the organization of certain public or private festivities since the hostilities are not over," and reminded the French that "all balls and public and private dances, except with dispensation, are prohibited" until further notice. The ordinance also prohibited the performance of jazz music in "public cafés, brasseries, restaurants, cabarets, and artistic organizations." Archives Départementales des Bouches-du-Rhône, séries 149 W 176.

58. Michel Adam, quoted in Coquart, *La France des GIs*, 168.

59. Coquart, *La France des GIs*, 166.

60. "Le coin des musiciens: A propos de la suppression de la danse," *Jazz Hot*, no. 1 (1945): 19.

61. I use the phrase "gender damage" in acknowledgment of the overuse of the term "gender crisis," a term that Mary Louise Roberts argues has been so frequently and uncritically applied that it has lost its analytic purchase. Roberts, *What Soldiers Do*, 85–86.

62. Panassié, *Monsieur Jazz*, 184.

63. Max Bengtsson, *Un été 44: De l'état de siège à la paix retrouvée* (Editions Grenet, 1994), 179.

64. Archives Départementales des Bouches-du-Rhône, séries 150 W 176, letter dated 12 March 1945.

65. Archives Départementales des Bouches-du-Rhône, séries 150 W 176, letter dated 22 March 1945.

66. Archives du Havre, Series I', letter dated 4 November 1944.

67. Archives du Havre, Series I', letter dated 23 November 1944.

68. Archives Départementales des Bouches-du-Rhône, séries 149 W 176, letter dated

13 February 1945.

69. Archives du Havre, Series I', box 30, letter dated 25 July 1945.

70. Archives Départementales des Bouches-du-Rhône, séries 149 W 176, letter dated 21 June 1945.

71. Archives Départementales des Bouches-du-Rhône, séries 149 W 176, letter dated 29 December 1944.

72. Bengtsson, *Un été 44*, 179.

73. Bengtsson, interviewed by Hamel, "Les Américains au Havre et dans sa region," n.p.

74. Testimony of Emilienne Ciesielski-Prevots, printed in *Votre histoire, c'est notre histoire: Récits des douze lauréats* (Centre Communal d'Action Sociale de la Ville du Havre, 2000), récit no. 11, page 2.

75. Ibid.

76. Roberts, *What Soldiers Do*, 86.

77. Archives Départementales des Bouches-du-Rhône, séries 149 W 176, letter dated 25 January 1945.

78. Testimony of Claude-Michel Langanay, printed in *Votre histoire, c'est notre histoire*, récit no. 5, page 3.

79. Panassié, *Monsieur Jazz*, 184.

80. Testimony of Jean Lerussé, printed in Bengtsson, *Un été 44*, 229.

81. Panassié, *Monsieur Jazz*, 184–85.

82. Drummer named Moustache, quoted in Coquart, *La France des GIs*, 165.

83. Frank Ténot, *Boris Vian: Le jazz et Saint-Germain* (Paris: Editions du May, 1993), 8.

84. Charles Delaunay, "Jazz 45," *Jazz Hot*, no. 1 (1945).

85. The one exception to this racialized list of heroes and villains is black musician Roy Eldridge. While Delaunay gives no explanation for this criticism, the fact that Eldridge played arranged jazz in Artie Shaw's symphonic band seems likely to have rendered him guilty by association.

86. Editorial, *Jazz Hot*, no. 1 (October 1945): 2.

87. Charles Delaunay, "André Ekyan," *Jazz Hot* (October 1945): 11.

88. Ibid.

89. "Revues de jazz américains et brittaniques," *Jazz Hot*, fascicule no. 3 (1945): 14.

90. Editorial, *Jazz Hot*, no. 1 (October 1945): 2.

91. *Jazz Hot*, numéro spécial de Noel (December 1945): 7.

92. René Belleau, "Ce que pensent du Hot Club de France les musiciens de jazz

français," *Jazz Hot*, no. 1 (1945): 10–11.

93. Ibid.

94. Ibid.

95. "Le jazz à Paris," *Jazz Hot*, no. 1 (October 1945): 23.

96. "Le jazz français à l'étranger," *Jazz Hot*, fascicule no. 3 (1945): n.p.

97. "Le disque au service de la Victoire," *Jazz Hot*, fascicule no. 3 (1945): 2.

98. Ludovic Tournès, "La réinterprétation du jazz: Un phénomène de contre-américanisation dans la France d'après-guerre," *Revue française d'études américaines* (hors-série): *Play It Again, Sim . . . Hommages à Sim Copans* (2001): 72–83.

99. *Jazz Hot* (March 1947), quoted in Tournès, "La réinterprétation du jazz," 78.

100. Fry, *Paris Blues*, 8.

101. Quoted in Ibid, 10.

102. *Marseille et les Américains*, 9.

CONCLUSION

1. Maurice Chevalier, *Ma route et mes chansons* (Paris: Flammarion, 1998), 565.

2. Ibid., 575.

3. For information about the *épuration sauvage* by region, see Philippe Bourdrel, *L'épuration sauvage, 1944–1945* (Paris: Perrin, 2002).

4. Julian Jackson, *France: The Dark Years, 1940–1944* (Oxford: Oxford University Press, 2001), 577–78.

5. Alan Riding writes that, in total, approximately 900,000 people were arrested on charges of collaboration and 124,613 stood trial. See Riding, *And the Show Went On: Cultural Life in Nazi-Occupied Paris* (New York: Alfred A. Knopf, 2010), 318. For estimates of the number of trials heard by each court, see Jackson, *France: The Dark Years*, 577–78.

6. Frederic Spotts, *The Shameful Peace: How French Artists and Intellectuals Survived the Nazi Occupation* (New Haven, CT: Yale University Press, 2008), 4, 230.

7. Riding, *And the Show Went On*, 320; and Spotts, *The Shameful Peace*, 257.

8. This is Julian Jackson's theory as to why action against authors was so swift and severe. Jackson, *France: The Dark Years*, 586.

9. Vercors, quoted in Gilles Ragache and Jean-Robert Ragache, *La vie quotidienne des écrivains et des artistes sous l'Occupation, 1940–1944* (Paris: Hachette, 1988), 288.

10. Riding, *And the Show Went On*, 329–30; and Karine Le Bail, *La musique au pas: Être musicien sous l'Occupation* (Paris: CNRS Editions, 2016), 214–15.

11. In 1949, the courts released Lubin from *dégradation nationale*. Le Bail, *La musique au pas*, 225–27; and Riding, *And the Show Went On*, 330.

12. Cluytens' sentence was also softened. In 1946, a court reduced his *dégradation nationale* to five years and lifted the professional ban on his public performance. Le Bail, *La musique au pas*, 222–24.

13. Riding, *And the Show Went On*, 331.

14. Ibid.

15. Le Bail, *La musique au pas*, 228.

16. Riding, *And the Show Went On*, 331.

17. Spotts, *The Shameful Peace*, 259.

18. Ibid.

19. See, for example, Guillaume Sbalchiero's online interview with Jacques Pessis, editor of a new, abridged version of Chevalier's memoirs. In the interview, published by the newspaper *L'Express*, Pessis argues that Chevalier never took a political position during the war, continuing to sing only to offer comfort to the French nation. "Maurice Chevalier collabo: 'Une rumeur montée par les nazis,'" http://www.lexpress.fr/culture/livre/maurice-chevalier-collabo-une-rumeur-montee-par-les-nazis_1070330.html.

20. Maurice Druon, quoted in Richard Raskin, "'Le Chant des Partisans': Functions of a Wartime Song," *Folklore* 102, no. 1 (1991): 75.

Bibliography

———•◆•———

PRIMARY SOURCES

Anthologies of Songs and Speeches

Barthoulot, T., et al., eds. *Paroles et musique: Les chansons et la Deuxième Guerre mondiale: Dossier documentaire*. Besançon: Musée de la Résistance et de la Déportation, 2003.

Chimello, Sylvain. *La Résistance en chantant*. Paris: Editions Autrement, 2004.

Maurin, Jean. *Résistance en Val D'Allier: Petites histoires de la grande histoire*. Langeac, 1992.

Pétain, Philippe. *Discours aux Français: 17 juin 1940–août 1944*. Edited by Jean-Claude Barbas. Paris: Albin Michel, 1989.

Films

Mademoiselle Swing. Directed by Richard Pottier. 1942. Paris: René Chateau, 2003. VHS.

Sous le Manteau. Clandestine film produced by the prisoners at Oflag XVII A. Armor Films. VHS.

Arrest Records

RESISTANCE FIGHTERS

Archives de la Préfecture de Police, Paris, series B/A, box 2361
Archives de la Préfecture de Police, Paris, series B/A, box 2105

ZAZOUS

Archives de la Préfecture de Police, Paris, series B/A, box 2097
Archives de la Préfecture de Police, Paris, series B/A, box 2433
Archives de la Préfecture de Police, Paris, series B/A, box 2436
Archives de la Préfecture de Police, Paris, series B/A, box 2437

Prisoner of War Diaries, Newspapers, Photographs, and Scripts

Archives Nationales, Paris, box F/9/2901
Archives Nationales, Paris, box F/9/2909
Archives Nationales, Paris, box F/9/2893
Archives Nationales, Paris, box F/9/2309
Archives Nationales, Paris, box 72 AJ/2633
Archives Nationales, Paris, box 72 AJ/2636
Archives Nationales, Paris, box 72 AJ 1798
Institut d'Histoire du Temps Présent, Paris, Fonds Georges Mongrédien
Institut d'Histoire du Temps Présent, Paris, box 72AJ.290.Captivité

Periodicals

Au Pilori, 1940–1944
Comeodia, 1941–1944
La Gerbe, 1941–1944
Les Nouveaux Temps, 1940–1944
L'Illustration, 1940–1944
Jazz Hot, 1945

Memoirs/Musical Treatises

Bengtsson, Max. *Un été 44: De l'état de siège à la paix retrouvée*. Editions Grenet, 1994.
Chevalier, Maurice. *Ma route et mes chansons*. Paris: Flammarion, 1998.
Christophe, Marcelle, and Robert Christophe. *Une famille dans la guerre: 1940–1945*.
    Paris: L'Harmattan, 1995.

Christophe, Robert. *Les années perdues: Journal de guerre, 1939–1945*. Chinon: Editions Anovi, 2008.

Delaunay, Charles. *De la vie et du jazz*. Paris: Editions Hot Jazz, 1941.

Gascar, Pierre. *Histoire de la captivité des Français en Allemagne: 1939–1945*. Paris: Gallimard, 1967.

Juif, Paul. *Théâtre et musique des temps de misère*. Aix-en-Provence: La Pensée Universitaire, 1958.

Meurisse, Paul. *Les éperons de la liberté*. Paris: Editions Robert Laffont, 1979.

Panassié, Hugues. *Monsieur Jazz*. Paris: Stock, 1975.

Votre histoire, c'est notre histoire: Récits des douze lauréats. Centre Communal d'Action Sociale de la Ville du Havre, 2000.

Franco-American Relations

Archives du Havre, series I'

Archives Départementales des Bouches-du-Rhône, séries 149 W 176.

Archives Départementales des Bouches-du-Rhône, séries 150 W 176.

SECONDARY SOURCES

Anderson, Benedict. *Imagined Communities: Reflections on the Origins and Spread of Nationalism*. London: Verso Editions, 1983.

Auslander, Leora. *Taste and Power: Furnishing Modern France*. Berkeley: University of California Press, 1996.

Austin, Roger. "Propaganda and Public Opinion in Vichy France: The Department of Hérault, 1940–44." *European Studies Review* 13 (1983): 455–82.

Austin, Roger, and H. R. Kedward, eds. *Vichy France and the Resistance: Culture and Ideology*. London: Croom Helm, 1985.

Bartlet, Elizabeth C. "The New Repertory at the Opéra during the Reign of Terror." In *Music and the French Revolution*, ed. Malcolm Boyd. Cambridge: Cambridge University Press, 1992.

Bauman, Richard. *Story, Performance, and Event*. Cambridge: Cambridge University Press, 1986.

Berenson, Edward, Vincent Duclert, and Christophe Prochasson. *The French Republic: History, Values, Debate*. Ithaca, NY: Cornell University Press, 2011.

Black, Edwin. "The Second Persona." *Quarterly Journal of Speech* 56 (1970): 109–19.

Bollon, Patrice. *Morale du masque*. Paris: Editions du Seuil, 1990.

Bordman, Gerald. *American Operetta: From H.M.S. Pinafore to Sweeney Todd*. Oxford: Oxford University Press, 1981.

Boswell-Kurc, Lilise. "Olivier Messiaen's Religious War-Time Works and Their Controversial Reception in France (1941–1946)." PhD diss., New York University, 2001.

Bourdrel, Philippe. *L'épuration sauvage, 1944–1945*. Paris: Perrin, 2002.

Boxwell, David A. "The Follies of War: Cross Dressing and Popular Theatre on the British Front Lines, 1914–1918." *Modernism/modernity* 9 (2002): 1–20.

Braggs, Rashida K. *Jazz Diasporas: Race, Music, and Migration in Post–World War II Paris*. Oakland: University of California Press, 2016.

Bret, David. *Piaf: A Passionate Life*. London: Robson Books, 1998.

Burch, Noel, and Geneviève Sellier. *La drôle de guerre des sexes du cinéma français, 1930–1956*. Paris: Editions Nathan, 1996.

Burrin, Philippe. *France under the Germans: Collaboration and Compromise*. Translated by Janet Lloyd. New York: New Press, 1993.

Butler, Judith. *Gender Trouble: Feminism and the Subversion of Identity*. New York: Routledge, 1999.

Campbell, Karlyn Kohrs. "Agency: Promiscuous and Protean." *Communication and Critical/Cultural Studies* 2 (2005): 1–19.

Campbell, Karlyn Kohrs, and Kathleen Hall Jamieson. *Deeds Done in Words: Presidential Rhetoric and the Genres of Governance*. Chicago: University of Chicago Press, 1990.

Capdevila, Luc. "The Quest for Masculinity in a Defeated France, 1940–1945." *Contemporary European History* 10 (2001): 423–45.

Carlson, Marvin. *Performance: A Critical Introduction*. New York: Routledge, 2004.

Carter, David A. "The Industrial Workers of the World and the Rhetoric of Song." *Quarterly Journal of Speech* 66 (1980): 365–74.

Catherine, Jean-Claude, ed. *La captivité des prisonniers de guerre (1939–1945): Histoire, art et mémoire: Pour une approche européenne*. Rennes: Presses Universitaires de Rennes, 2008.

Charland, Maurice. "Constitutive Rhetoric: The Case of the Peuple Québécois." *Quarterly Journal of Speech* 73 (1987): 133–50.

Chidester, Phil. "May the Circle Stay Unbroken: *Friends*, the Presence of Absence, and the Rhetorical Reinforcement of Whiteness." *Critical Studies in Media Communication* 25 (2008): 157–74.

Chimènes, Myriam, ed. *La vie musicale sous Vichy*. Brussels: Complexe, 2001.

Conquergood, Dwight. "Ethnography, Rhetoric, and Performance." *Quarterly Journal of Speech* 78 (1992): 80–123.

———. "Performance Studies: Interventions and Radical Research." *Drama Review* 46 (2002): 145–56.

Conway, Kelley. *Chanteuse in the City: The Realist Singer in French Film*. Berkeley: University of California Press, 2004.

Coquart, Elizabeth. *La France des GIs: Histoire d'un amour déçu*. Paris: Albin Michel, 2003.

Cosgrove, Stuart. "The Zoot-Suit and Style Warfare." *History Workshop* 18 (Autumn 1984): 77–91.

Dauncey, Hugh, and Steve Cannon, eds. *Popular Music in France from Chanson to Techno: Culture, Identity and Society*. Aldershot, UK: Ashgate, 2003.

Delgado, Fernando. "All along the Border: Kid Frost and the Performance of Brown Masculinity." *Text and Performance Quarterly* 20 (2000): 388–401.

———. "Chicano Ideology Revisited: Rap Music and the (Re)Articulation of Chicanismo." *Western Journal of Communication* 62 (1998): 95–113.

Diamond, Elin, ed. *Performance and Cultural Politics*. London: Routledge, 1996.

Dimitriadis, Greg. "Hip Hop to Rap: Some Implications of an Historically Situated Approach to Performance." *Text and Performance Quarterly* 19 (1999): 355–69.

Dobuzinskis, Laurent. "Defenders of Liberal Individualism, Republican Virtues and Solidarity: The Forgotten Intellectual Founding Fathers of the French Third Republic." *European Journal of Political Theory* 7 (2008): 287–307.

Dompnier, Nathalie. *Vichy à travers chants*. Paris: Editions Nathan, 1996.

Durand, Yves. *Prisonniers de guerre dans les Stalags, les Oflags et les Kommandos, 1939–1945*. Paris: Hachette, 1994.

Dyer, Richard. "White." *Screen* 29 (1988): 44–64.

Ehrlich, Evelyn. *Cinema of Paradox: French Filmmaking under the German Occupation*. New York: Columbia University Press, 1985.

Fauser, Annegret. *Sounds of War: Music in the United States during World War II*. Oxford: Oxford University Press, 2013.

Ferris, Lesley, ed. *Crossing the Stage: Controversies on Cross-Dressing*. London: Routledge, 1993.

Fishman, Sarah. *The Battle for Children: World War II, Youth Crime, and Juvenile Justice in Twentieth-Century France*. Cambridge, MA: Harvard University Press, 2002.

———. "Grand Delusions: The Unintended Consequences of Vichy France's Prisoner of War Propaganda." *Journal of Contemporary History* 26 (1991): 229–54.

———. *We Will Wait: Wives of French Prisoners of War, 1940–1945.* New Haven, CT: Yale University Press, 1991.

Foster, Lisa. "Populist Argumentation in Bruce Springsteen's *The Rising.*" *Argumentation and Advocacy* 48 (2011): 61–80.

———. "The Rhetoric of Heavy Metal Resistance: Musical Modalities in Iraqi Public Life." *Middle East Journal of Culture and Communication* 4 (2011): 320–38.

Francesconi, Robert. "Free Jazz and Black Nationalism: A Rhetoric of Musical Style." *Critical Studies in Mass Communication* 3 (1986): 36–49.

Frith, Simon. *Performing Rites: On the Value of Popular Music.* Cambridge, MA: Harvard University Press, 1996.

Fry, Andy. *African American Music and French Popular Culture, 1920–1960.* Chicago: University of Chicago Press, 2014.

Fulcher, Jane. "French Identity in Flux: Vichy's Collaboration and Antigone's Operatic Triumph." *Proceedings of the American Philosophical Society* 150 (2006): 261–95.

———. "Musical Style, Meaning, and Politics in France on the Eve of the Second World War." *Journal of Musicology* 13 (1995): 425–53.

———. "The Preparation for Vichy: Anti-Semitism in French Musical Culture between the Two World Wars." *Musical Quarterly* 79 (1995): 458–75.

Gencarella, Stephen Olbrys, and Phaedra C. Pezzullo, eds. *Readings on Rhetoric and Performance.* State College, PA: Strata Publishing, 2010.

Gervereau, Laurent, and Denis Peschanski, eds. *La propagande sous Vichy, 1940–1944.* Paris: Bibliothèque de Documentation Internationale Contemporaine, 1990.

Gessele, Cynthia M. "The Conservatoire de Musique and National Music Education in France, 1795–1801." In *Music and the French Revolution*, ed. Malcolm Boyd, 201–2. Cambridge: Cambridge University Press, 1992.

Gonzalez, Alberto, and John J. Makay. "Rhetorical Ascription and the Gospel According to Dylan." *Quarterly Journal of Speech* 69 (1983): 1–14.

Goodale, Greg. *Sonic Persuasion: Reading Sound in the Recorded Age.* Urbana: University of Illinois Press, 2011.

Gray, Jonathan. *Watching with the Simpsons: Television, Parody, and Intertextuality.* New York: Routledge, 2006.

Griffiths, Dai. "What Was, or Is, Critical Musicology?" *Radical Musicology* 5 (2010–2011).

Gross, Alan G., and William M. Keith, eds. *Rhetorical Hermeneutics: Invention and Interpretation in the Age of Science.* Albany: State University of New York Press, 1997.

Grossberg, Lawrence. "Another Boring Day in Paradise: Rock and Roll and the

Empowerment of Everyday Life." *Popular Music* 4 (1984): 225–58.

Gunn, Joshua. "Mourning Speech: Haunting and the Spectral Voices of Nine-Eleven." *Text and Performance Quarterly* 24 (2004): 91–114.

Halimi, André. *Chantons sous l'Occupation*. Paris: Marabout, 1976.

Halls, W. D. *The Youth of Vichy France*. Oxford: Clarendon Press, 1981.

Hamel, Ludivine. "Les Américains au Havre et dans sa region, 1944–1946: Réalisations et impacts." Mémoire de daîtrise d'histoire, Université du Havre, 2001.

Hariman, Robert. "Political Parody and Public Culture." *Quarterly Journal of Speech* 94 (2008): 247–72.

Harpine, William D. "'We Want Yer, McKinley': Epideictic Rhetoric in Songs from the 1896 Presidential Campaign." *Rhetoric Society Quarterly* 34 (2004): 73–88.

Hebdige, Dick. *Subculture: The Meaning of Style*. London: Routledge, 1979.

Hennion, Antoine, ed. *1789–1989: Musique, histoire, démocratie*. Paris: Fondation de la Maison des Sciences de l'Homme, 1992.

Hill, Mike. *After Whiteness: Unmaking an American Majority*. New York: New York University Press, 2004.

Hutcheon, Linda. *A Theory of Parody: The Teachings of Twentieth-Century Art Forms*. New York: Methuen, 1986.

Irvine, James R., and Walter G. Kirkpatrick. "The Musical Form in Rhetorical Exchange: Theoretical Considerations." *Quarterly Journal of Speech* 58 (1972): 272–84.

Jackson, Jeffrey H. *Making Jazz French: Music and Modern Life in Interwar Paris*. Durham, NC: Duke University Press, 2003.

Jackson, Julian. *France: The Dark Years, 1940–1944*. Oxford: Oxford University Press, 2001.

Jordan, Matthew F. *Le Jazz: Jazz and French Cultural Identity*. Urbana-Champaign: University of Illinois Press, 2010.

Jorgensen-Earp, Cheryl R. *Discourse and Defiance under Nazi Occupation: Guernsey, Channel Islands, 1940–1945*. East Lansing: Michigan State University Press, 2013.

Josse, Raymond. "La naissance de la Résistance étudiante à Paris et la manifestation du 11 novembre 1940." *Revue d'histoire de la Deuxième Guerre mondiale* 47 (1962): 1–31.

Kater, Michael H. *Different Drummers*. Oxford: Oxford University Press, 1992.

Kedward, H. R. *Occupied France: Collaboration and Resistance, 1940–1944*. Oxford: Blackwell, 1985.

———. "Patriots and Patriotism in Vichy France." *Transactions of the Royal Historical Society* 32 (1982): 175–92.

————. *Resistance in Vichy France: A Study of Ideas and Motivation in the Southern Zone, 1940–1944*. Oxford: Oxford University Press, 1978.

Kosokoff, Steven, and Carl W. Carmichael. "The Rhetoric of Protest: Song, Speech, and Attitude Change." *Southern Speech Journal* 35 (1970): 295–302.

Le Bail, Karine. *La musique au pas: Être musicien sous l'Occupation*. Paris: CNRS Editions, 2016.

Lebovics, Herman. *Mona Lisa's Escort: André Malraux and the Reinvention of French Culture*. Ithaca, NY: Cornell University Press, 1999.

Lowe, Lisa. *Critical Terrains: French and British Orientalisms*. Ithaca, NY: Cornell University Press, 1991.

Mackinlay, Sterling. *Origin and Development of Light Opera*. Philadelphia: David McKay Co., 1927.

Marly, Anna. *Mémoires*. Paris: Little Big Man, 2000.

Marseille et les Américains. Marseille: Musée d'Histoire de Marseille, 1996.

Martin, Denis-Constant, and Olivier Roueff. *La France du jazz: Musique, modernité et identité dans la première moitié du XXᵉ siècle*. Marseille: Editions Parenthèses, 2002.

Mason, Laura. *Singing the French Revolution: Popular Culture and Politics, 1787–1799*. Ithaca, NY: Cornell University Press, 1996.

Matore, Daniel. "Le modernisme musical français à la veille de la Seconde Guerre mondiale." *Revue internationale de musique française* 18 (1985): 69–78.

McCann, Bryan. "Contesting the Mark of Criminality: Race, Place, and the Prerogative of Violence in N.W.A.'s Straight Outta Compton." *Critical Studies in Media Communication* 29 (2012): 367–86.

McGee, Michael C. "In Search of 'The People': A Rhetorical Alternative." *Quarterly Journal of Speech* 61 (1975): 235–49.

Mohrmann, G. P., and F. Eugene Scott. "Popular Music and World War II: The Rhetoric of Continuation." *Quarterly Journal of Speech* 62 (1976): 145–56.

Mulvey, Laura. "Visual Pleasure and Narrative Cinema." *Screen* 16 (1975): 6–18.

Nakayama, Thomas K., and Robert L. Krizek. "Whiteness: A Strategic Rhetoric." *Quarterly Journal of Speech* 81 (1995): 291–309.

Nettelbeck, Colin. *Dancing with de Beauvoir: Jazz and the French*. Carlton, Victoria, Australia: Melbourne University Press, 2004.

Ozouf, Mona. *Festivals and the French Revolution*. Translated by Alan Sheridan. Cambridge, MA: Harvard University Press, 1991.

Pells, Richard. *Not Like Us: How Europeans Have Loved, Hated, and Transformed American Culture since World War II.* New York: Basic Books, 1997.

Phillips, Kendall R. "Rhetorical Maneuvers: Subjectivity, Power, and Resistance." *Philosophy and Rhetoric* 39 (2006): 310–32.

Pollard, Miranda. *Reign of Virtue: Mobilizing Gender in Vichy France.* Chicago: University of Chicago Press, 1998.

Potter, Caroline. "French Music and the Second World War." In *French Music since Berlioz,* ed. Richard Langham Smith and Caroline Potter. Aldershot, UK: Ashgate, 2006.

Poulin, D. "Zazous and Swing Jazz: Cultural Resistance under the Vichy Regime, 1940–1943." Master's thesis, Université du Québec à Montréal, 1995.

Rachamimov, Alon. "The Disruptive Comforts of Drag: (Trans)Gender Performances among Prisoners of War in Russia, 1914–1920." *American Historical Review* 111 (2006): 362–82.

Ragache, Gilles, and Jean-Robert Ragache. *La vie quotidienne des écrivains et des artistes sous l'Occupation, 1940–1944.* Paris: Hachette, 1988.

Raskin, Richard. "'Le Chant des Partisans': Functions of a Wartime Song." *Folklore* 102, no. 1 (1991): 62–76.

Rearick, Charles. *The French in Love and War: Popular Culture in the Era of the World Wars.* New Haven, CT: Yale University Press, 1997.

Régnier, Gérard. "Jazz et société en France sous l'Occupation (1940–1944)." PhD diss., Université de Paris 1 Panthéon–Sorbonne, January 2006.

Riding, Alan. *And the Show Went On: Cultural Life in Nazi-Occupied Paris.* New York: Alfred A. Knopf, 2010.

Rioux, Emmanuelle. "Les zazous: Enfants terribles de Vichy." *L'Histoire* 165 (1993).

———. "Les zazous: Un phénomène socio-culturel pendant l'Occupation." Mémoire de maîtrise, Université de Paris X-Nanterre, 1987.

Roberts, Mary Louise. *Civilization without Sexes: Reconstructing Gender in Postwar France, 1917–1927.* Chicago: University of Chicago Press, 1994.

———. *What Soldiers Do: Sex and the American GI in World War II France.* Chicago: University of Chicago Press, 2013.

Roberts, Sophie. "A Case for Dissidence in Occupied Paris: The Zazous, Youth Dissidence, and the Yellow Star Campaign in Occupied Paris (1942)." *French History* 24 (2010): 82–103.

Roger, Philippe. *L'ennemi américain: Généalogie de l'antiaméricanisme français.* Paris:

Editions du Seuil, 2002.

Rosenberg, Emily. *Spreading the American Dream: American Economic and Cultural Expansion, 1890–1945*. New York: Hill and Wang, 1982.

Said, Edward. *Orientalism*. New York: Pantheon Books, 1978.

Samson, Michel, Gilles Suzanne, and Elisabeth Cestor. *A fond de cale: 1917–2011, un siècle de jazz à Marseille*. Marseille: Wildproject, 2012.

Savage, Jon. *Teenage: The Creation of Youth Culture*. London: Chatto & Windus, 2007.

Schneider, Herbert. "The Sung Constitutions of 1792: An Essay on Propaganda in the Revolutionary Song." In *Music and the French Revolution*, ed. Malcolm Boyd, 236–75. Cambridge: Cambridge University Press, 1992.

Schulman, Seth. "The Celebrity Culture of Modern Nightlife: Music-Hall, Dance, and Jazz in Interwar Paris, 1918–1930." PhD diss., Brown University, 2000.

Scott, James C. *Domination and the Arts of Resistance: Hidden Transcripts*. New Haven, CT: Yale University Press, 1990.

Scott, Joan. *The Politics of the Veil*. Princeton, NJ: Princeton University Press, 2007.

Sears, Richard S. *V-Discs: A History and Discography*. Westport, CT: Greenwood Press, 1980.

Sedgwick, Eve. *Between Men: English Literature and Male Homosocial Desire*. New York: Columbia University Press, 1985.

Sellnow, Deanna, and Timothy Sellnow. "'The Illusion of Life' Rhetorical Perspective: An Integrated Approach to the Study of Music as Communication." *Critical Studies in Media Communication* 18 (2001): 395–415.

———. "John Corigliano's 'Symphony No. 1' as a Communicative Medium for the AIDS Crisis." *Communication Studies* 44 (1993): 87–101.

Shack, William A. *Harlem in Montmartre: A Paris Jazz Story between the Great Wars*. Berkeley: University of California Press, 2001.

Shulman, Holly Cowan. *The Voice of America: Propaganda and Democracy, 1941–1945*. Madison: University of Wisconsin Press, 1990.

Simeone, Nigel. "Messiaen and the Concerts de la Pléiade: 'A Kind of Clandestine Revenge against the Occupation.'" *Music and Letters* 81 (2000): 551–84.

Simon, Yannick. "Les périodiques musicaux français pendant la Seconde Guerre mondiale." *Fontes Artis Musicae* 49 (2002): 67–78.

Small, Christopher. *Musicking: The Meanings of Performing and Listening*. Hanover, NH: University Press of New England, 1998.

Spotts, Frederic. *The Shameful Peace: How French Artists and Intellectuals Survived the Nazi Occupation*. New Haven, CT: Yale University Press, 2008.

Sprout, Leslie. *The Musical Legacy of Wartime France.* Berkeley: University of California Press, 2013.

———. "Music for a 'New Era': Composers and National Identity in France, 1936–1946." PhD diss., University of California Berkeley, 2000.

Storey, John, ed. *Cultural Theory and Popular Culture: A Reader.* London: Pearson Education Ltd., 2009.

Stovall, Tyler. *Paris Noir: African Americans in the City of Light.* Boston: Mariner Books, 1996.

Sweeney, Regina M. *Singing Our Way to Victory: French Cultural Politics and Music during the Great War.* Middletown, CT: Wesleyan University Press, 2001.

Sweets, John F. *The Politics of Resistance in France, 1940–1944.* Dekalb: Northern Illinois University Press, 1976.

Taylor, Lynne. "The Black Market in Occupied Northern France, 1940–4." *Contemporary European History* 6 (1997): 153–76.

Ténot, Frank. *Boris Vian: Le jazz et Saint-Germain.* Paris: Editions du May, 1993.

Thomson, Andrew A. "'Over There' 1944/45—Americans in the Liberation of France: Their Perceptions of and Relations with France and the French." PhD diss., University of Kent at Canterbury, 1996.

Torrent, Régine. *La France américaine: Controverses de la Libération* (Brussels: Editions Racine, 2004.

Tournès, Ludovic. *New Orleans sur Seine: Histoire du jazz en France.* Paris: Fayard, 1999.

———. "La réinterprétation du jazz: Un phénomène de contre-américanisation dans la France d'après-guerre." *Revue française d'études américaines* (hors-série): *Play It Again, Sim . . . Hommages à Sim Copans* (2001): 72–83.

Traubner, Richard. *Operetta: A Theatrical History.* New York: Doubleday and Co., 1983.

Turner, Victor. *From Ritual to Theatre: The Human Seriousness of Play.* New York: Performing Arts Journal Publications, 1982.

Ullman, Sharon R. *Sex Seen: The Emergence of Modern Sexuality in America.* Berkeley: University of California Press, 1997.

Walton, Whitney. *France at the Crystal Palace: Bourgeois Taste and Artisan Manufacture in the Nineteenth Century.* Berkeley: University of California Press, 1992.

Weber, Eugene. *Peasants into Frenchmen: The Modernization of Rural France, 1870–1914.* Stanford, CA: Stanford University Press, 1976.

Valérin, Patrick. *Chansons et chanteurs des années noires: Une approche de l'histoire au travers de la chanson et de ses serviteurs.* Malemort: Proanima, 1996.

Veillon, Dominique. *La mode sous l'Occupation: Débrouillardise et coquetterie dans la*

France en guerre, 1939–1945. Paris: Editions Payot, 1990.

Virgili, Fabrice. *Naître ennemi: Les enfants de couples franco-allemands nés pendant la Seconde Guerre mondiale*. Paris: Payot, 2009.

———. *Shorn Women: Gender and Punishment in Liberation France*. Oxford: Berg, 2002.

Index

Page numbers in italics refer to figures.